ON JUNG

Anthony Stevens has worked as a Jungian analyst for the last thirty years and is an experienced psychiatrist. He is a graduate of Oxford University and in addition to his DM has two degrees in psychology. His other books include *Archetype: A Natural History of the Self* (1982), *The Two Million-Year-Old Self* (1993), *Jung* (1994), *Private Myths: Dreams and Dreaming* (Penguin, 1996), *Ariadne's Clue* (Allen Lane, 1998) and, most recently, *An Intelligent Person's Guide to Psychotherapy* (1998).

CONTENTS

FIGURES

PREFACE

In the nine years that have elapsed since the original publication of this book a change has occurred in public perception of the founders of the major analytic traditions. Attacks on Sigmund Freud by such writers as Frederick Crews, Malcolm Macmillan and Richard Webster have left his scientific reputation in tatters, and highly critical books about Jung have received wide notice and not a little acclaim. However, while many of the criticisms of Freud have been well substantiated, those levelled against Jung have not. Accordingly, I have added a new chapter to the end of the present volume in which I summarize the accusations made by Jung's severest critic, Richard Noll, and examine them in greater detail than they have received elsewhere.

On the whole, Jung's ideas have stood the test of time better than Freud's. Jung's view of dreams as being transparent statements of normal psychic functioning (rather than disguises of repressed wishes as Freud conceived them) has been confirmed by dream researchers of the stature of J. Allan Hobson of Harvard. Jung's view of the unconscious as made up of archetypal propensities shaped by evolution (as opposed to the Freudian view that it is made up of repressed sexual urges) has been confirmed by the new breed of evolutionary psychologists and psychiatrists, who have rediscovered Jung's 'archetypes' in the form of their own 'evolved psychological mechanisms'. Jung's insistence on the crucial therapeutic contribution made by establishing a warm, accepting and reciprocal alliance between analyst and patient (as opposed to Freud's advocacy of a 'surgical' approach to patients, characterized by cold objectivity and personal reticence) has been supported by the latest studies of successful outcome in the practice of psychotherapy.

In recent years there has been some dispute about the status of Jung's memoir *Memories, Dreams, Reflections.* At the time of publication of the first edition of *On Jung,* it was generally assumed that those parts of the memoir which were not actually written by Jung himself were dictated by him to his secretary, Aniela Jaffé. It now appears that Jaffé's role was more active than this. Rather in the manner of a ghost writer, she jogged Jung's memory and stimulated his thoughts by putting to him a large number of questions to which he responded. The material gathered in this way required a good deal of reorganizing and editing to make it suitable for publication, and it was to this labour that Aniela Jaffé devoted herself, thus putting posterity for ever in her debt.

Researchers such as Alan Elms and Sonu Shamdasani have established that the original manuscript of *Memories, Dreams, Reflections* was a good deal longer than the published version. Certain passages concerning Jung's travels in Africa, and his relations with such figures as William James and Theodore Flournoy, were edited out on grounds of excessive length, while material relating to Jung's relationship with his mistress, Toni Wolff, was dropped in the interests of confidentiality and on the insistence of Jung's heirs.

As as result of these omissions and of Aniela Jaffé's contribution, some critics, especially Richard Noll, have attempted to discredit *Memories, Dreams, Reflections* as Jung's 'pseudo-autobiography', as if it were a figment of Jaffé's imagination. This is patently absurd. One might as well argue that the famous *Life of Samuel Johnson* was valueless because the great man's words were written down, organized, selected, and edited by James Boswell. Far from being a piece of posthumous hagiography, the manuscript of Jung's memoirs was completed before his death and was authenticated by him. As Jaffé says in her personal introduction, 'Jung read through the manuscript of this book and approved it.' It still stands as a rich and profoundly moving account of the life of one of the truly great personalities of the twentieth century: as Jung's close friend and biographer, Barbara Hannah, wrote, '[it] will always remain the deepest and most authentic source concerning Jung'. I make no apology, therefore, for drawing on it in the course of the pages which follow.

ACKNOWLEDGEMENTS

I would like to express my thanks to Routledge and to Princeton University Press for permission to quote from *The Collected Works of C.G. Jung*; to Routledge and to Harcourt Brace Jovanovich (New York) for permission to quote from Cary Baynes's translation of C.G. Jung's Foreword to *The Secret of the Golden Flower*; to Leslie Kenton for permission to quote from 'All I Ever Wanted Was a Baby'; and to Routledge, William Collins and Random House, Inc. for permission to quote from *Memories, Dreams, Reflections* by C.G. Jung, recorded and edited by Aniela Jaffé.

The final chapter of this second edition is based on reviews written by me which originally appeared in the *Journal of Analytical Psychology*, and I am grateful to the editors for their permission to make use of this material.

I am also indebted to Dr John-Raphael Staude and to Routledge for permission to use the diagram on p. 62, and to Dr Edward S. Edinger, the C.G. Jung Foundation for Analytical Psychology, New York, and G. P. Putnam's Sons, New York, for permission to use the diagram on p. 67.

Among those who read the first draft of this book I am particularly grateful to the following for their helpful comments and suggestions: Christopher Booker, Salley Brown, Julian David, Nicholas de Jongh, Jane Mayers, Chuck Schwartz, Bani Shorter, and, sternest critic of all, Andrew Franklin.

I must also thank my secretary, Norma Luscombe, for producing the final typescript with patience, accuracy and infinite good nature. The book was copy-edited by Elizabeth Bland and proof-read by John Carville and I am immensely grateful to them for their skill and their care.

Finally, my special thanks are due to Dr Anne De Vore of Colorado, for it was during March 1985, when I had the good fortune to be a snow-bound guest in her house in the Rocky Mountains, that the structure of this book took shape within my mind.

Part I

JUNG'S PSYCHOLOGY

Chapter One

THE PERSONAL EQUATION

Every so often in the history of ideas, an individual makes a contribution of such outstanding importance that a whole intellectual discipline becomes identified with his name. This is as true of Jungian analytical psychology as it is of Freudian psychoanalysis, Darwinian biology, Copernican astronomy or Newtonian physics. Each bears the stamp of its creator's personality. But whereas in natural science the stamp tends to erode with time as the discipline grows beyond the vision of its creator, in depth psychology the stamp makes a lasting and indelible impression.

The ideas at the heart of the psychotherapeutic systems devised by that impressive triumvirate of analysts, Sigmund Freud, Alfred Adler and Carl Gustav Jung, arose directly out of the personal lives of their originators, and none of them was more aware of this than Jung. When on the eve of the outbreak of the First World War this Big Three parted company after years of fruitful collaboration, Jung recognized that the rupture was due more to personal than to intellectual differences between them. Each possessed a different type of personality which gave him an individual set of biases which influenced his perception of reality. Jung's theory of psychological types grew out of this insight, as did his understanding that every psychological system, including his own, must be in the nature of a subjective confession. 'Even when I am dealing with empirical data,' he wrote, 'I am necessarily speaking about myself' (*CW* 4, para. 774). In advanced old age, he added: 'My life is what I have done, my scientific work; the one is inseparable from the other. The work is an expression of my inner development' (*MDR*, p. 211).

When Jung insisted that all those who wished to become analysts must themselves be analysed it was because he knew that, if they were to attain any degree of objectivity in their work, they must become conscious of the personal biases they carried with them. Altogether these biases added up to what he called 'the personal equation'.

That psychiatry demands intense personal engagement on the part of the physician was what attracted Jung into the profession in the first place – this and the realization that psychiatry was the one branch of medicine which embraced the two passionate interests of his life: nature and the life of the spirit. In his extraordinary memoir, *Memories, Dreams, Reflections,* he tells us of his excitement when, as a medical student, he dipped into Krafft-Ebing's *Textbook of Psychiatry.*

Beginning at the preface, he read: 'It is probably due to the peculiarity of the subject and its incomplete state of development that psychiatric textbooks are stamped with a more or less subjective character.' A few lines further on, the author referred to the psychoses as 'diseases of the personality', and it was this that galvanized Jung.

> My heart suddenly began to pound. I had to stand up and draw a deep breath. My excitement was intense, for it had become clear to me, in a flash of illumination, that for me the only possible goal was psychiatry. Here alone the two currents of my interest could flow together and in a united stream dig their own bed. Here was the empirical field common to biological and spiritual facts, which I had everywhere sought and nowhere found. Here at last was the place where the collision of nature and spirit became a reality.
>
> My violent reaction set in when Krafft-Ebing spoke of the 'subjective character' of psychiatric textbooks. So, I thought, the textbook is in part the subjective confession of the author. With his specific prejudice, with the totality of his being, he stands behind the objectivity of his experiences and responds to the 'disease of the personality' with the whole of his own personality.

This, says Jung, cast such a transfiguring light on psychiatry that he was irretrievably drawn under its spell (*MDR*, p. 111).

To speak of Jung's psychology is, therefore, to use an innocent *double entendre*, since the analytical psychology devised by Jung in all important respects grew out of his own psychology. This interpenetration of the life and work is reflected in the structure of this book, which seeks to outline the basic principles of Jungian psychology in the context of the life which gave rise to them. It is hoped that this will provide the reader with a richer experience of the meaning and quality of Jungian psychology than an account which sought to separate – artificially, in my view – the psychological discipline from the personal history of its creator.

By adopting this approach, however, I would not wish to imply that analytical psychology is merely an aid to understanding Jung's biography. The single most important fact about Jung is that he was an introspective genius. Through rigorous self-examination, and what can only be described as a *religious* commitment to his inner life, he was able to enter and illuminate that inaccessible hinterland of the human spirit where all meanings originate. By turning inwards, he, the individual man, was able to reveal the universal man lurking in the dark recesses of his own soul. For this reason both he and his Psychology deserve equal attention.

THE LIFE

Carl Gustav Jung was born in 1875 in the village of Kesswil on the Swiss shore of Lake Constance. He was the only son of the Reverend Paul Achilles Jung (1842–96), a kindly but undistinguished country pastor, and his wife Emilie, youngest daughter of Samuel Preiswerk (1799–1871), the professor who taught Paul Jung Hebrew as a theology student.

In later life, Jung was to maintain that grandparents can exert as great an influence as parents over the destiny of an individual, and this was probably true in his own case. Certainly, both his grandfathers were unusual men. Samuel Preiswerk, a distinguished theologian and Hebraist, was president of the pastors of Basel and an early advocate of Zionism. The reason why he devoted his life to the study of Hebrew was apparently his belief that it was the language spoken in Heaven. He was a convinced spiritualist who held regular conversations with his first wife after her death, and when he composed his sermons, he insisted that Emilie sat behind him to ward off evil spirits. Jung's grandmother, Samuel Preiswerk's second wife, was also said to be clairvoyant, as were other members of her family, most of whom seem to have lived in houses where things were forever going bump in the night. Such phenomena never ceased to fascinate Jung, and religious questions preoccupied him to the end of his life.

Jung's paternal grandfather was an even greater influence. Also named Carl Gustav, this august figure was something of a legend in Basel, where he practised as a physician until his death in 1864 at the age of seventy. He was Rector of Basel University, Grand Master of the Freemasons of Switzerland, and the author of numerous plays and scientific works. Twice married, and the father of fourteen children, he was himself rumoured to be the illegitimate son of Goethe, to whom he bore a physical resemblance. He was also interested in the treatment of mental illness: he tried, unsuccessfully, to promote the endowment of a Chair of Psychiatry at Basel, and he founded a home for retarded children, whom he attended with much care and devotion.

Jung was evidently intrigued by the thought that Goethe might have been his great-grandfather and, although he referred to it as 'this annoying legend', he did little to stress the fact of its implausibility. On the whole, he seems not to have believed in the Goethe connection, but there can be no doubt that the image of his grandfather Jung exercised a powerful attraction for him, and may well have enticed him into medicine and sustained him in his choice of a psychiatric career.

The actual circumstances of Jung's life are soon recounted. When he was six months old, his family moved to Laufen, near the Falls of the Rhine, where they remained until he was four. In 1879 they moved to a village just outside Basel (now a suburb) called Klein-Hüningen, where they lived in a fine old parsonage. In addition to ministering to his parishioners, Paul Jung became Chaplain to the Friedmatt Mental Hospital. Carl attended the village school, and progressed from there to the Gymnasium in Basel in 1884, the year his sister, Gertrud, was born. In 1895 he enrolled as a student at Basel University to study natural science and medicine. He graduated in 1900 and, having decided to specialize in psychiatry, became assistant to Eugen Bleuler, one of the outstanding psychiatrists of his time, at the Burghölzli Mental Hospital, which had attained international repute as the Psychiatric Clinic of Zürich University.

In 1903 Jung married Emma Rauschenbach (1882–1955), daughter of a rich Schaffhausen industrialist. Between 1904 and 1914 they had five children: four daughters and a son. In 1905 Jung was appointed lecturer in psychiatry at the University of Zürich and senior staff physician at the Burghölzli. He began to establish a reputation for himself in the psychological world as a result of research based on Galton's word-association test. When this work was published in 1906 he made contact with Sigmund Freud and, in March 1907, went to visit him in Vienna. On this occasion they conversed for thirteen hours without a break and seem to have been greatly impressed with one another. A period of collaboration ensued, mostly by correspondence.

In 1909 both men were invited to Clark University, Worcester, Massachusetts, Freud to lecture on psychoanalysis and Jung on the word-association test. They travelled to the United States together, and during the journey they had long discussions and analysed each other's dreams. The next year, 1910, saw the foundation of the International Psychoanalytic Association, and Jung served as its first President until his resignation in 1914, when he finally broke with Freud. He also gave up his lectureship at the University of Zürich and, no longer holding an appointment at the Burghölzli, retreated to his house beside the lake at Küsnacht to concentrate on his private practice and his own research.

During the period 1914–18 he underwent a protracted episode of psychological disturbance, which has been variously described as a mid-life crisis, a breakdown, a psychosis, a creative illness and a hierophantic realization. Whatever it was that afflicted him, he used the experience to further his psychological understanding and made a painstaking record of the copious material which erupted from his unconscious throughout this prolonged illness. He recovered during the year immediately following the Armistice of 1918, when he served as Commandant of a camp for British internees at Château d'Oex.

He spent the rest of his life reseaching into the significance of what had happened to him during what he described as his 'experiment with the unconscious'. This research led him into a detailed study of Gnosticism, comparative religion, mythology and alchemy. He also made anthropological expeditions to the Pueblo Indians of New Mexico in 1924–5 and to the Elgoni of Kenya in 1925–6.

Throughout the second half of his life and far into old age he wrote prolifically and published most of the books, articles and learned papers which made up the eighteen volumes of his *Collected Works*. He continued to see patients into his late seventies and kept up an extensive correspondence with people all over the world until the end of his life. He died at his home in Küsnacht on 6 June 1961 at the age of 85, his wife having died six years earlier.

On the whole, it was a fairly uneventful life; and those who turn to *Memories, Dreams, Reflections* in the hope of filling out the bare facts given above with intimate details of Jung's personal relationships, or of his encounters with the many important people who came to see him, will be disappointed. For although he greatly enjoyed human contacts, what was of primary concern to him was 'the work'. By this he meant working to record and comprehend the images and symbols arising from the unconscious. To this day, Jungians seldom talk of *analysing* people: they *work* with them.

THE WORK

In the course of his life Jung worked as a psychologist and psychiatrist as well as becoming one of the world's most brilliant analysts. Since people are not always sure about the differences between these specialities, it is perhaps as well to begin with some definitions. A *psychiatrist* is a physician who specializes in the treatment of all kinds of mental illness; an *analyst* is a therapist (who may or may not be medically qualified) who concentrates on the treatment of one group of mental disorders – the neuroses – through a long and careful examination of largely unconscious processes; while a *psychologist* is a pure scientist who studies all states of mind and all forms of behaviour, whether normal or abnormal, human or animal.

During Jung's time as a psychiatrist on the staff of the Burghölzli Hospital, Zürich, from 1900 to 1909, he was responsible, as I have mentioned, for an important piece of pure psychological research using the word-association test. This demonstrated the existence and mode of functioning of unconscious complexes. His work as an analyst began with his collaboration with Sigmund Freud, during which he helped to establish psychoanalysis as an international movement, and reached its apogee after his mid-life crisis when he developed his own therapeutic system, which he called at first 'complex psychology' and later 'analytical psychology', so as to distinguish it from Freudian 'psychoanalysis'.

Analysts of both schools are sometimes called 'depth psychologists', the 'depth' referring to what is the central preoccupation of their work – the unconscious mind. On the whole, Jung and his followers have always preferred to use the terms 'psyche' and 'psychic' rather than 'mind' or 'mental', because *psyche* refers to the entire mental apparatus, unconscious as well as conscious, whereas *mind* is used in common parlance to designate that aspect of mental functioning which is completely conscious.

Other schools of analysis have evolved out of the original disciplines established by Freud, Adler and Jung, but all of them agree in conceiving consciousness as the tip of the psychic iceberg. They proceed on the assumption that all human behaviour is motivated, and largely determined, by portions of the psyche which are not directly accessible to consciousness. These inaccessible portions are covered by the generic term 'the unconscious'.

This is, in many ways, an unfortunate piece of nomenclature, for it implies that the unconscious is a thing like the pineal gland or a place like Paris or the Caspian Sea. In fact, it is neither thing nor place: it is a process, possessing a dynamism all its own, on which the conscious ego rides like a jockey. 'The unconscious', therefore, is but a hypothesis. Its existence cannot be decisively proved, only inferred from its manifestations in symbols, symptoms and behaviour. However, it has proved to be a useful hypothesis, which no analyst can work without.

In the Jungian view, mental health (or illness) depends on the functional relationship, achieved in the course of individual development, between conscious and unconscious processes. Progress in the therapeutic application of depth psychology has resulted from study of this relationship and the creation of techniques designed to bring about its readjustment when the relationship shows signs of going wrong. Moreover, conscious–unconscious interaction is important not only in the maintenance of mental health but also in the achievement of all creative activity, whether artistic, literary or scientific, and on it depends what Jung came to regard as the highest of all human attainments, the development of the personality, whereby an individual becomes as complete a human being as it is possible for him or her to be. He called this 'individuation', and, on the basis of his own experience during the years after his break with Freud, he asserted that it could be achieved by opening oneself up to a profound experience of one's own unconscious processes. He summed it up in the first sentence of his autobiography, which he commenced at the age of eighty-two: 'My life,' he wrote, 'is a story of the self-realization of the unconscious' (*MDR*, p. 17).

Since the unconscious is so fundamental to our theme, it is crucial that we trace the origins and history of its evolution as a concept, for only then shall we be able to assess the true significance of Jung's life and work. That Jung was one of the great pioneers in the exploration of the unconscious there is little dispute, but it would be incorrect to assume that he was one of the first. All individual contributions, great and small, flow out of a stream that has its origins in the remote foothills of antiquity, and if we are to understand Jung's contribution in the context of his life, then it is no less important that we should understand his life in the context of his culture. This in itself could take many books. Here limitations of space must confine us to a very brief examination of the emergence of the unconscious as an idea. When we have determined what Jung inherited, we shall be better able to appreciate the importance of his personal contribution, and the value of what he has bequeathed us.

SUGGESTIONS FOR FURTHER READING

Vincent Brome, *Jung: Man and Myth*
C. G. Jung, *Memories, Dreams, Reflections*
Anthony Storr, *Jung*
Laurens van der Post, *Jung and the Story of Our Time*
Marie-Louise von Franz, *C. G. Jung: His Myth in Our Time*
Gerhard Wehr, *Jung: A Biography*

Chapter Two

THE UNCONSCIOUS

The unconscious was not 'discovered' by Freud, as some of his popularizers would have us believe. As the researches of Henri Ellenberger (1970) and Lancelot Whyte (1979) have made clear, it has long been recognized that there are parts of the psyche which elude the grasp of consciousness. Awareness that there are different degrees of consciousness is to be found among the ancient Egyptians, Hebrews, Hindus and medieval Christians, and it is evident that those aspects of life which are hidden from our view have intrigued original minds since the beginnings of civilization. St Augustine (354–430), the early Christian theologian, put the case for the unconscious with his customary precision when he observed: 'I cannot grasp all that I am.' That he had experiences which were beyond his control greatly worried him because, among other things, he wondered how far he could be held morally responsible for his dreams.

In the development of an idea like 'the unconscious' three stages are discernible: in the first place, it has to be *conceivable*; then, once it has been propounded, and provided it catches on, it becomes *topical*; finally, if it stands the test of time, it becomes *effective*. When we apply these stages to the history of the idea of the unconscious, it is apparent that it was conceivable around 1700, topical around 1800 and effective around 1900 (Whyte, 1979). During the period 1700 to 1900, therefore, the *existence* of the unconscious was established. However, investigation of its *structure* and *function* did not begin until the 1890s with Sigmund Freud – and that is a measure of his genius.

Since the number of those who have contributed to our knowledge of the unconscious is legion, it is convenient to consider them under four headings: the philosophers, the hypnotists, the psychologists and the analysts. We will begin with the philosophers because they did more than anyone else to distil and clarify the idea.

THE PHILOSOPHERS

The first modern thinker to be credited with a clear formulation of the idea of the unconscious was Gottfried von Leibniz (1646–1716). However, full recognition of the unconscious as a dynamic principle underlying consciousness was not achieved until the nineteenth century, when it became a central issue for the German philosophers von Schelling, Hegel, Schopenhauer and Nietzsche. Each of these thinkers influenced Jung, and many of the tenets of analytical psychology are prefigured in their works.

A major landmark was the publication in 1868 of *The Philosophy of the Unconscious* by Eduard von Hartmann (1842–1906). This massive work was a compendium of all that had been written about the unconscious up to that time. It was translated into French and English from the original German and went through many editions in all three languages. Its influence on European culture would be hard to overestimate, and von Hartmann's work, combined with the great popular esteem attained by Schopenhauer and Nietzsche, meant that by the close of the nineteenth century the idea of the unconscious was both familiar and accepted and that the philosophical ground was well prepared to receive and nurture the fertile genius of Sigmund Freud.

THE HYPNOTISTS

While the philosophers were responsible for shaping the idea of the unconscious, it was those involved in the treatment of mental illness who provided the empirical evidence necessary to lend the hypothesis some degree of scientific respectability. Modern dynamic psychiatry may be said to have begun with the introduction of the controversial technique devised by the Viennese physician Franz Anton Mesmer (1734–1815). Mesmer achieved great fame and notoriety through his success in treating a variety of nervous maladies by what is now called hypnotism but which Mesmer termed 'animal magnetism'. The techniques devised by Mesmer were taken up by others, freed of their mystical connotations and applied successfully in both England and France.

The most famous exponent of hypnotism was the eminent French neurologist Jean-Martin Charcot (1825–93), who used it in the study and treatment of hysteria. He was able to demonstrate the psychological origin of hysterical paralysis by inducing identical forms of paralysis in healthy subjects through hypnotic suggestion. He also showed that subjects could, on command, turn blind, deaf, hallucinated, spastic and cataleptic, as well as exhibiting the curious phenomenon of *multiple personality*, whereby two or more apparently separate personalities are revealed in the same person.

Interest in multiple personality is extremely ancient and goes back to the notion of 'possession' by alien spirits. Right up to the present, it has been regarded as the proper domain of the exorcist. When the condition became a subject for scientific inquiry in the nineteenth century it was originally thought that multiple personalities were 'dual' only, but later it was recognised that the unconscious behaves as a matrix out of which whole sets of subpersonalities can emerge. Charcot believed that dissociated or split-off fragments of the total personality could follow an unconscious development of their own and that they could then appear under hypnosis or manifest themselves spontaneously in clinical disturbance.

This important idea was taken up by Charcot's pupil Pierre Janet (1859–1947), who linked these 'simultaneous psychological existences' with what he called 'subconscious fixed ideas'. 'The idea,' wrote Janet, 'like a virus, develops in a corner of the personality inaccessible to the subject, works subconsciously, and brings about all disorders of hysteria and mental disease.' When Jung later defined and introduced the term 'complex' into psychology, he equated it with Janet's *idée fixe subconsciente*. Jung also embraced the view that the personal psyche is made up of a number of subpersonalities which 'personate' in dreams and fantasies.

The work of Charcot and Janet was indispensable to the foundation of depth psychology, Freud having studied under the former in 1885 and Jung under the latter during the winter semester of 1902–3. As a result of Charcot's influence Freud ceased to be a clinical neurologist, became a dynamic psychologist and began his collaboration with Joseph Breuer (1842–1925) in Vienna.

Breuer had made successful use of hypnosis for some time in the treatment of hysterical illness and claimed great success from the technique of *abreaction*, by which the hypnotized patient is encouraged to relive traumatic experiences responsible for the illness and to discharge the powerful emotions associated with them (a process which resulted in 'catharsis'). Freud was much impressed with Breuer's results and himself dated the beginning of psychoanalysis from Breuer's treatment of a patient called Anna O., 'whose numerous hysterical symptoms disappeared one by one, as Breuer was able to make her evoke the specific circumstances that had led to their appearance'. Thus, for example, her difficulty in swallowing disappeared when she remembered (and 'abreacted' to Breuer) her feeling of aversion when a dog had lapped water from her glass.

As we shall see, Freud soon abandoned hypnotism in favour of his own procedure of *free association*, by which patients were able to recover forgotten or repressed memories in full consciousness Nevertheless, it is true to say that the use of hypnosis and the study of its effects played a fundamentally important role in revealing the power of unconscious forces and in developing the therapeutic techniques necessary to render these unconscious components accessible to consciousness. Although Jung made little use of hypnotism himself, he would not have been in a position to formulate his theories had others not used it before him.

THE PSYCHOLOGISTS

Psychology was a late arrival on the scientific stage, emerging as an independent discipline only in the second half of the nineteenth century. The practitioner of this new science who contributed most to the experimental investigation of the unconscious was the English physician, chemist and mathematician Francis Galton (1822–1911). It was Galton who devised the word-association test, which Jung was later to put to good use in his study of complexes, and which, as it happened, was instrumental in starting off his association with Freud. In the test, the subject is read a series of words and asked to respond to each stimulus word with the first word that comes into his head. Galton found that responses were not given randomly, or through conscious intervention of the will, but were automatic expressions of thoughts, feelings and memories which the subject associated with the stimulus word. As already mentioned, we owe to Jung the insight that these thoughts, feelings and memories group themselves into dynamic clusters ('complexes'), which function like subpersonalities or Janet's 'fixed ideas'.

From the standpoint of Jung's psychology as a whole, however, the most important psychological study was that of Théodore Flournoy (1854–1920), who devoted five years to a painstaking investigation of one woman, a spiritualist medium called Catherine Muller (better known under her pseudonym, Helen Smith). In the trance state, Helen Smith gave detailed descriptions of her previous lives as Queen Simandini from fifteenth-century India, Queen Marie-Antoinette and an inhabitant of the planet Mars, whose language she spoke fluently. Many believed her to be genuine; others thought her to be a fraud. Flournoy concluded that she was neither. He maintained that her utterances were 'romances of the subliminal imagination', and that they were proof of the mythopoeic capacities of the unconscious. He recorded and analysed everything that Helen said and demonstrated that the content of her trance performances could be traced to forgotten memories (e.g., books read in childhood, etc.) – a phenomenon for which Flournoy coined the term *cryptomnesia* (literally 'hidden memory'). When her 'Martian' utterances were subjected to philological examination, they were found to be made up of distorted Hungarian words (Helen's father was Hungarian) based on French grammatical constructs (French being her mother tongue).

Other psychologists investigated parallel phenomena such as table turning, water divining and use of the ouija board, concluding that the phenomena were due not to 'spirits' but to unconscious thoughts causing unconscious movements on the part of the participants. One technique beloved of the spiritualists, automatic writing, was actually borrowed by psychologists as a useful means of investigating the unconscious.

Jung, who had a lifelong interest in the paranormal, was clearly intrigued by all these studies, and was heavily influenced by Flournoy's examination of Helen Smith when choosing the subject of his own doctoral dissertation, which he presented in 1902, with the title 'On the Psychology and Pathology of So-Called Occult Phenomena'. Freud, on the other hand, had no interest in such matters. If anything, he was repelled by them. But, if nothing else, the psychologists provided the analysts with empirical evidence for the existence of dynamic components in the unconscious.

THE ANALYSTS

By the end of the nineteenth century a number of conclusions had been reached about the nature and function of the unconscious mind. These conclusions can be summarized by the following propositions:

1. that many of our perceptual and ideational processes occur beneath the threshold of consciousness – an idea summed up by such terms as Helmholtz's 'unconscious inference' and W. B. Carpenter's (1813–85) 'unconscious cerebration';
2. that there are stored up in the unconscious numerous memories and perceptions of which the conscious individual knows nothing, and that these may be recovered through hypnosis, giving rise to the astonishing phenomenon of hypnotic hypermnesia (in which the subject recalls memories in extraordinary detail);
3. that skills acquired through conscious effort – such as riding a bicycle or speaking a foreign language – become automatic and then proceed unconsciously;
4. that the unconscious possesses a creative, mythopoeic function which is limitlessly productive of dreams, myths, stories, images, symbols and ideas, and, in psychopathological states, can give rise to delusions, hallucinations and the various manifestations of hysteria;
5. that the unconscious functions as a dynamic agency, Mesmer's original concept of 'magnetic fluid' being replaced by the notion of psychic energy, and that this energy can be inhibited, sublimated and transferred from one psychic component to another;

6 that beneath the threshold of consciousness, subpersonalities exist which either develop spontaneously or are parts of the conscious personality which have become 'dissociated', or split-off from consciousness, and that these subpersonalities may appear in dreams or fantasies, or be exhibited in hypnotic or mediumistic trance states or in states of multiple personality.

When Freud started his practice in Vienna in 1886, therefore, appreciation of the clinical significance of the unconscious was already well advanced. We have noted the important influence of Charcot and Breuer on Freud's early thinking. Where Freud moved beyond these pioneers was in his realization that neurosis is an altogether more complicated condition than either of them seemed to recognize, and that hypnosis is not a technique likely to produce a lasting cure. Two facts about neurotic patients impressed Freud: one was the frequency with which real or imagined sexual trauma, suffered early in life, was found to be the cause of the illness, and the other was the patient's unwillingness to acknowledge the nature of the trauma. Evidently, the traumatic memory was so painful that the patient had to defend himself or herself against it by *repressing* it into the unconscious. Freud believed this defence could be more readily removed, and the memory more lastingly recovered, if the patient was fully awake rather than hypnotized. Moreover, in the waking state the patient actually *experienced* the discharge of the emotion involved.

As a result, Freud ceased to use hypnosis, and replaced it with his own technique of *free association*, which for him became the key for unlocking the unconscious, and it was established as the 'basic rule' of the therapeutic procedure which came to be known as psychoanalysis. The patient relaxed on a couch and was instructed to associate freely – i.e., to give frank and open expression to whatever came into his mind, however absurd, embarrassing or obscene it might be. Not surprisingly, patients often experienced some inhibition about doing this, and such inhibition Freud termed *resistance*. When resistance occurred, Freud *interpreted* it to the patient, so that the cause of the resistance was understood and the resistance itself overcome. As sessions continued, Freud discovered that patients would begin to experience irrational feelings of love or hostility for him, which on analysis proved to be recapitulations of similar feelings experienced in relation to important figures – usually parental figures – in the past. These Freud called *transference* feelings – since they were *transferred* from the parents to himself. These, too, he would interpret. Together, these original techniques formed the basis of psychoanalytic treatment.

Thus, although Freud took over and adapted many of the ideas which had developed before him, he was, nevertheless, a brilliant innovator. Not only did he produce a new synthesis of earlier ideas, but he invented an entirely new mode of dealing with the unconscious (and of treating neurotic illness) – namely, the analytic situation, the basic rule of free association and the analysis of resistance and transference.

Freud also used free association to unravel the mystery of dreams. He became certain that the same psychic agency that caused patients to resist the expression of obscene thoughts on the couch also *censored* similar thoughts in dreams. What we recall as the *manifest* content of a dream is, Freud believed, a disguised or bowdlerized version of its *latent* content, which is invariably a sexual or incestuous wish. He concluded that dreams are a vicarious means of fulfilling repressed sexual desires. Their manifest content is a distorted expression of these desires, which are altered by the censor in such a way as to make them 'acceptable' to the dreamer. Thus, instead of dreaming of having sexual intercourse with his mother, the dreamer might see a train, carrying him home, plunging in and out of a series of tunnels. Free association round these images outwits the censor, and makes the true meaning of the dream apparent.

Two important assumptions about the nature of the unconscious are evident, therefore, in Freud's thinking: first, that it consists of memories peculiar to the individual; second, that when these memories are repressed they are invariably of a sexual nature. Freud added to these a third assumption, namely that the energy driving the whole psychic apparatus and responsible for its development in childhood is sexual in origin. He called this sexual energy *libido*. It is necessary to stress these assumptions because they were to become sources of contention between Freud and the most brilliant of his collaborators, Adler and Jung.

During the 1890s Freud himself suffered from neurotic symptoms, which he dealt with in two ways: he sought the advice of an ear, nose and throat specialist called Wilhelm Fliess, who was destined to become a close friend and confidant, and, between 1894 and 1899, he conducted an extensive self-analysis, using his own techniques of dream analysis and free association. Fliess was a great support to him during this time. Freud emerged from the episode free of symptoms and convinced that he had discovered the basic principles of psychic functioning, the aetiology of neurotic illness and the therapy necessary for its cure.

All the essential features of psychoanalytic theory were elaborated during this period – infantile sexuality, the stages of libidinal development in childhood, the Oedipus complex and castration complex, principles governing the fixation and transformation of libido, the theory of dreams, parapraxes and screen memories, the notion that early fantasies, as well as early sexual experiences, play a crucial role in determining later development, the understanding of symptoms as vicarious realizations of repressed sexual wishes and so on.

This six-year period of neurotic affliction and self-healing seems, therefore, to have been a 'creative illness' for Freud, much in the same way as the 'breakdown' of 1913–18 was for Jung. Interestingly, both men were approximately the same age when these episodes of illness and self-treatment occurred: Freud's illness struck him between the ages of thirty-eight and forty-four, Jung's between thirty-eight and forty-three – a time of life which Jung was to refer to as the 'mid-life crisis'. Both emerged convinced that they had made major discoveries which they must share with mankind. In both instances, their suffering and its outcome would seem to bear witness to the truth of St Augustine's dictum 'Seek not abroad, turn back into thyself, for in the inner man dwells the truth.' On their recovery, both men published major and profoundly original works: Freud's *The Interpretation of Dreams* appeared in 1900, Jung's *Psychological Types* in 1921.

One of the first disciples to be attracted to Freud was Alfred Adler (1870–1937), a Viennese physician who remained an active member of Freud's psychoanalytic circle until 1911. Like Jung, Adler came to disagree with the exclusive emphasis Freud placed on sexual development in the aetiology of neurosis, and became increasingly convinced that social instincts, and compensatory power strivings, were more fundamental motivations than sexuality. Adler parted company with Freud when the theoretical differences between them grew so wide as to be irreconcilable.

As we have seen, Jung joined the psychoanalytic movement after the publication of his *Studies in Word Association* (1906) and his meeting with Freud in Vienna in March 1907. For both of them, this meeting was one of the most important of their lives. The intensely personal quality of their relationship was apparent from the start. 'We met at 1 o'clock in the afternoon,' recalled Jung, 'and talked virtually without pause for thirteen hours. Freud was the first man of real importance I had encountered; in my experience up to that time, no one else could compare with him. There was nothing in the least trivial in his attitude. I found him extremely intelligent, shrewd, and altogether remarkable' (*MDR*, p. 146).

But even at this stage in their burgeoning friendship Jung had doubts about the fundamental place attributed by Freud to sexuality. He observed that Freud seemed committed to his sexual theory to an almost fanatical degree. 'When he spoke of it his tone became urgent,' Jung noted. 'A strange, deeply moved expression came over his face' (*MDR*, p. 147). It was as if the subject had assumed a *religious* meaning for Freud, who was an atheist – he had rejected God and put sex in His place.

As their friendship grew, Jung owned up to his reservations about Freud's sexual theory, but Freud dismissed these as due to inexperience, and Jung decided to keep his doubts to himself rather than damage a relationship which, for both men, was of the highest emotional and professional importance.

During their trip to America in 1909, however, new difficulties began to arise between them. These concerned their differing views on the nature of the unconscious, and raised the question of Freud's authority as leader of the psychoanalytic movement.

For nine years Jung had been conducting a careful study of schizophrenic delusions and hallucinations among patients at the Burghölzli Hospital in Zürich. This had convinced him that there must exist a collective or universal foundation to the human psyche. Not only did the strange ideas, hallucinations and visual images reported by individual schizophrenics resemble those reported by others, but they also bore a startling similarity to the mythologems and religious images which had been widely reported by students of cultural history from all over the world. Jung gathered a wealth of evidence which persuaded him that this universal symbolism was due less to individual experience or cultural dissemination than to the structure of the human brain and to a fundamental component of the unconscious psyche which was shared by all humankind.

This tremendous idea Jung also refrained from passing on to Freud, for the same reason that he shielded the older man from criticisms of the sexual theory. But during the course of their journey, Jung had a dream which brought matters to a head for him, though Freud did not appreciate its significance. This is the dream:

> I was in a house I did not know, which had two storeys. It was 'my house'. I found myself in the upper storey where there was a kind of salon furnished with fine pieces in rococo style. On the walls hung a number of precious old paintings. I wondered that this should be my house, and thought, 'Not bad.' But then it occurred to me that I did not know what the lower floor looked like. Descending the stairs, I reached the ground floor. There everything was much older, and I realized that this part of the house must date from about the fifteenth or sixteenth century. The furnishings were medieval; the floors were of red brick. Everywhere it was rather dark. I went from one room to another, thinking, 'Now I really must explore the whole house.' I came upon a heavy door, and opened it. Beyond it, I discovered a stone stairway that led down into the cellar. Descending again, I found myself in a beautifully vaulted room which looked exceedingly ancient. Examining the walls, I discovered layers of brick among ordinary stone blocks, and chips of brick in the mortar. As soon as I saw this I knew that the walls dated from Roman times. My interest by now was intense. I looked more closely at the floor. It was of stone slabs, and in one of these I discovered a ring. When I pulled it, the stone slab lifted, again I saw a stairway of narrow stone steps leading down into the depths. These, too, I descended, and entered a low cave cut into the rock. Thick dust lay on the floor, and in the dust were scattered bones and broken pottery, like remains of a primitive culture. I discovered two human skulls, obviously very old and half disintegrated. Then I awoke. (*MDR*, p. 155.)

He told the dream to Freud, who was particularly exercised by the two skulls, and he pressed Jung for his associations to them, in order to identify what he thought must be an unconscious death wish against two people in Jung's life. This interpretation struck Jung as very wide of the mark, but again, for the sake of peace, he named two people to keep Freud happy. Privately, however, he thought over the dream, and its meaning became very clear to him:

> It was plain to me that the house represented a kind of image of the psyche – that is to say, of my then state of consciousness, with hitherto unconscious additions. Consciousness was represented by the salon. It had an inhabited atmosphere, in spite of its antiquated style.
>
> The ground floor stood for the first level of the unconscious. The deeper I went, the more alien and the darker the scene became. In the cave, I discovered remains of a primitive culture, that is the world of the primitive man within myself – a world which can scarcely be reached or illuminated by consciousness. The primitive psyche of man borders on the life of the animal soul, just as the caves of prehistoric times were usually inhabited by animals before men laid claim to them. (*MDR*, p. 156.)

This dream, and its interpretation, marked a turning point in Jung's relationship with Freud. It intensified his interest in archaeology, mythology and comparative religion, and he spent most of 1910 collecting material for a book, which was published in two parts in 1911 and 1912. This book, *Metamorphoses and Symbols of the Libido* (published in English in 1916 with the title *The Psychology of the Unconscious*, and now available as *Symbols of Transformation*, Volume 5 of the *Collected Works*), was to inaugurate his departure from the psychoanalytic movement. It consisted of Jung's reflections on a series of fantasies recorded by an American woman, pseudonymously called Miss Miller. In the course of this work Jung not only announced his hypothesis of a collective unconscious, educing many mythological parallels to Miss Miller's fantasies, but he also decisively rejected Freud's view of libido as exclusively sexual. Instead, Jung hypothesized that libido is non-specific psychic energy akin to Henri Bergson's (1859–1941) *élan vital*, arguing that sexuality is but one form in which this energy can be channelled. He also rejected another cardinal doctrine of psychoanalytic theory, namely that the Oedipus or Elektra complex was a developmental stage through which all boys and girls passed. While he acknowledged that boys became powerfully attached to their mothers, and that this could bring them into jealous conflict with their fathers, Jung denied that either the attachment or the conflict was inevitably sexual. On the contrary, he regarded the mother as a protective, nurturant figure rather than an object of incestuous desire. To Jung, the son's longing for his mother was spiritual rather than sexual, and any desire a boy may have to return to the womb was, *au fond*, a need to be 'reborn' in a renewed act of self-realization. In other words, Jung regarded psychological incest not as a quest for a physical goal but as a means to spiritual development.

Jung recognized that these views were so fundamentally incompatible with Freud's that he hesitated for several months before completing the book and sending it for publication, fearful that its appearance would cost him Freud's friendship. Eventually he decided to press on, but his fears proved justified.

As this and later chapters will make clear, the reasons for rupture in relations between the early psychoanalysts were indeed more personal than intellectual, as Jung later concluded. As it happened, neither Freud nor Jung was a particularly easy man to get on with. With Freud there was always a tendency for enmity to follow friendship, not only in the case of Jung and Adler, but also with other colleagues such as Meynert, Breuer, Fliess and Stekel. Nor was Jung alone in the severity of his reaction to Freud's rejection: in similar circumstances, Victor Tausk committed suicide in 1919; Herbert Silberer fell into a deep depression and hanged himself in 1923; and Wilhelm Reich, like Jung, suffered from a nervous breakdown from which he subsequently recovered, though, in Reich's case, the recovery was only temporary.

For his part Jung had considerable difficulty in relating to men, and had few male friends except a companion from childhood, Albert Oeri, the sinologist Richard Wilhelm and, in late maturity, the British analyst E. A. Bennet and writer Laurens van der Post. Jung was always much more at home in the company of women, who were powerfully attracted to him and gathered round him to form a sizeable coterie, known to Zürich wits as the *Jungfrauen*.

In Freud's case, part of the problem was his prickliness over the question of his authority. As time went by, Jung grew increasingly impatient with what he saw as Freud's dogmatic authoritarianism, and in old age he could still vividly remember how Freud had said to him: 'My dear Jung, promise me never to abandon the sexual theory. That is the most essential thing of all. You see, we must make a dogma of it, an unshakeable bulwark.' It was said with great emotion, in the tone, Jung thought, of a father begging his son always to go to church on Sundays. In some astonishment Jung asked him, 'A bulwark – against what?', to which Freud replied, 'Against the black tide of mud – of occultism.'

Jung knew he could never accept such an attitude. By 'occultism' Freud seemed to mean 'everything that philosophy and religion, including the rising contemporary science of parapsychology, had learned about the psyche'. To Jung, Freud's sexual theory seemed no less 'occult' (*MDR*, pp. 147–8).

On one occasion during their American trip, when Jung was attempting to analyse one of Freud's dreams, he asked Freud for associations to a certain part of the dream. Freud refused to oblige. 'I cannot risk my authority!' he said. Jung was appalled by this reply. At that moment, Jung comments, Freud lost his authority altogether. 'That sentence burned itself into my memory; and in it the end of our relationship was already foreshadowed. Freud was placing personal authority above the truth' (*MDR*, p. 154).

It was this quality in Freud which, for all his great intelligence and charm, caused him on occasion to stand aloof and be intolerant of dissent among the ranks of his followers. As his loyal disciple and biographer, Ernest Jones, rather stuffily remarks, Freud insisted, 'The founder of psychoanalysis must be the person best qualified to judge what was psychoanalysis and what was not.' This statement hardly has about it the ring of scientific objectivity.

Jung's suggestion that his differences with Freud were due to his own introverted approach to reality, as opposed to Freud's extraverted orientation, is valid as far as it goes, but it does not take sufficient account of their different origins. Whereas Freud had an urban Jewish background, and an education which led him into empirical science, Jung was a rural Protestant, whose young mind had been steeped in Romantic idealism and the *Naturphilosophie* of Friedrich von Schelling (1775–1854). Whereas Freud's mother had been a beautiful young woman who lavished love and attention on him, Jung's mother was a homely soul who was prone to what seem to have been attacks of depression, which caused her to spend at least one long period in hospital during her son's early childhood. Freud's concept of the Oedipus complex and its central role in human development grew directly out of his analysis of his own childhood experience. That neither Jung nor Adler accepted the universality of the Oedipus complex was due to their quite different childhood circumstances. Events in Adler's early history caused him to place great emphasis on the developmental influence of birth order in siblings, and on the individual's need to compensate for early feelings of inferiority, while Jung's sense of maternal deprivation, and a religious crisis experienced during adolescence in relation to his father, caused him to turn inwards and seek spiritual security within himself. Their childhood circumstances predisposed both Freud and Jung to breakdown in mid-life, and these, together with the techniques and insights which both men believed to be responsible for their recovery, were to be firmly incorporated in the therapeutic systems that bear their names.

When one ponders these facts one begins to appreciate the truth of Jung's words, referred to at the begining of Chapter One, when in an article describing his differences with Freud, published in 1929 when he was fifty-four, he wrote: 'Philosophical criticism has helped me to see that every psychology – my own included – has the character of a subjective confession' (*CW* 4, para. 774).

Although both men created therapeutic systems of great originality, this subjective quality of confession – the personal equation – has to be taken into account when evaluating any part of their creation.

Having outlined some aspects of Freud's system, we must now examine Jung's in greater detail.

SUGGESTIONS FOR FURTHER READING

Alfred Adler, *The Practice and Theory of Individual Psychology*
Henri F. Ellenberger, *The Discovery of the Unconscious*
Sigmund Freud, *On the History of the Psycho-analytic Movement*
—— *The Interpretation of Dreams*
Ernest Jones, *The Life and Work of Sigmund Freud*
C. G. Jung, *Freud and Psychoanalysis* (*CW* 4)

William McGuire, *The Freud/Jung Letters*
Bertrand Russell, *A History of Western Philosophy*
Robert Thompson, *The Pelican History of Psychology*
L. L. Whyte, *The Unconscious Before Freud*

Chapter Three

METAPSYCHOLOGY: JUNG'S MODEL OF THE PSYCHE

'Metapsychology' is the term Freud used to cover his theories about the structure and function of the psyche. If an analogy is drawn with medical science, then metapsychology is the 'anatomy and physiology' of the mind. It is important, however, not to take this analogy literally, for literalism kills.

An ancient image of the psyche is the butterfly. It is a beautiful symbol, for the psyche, like the butterfly, is a living manifestation of the principle of metamorphosis. We must be careful, when we approach it scientifically, that we do not kill it and, like some obsessive entomologist, pin it down on a specimen board to be stored in a museum.

Moreover, metapsychology consists of abstractions, not directly observable entities. Freud readily admitted that metapsychology is a 'fiction': we invent a vocabulary which enables us to talk about the psyche *as if* it possessed a structure, so that we can create a working model as an aid to comprehension. But this imaginary model does not represent concrete reality. It is a metaphor. The only way in which we can *know* the psyche is by *living* it. All else is inference.

Doubtless, future generations of psychologists will regard Jung's model of the psyche as extraordinarily crude – as crude, say, as an early astronomer's model of the universe or an early cartographer's map of the world. But crude models are at least a beginning, and ignorance should not deter us from constructing them, always provided we do not become bewitched by them and confuse them with reality. One must never forget that the devil enters psychology through *reification* – the process by which we are beguiled into treating a concept as if it were the real thing.

The intention behind this chapter is to provide a guide to the Jungian 'fiction', so that the reader can enter into the imaginative conspiracy that all Jungians share with each other and with their patients. This will provide us with a common language and a series of assumptions through which it will be possible to communicate in the chapters which follow.

We can represent Jung's model of the psyche in the form of a diagram (see Figure 1). The *ego* is shown orbiting in a band of consciousness round a central nucleus – the *Self*. They are linked by the ego–Self axis. The inner and middle concentric bands represent the *collective* and the *personal unconscious* respectively. The functional units making up the personal unconscious are *complexes*, and those of which the collective unconscious is composed are *archetypes*. These functional 'components' are to be conceived not as fixed or static but as dynamic 'systems' in constant process of interaction and change. All are under the co-ordinating influence of the Self.

As we have noted, a complex is a group of associated ideas bound together by a shared emotional charge: it exerts a dynamic effect on conscious experience and on behaviour. An archetype, on the other hand, is an innate 'centre' or 'dominant', common to both the brain and the psyche, which has the capacity to initiate, influence and mediate the behavioural characteristics and typical experiences of all human beings, irrespective of race, culture, historical epoch or geographical location. A close functional relationship exists between complexes and archetypes, in that complexes are 'personifications' of archetypes: complexes are the means through which archetypes manifest themselves in the personal psyche.

The model is divisible into three concentric spheres, like a three-layered onion, if so uncomplicated a vegetable can be said to exist. The outer layer represents consciousness with its focal ego, the middle layer the personal unconscious with its complexes, the central sphere the collective unconscious with its archetypes, and, at its core, the co-ordinating nucleus of the entire system, the Self. Together these components make up the 'anatomy' of the psyche, and we shall consider each of them in turn.

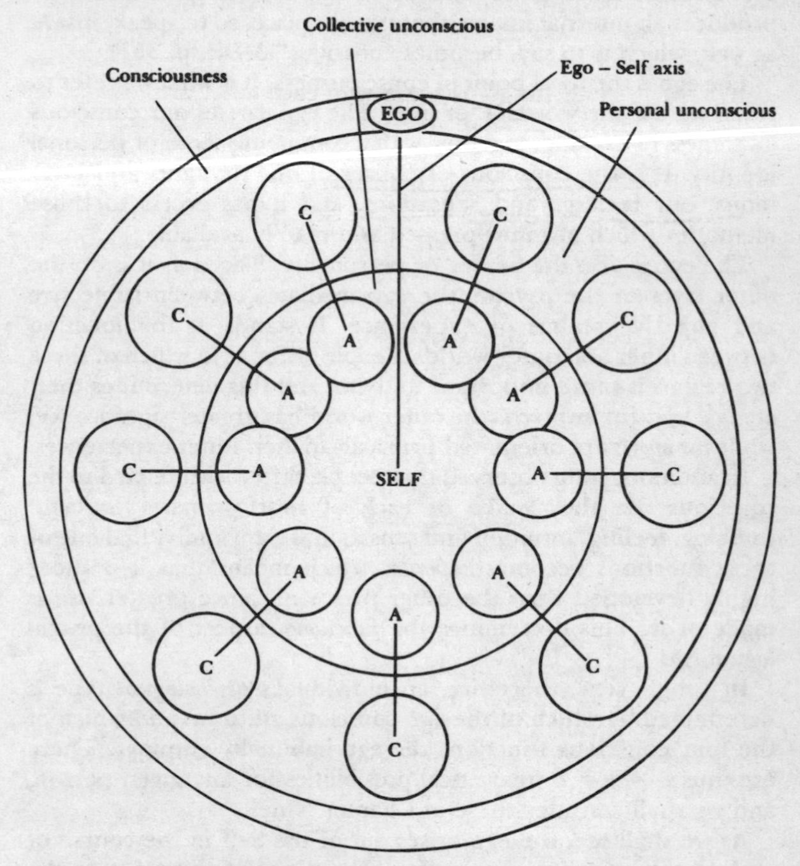

Figure 1 Schematic diagram of Jung's model of the psyche

EGO-CONSCIOUSNESS AND THE PSYCHOLOGICAL TYPE

The phenomenon of human consciousness was a recurrent source of wonder to Jung. He saw it as the most remarkable achievement of the cosmos, and he detected a purposive element in its evolution. It was as if the cosmos had *wished* to become conscious of itself, and *created* consciousness as a means to achieve this goal. 'When one reflects upon what consciousness really is, one is profoundly impressed by the extreme wonder of the fact that an event which takes place outside in the cosmos simultaneously produces an internal image, that it takes place, so to speak, inside as well, which is to say, becomes conscious' (*MDR*, p. 351).

The ego is the focal point of consciousness. It is what we refer to when we use the words 'I' or 'me'. The ego carries our conscious awareness of existing, together with a continuing sense of personal identity. It is the conscious organizer of our thoughts and intuitions, our feelings and sensations, and it has access to those memories which are unrepressed and readily available.

The ego is also the bearer of personality. Placed as it is on the outer layer of the psyche, the ego mediates between subjective and objective realms of experience. It stands at the junction between inner and outer worlds. People differ as to which of these two realms is more important to them, and this determines their *attitude type*: for *extraverts* the outer world has greater significance, while *introverts* are orientated primarily to their inner experiences.

In addition, Jung observed that people differ with regard to the conscious use they make of each of four primary *functions*: thinking, feeling, intuition and sensation. In any individual one of these functions becomes *superior*, which means that it is more highly developed than the other functions, since greater use is made of it. This determines the *functional* aspect of the *psychological type*.

In Jung's view, therefore, an individual's *psychological* type is determined by which of the two conscious attitudes and which of the four conscious functions the ego habitually employs. There are thus 2 × 4 = 8 theoretical possibilities for any given person, and we shall consider these in Chapter Nine.

As we shall see, the ego arises out of the Self in the course of early development, rather as the moon dissociated itself from the earth early in the history of our planet. Unlike the moon, however, the ego possesses an executive function: it is mediator of the Self to the world and of the world to the Self. The ego also performs other crucial roles: it is the perceiver of meaning and the assessor of value, activities which not only promote survival but also make life worth living. It is to be conceived, however, as subordinate to the Self. For the ego orbits the Self like the moon orbiting the earth or the earth the sun. Yet it is at the same time an expression of the Self. Jung wrote of the Self: 'It is not only the centre but also the whole circumference which embraces both consciousness and unconsciousness; it is the centre of this totality, just as the ego is the centre of the conscious mind' (*CW* 12, para. 41).

COMPLEXES AND THE PERSONAL UNCONSCIOUS

The personal unconscious is the product of interaction between the collective unconscious and the environment in which the individual grows up. 'Everything of which I know, but of which I am not at the moment thinking; everything of which I was once conscious but have now forgotten; everything perceived by my senses, but not noted by my conscious mind; everything which, involuntarily and without paying attention to it, I feel, think, remember, want, and do; all the future things which are taking shape in me and will sometime come to consciousness; all this is the content of the unconscious' (*CW* 8, para. 382). 'Besides these we must include all more or less intentional repressions of painful thoughts and feelings. I call the sum of these contents the "personal unconscious"' (*CW* 8, para. 270).

The functional units of which the personal unconscious is composed are complexes, and this is as true of healthy people as it is of people who are neurotic or psychotic. While Freud conceived of complexes as involved solely in illness, Jung saw them as essential parts of the healthy mind.

What impressed Jung most about the complex is its *autonomy* (Greek, *auto* = self, *nomos* = law): it is a law unto itself. Complexes seem to possess a will, a life and a personality of their own: 'Complexes behave like independent beings,' wrote Jung, 'a fact equally evident in abnormal states of mind' – by which he meant their expression in such phenomena as the hallucinatory voices 'heard' by schizophrenics, the 'spirits' which 'control' mediums in the trance state, the multiple personalities apparent in hysterics, etc.

His work with the word-association test convinced Jung that at the heart of every complex there exists a 'nuclear element' which functions beyond the reach of the conscious will. It is round this nucleus that the emotionally charged associated ideas cluster. What provides the nucleus? In the case of the major complexes – for example, the mother and father complexes and what he later identified as the persona, shadow, ego, anima and animus – he came to the conclusion that this nuclear element was a component of the collective unconscious. From 1912 he referred to these elements as 'primordial images', and after 1919 he called them 'archetypes'.

How does an archetype of the collective unconscious become a complex in the personal psyche? This is a crucial question because the answer must tell us something of how, in each and everyone of us, our personal life becomes grafted, so to speak, onto the collective history of the species.

The *laws of association*, worked out by academic psychologists at the end of the nineteenth century, give at least a partial answer. There are two of these laws: the *law of similarity* and the *law of contiguity*. Applying these laws, it can be hypothesized that an archetype becomes active in the psyche when an individual comes into proximity (*contiguity*) with a situation or a person whose characteristics possess *similarity* to the archetype in question. When an archetype is successfully activated, it accrues to itself ideas, percepts and emotional experiences associated with the situation or person responsible for its activation, and these are built into a complex which then becomes functional in the personal unconscious.

Let us take, for example, the development of the mother complex in the child's maturing psyche. The complex is formed and becomes active as a consequence of the child's living in close *contiguity* to a woman (usually the mother) whose behaviour is *similar* to the child's built-in anticipation of maternity (the mother archetype). In the absence of the personal mother, the archetype can be activated by any other female who is consistently *in loco parentis* – an aunt, grandmother, nanny or older sister. Later in life, the same complex can be *projected* onto other older women, or onto institutions or public figures, which perform a maternal role – the Church, the Queen, the university or even the Army. The religious manifestations of the archetype are legion – the earth goddesses of the Mediterranean region, for example, culminating in the Holy Virgin, Mother of God – all of whom could activate the mother complex and release powerful feelings of devotion in believers. Similarly, in adults, arousal of the sexual archetypal system depends on the presence, either in fact or in fantasy, of a partner whose characteristics and behaviour possess erotic interest for the individual.

The activation of an archetypal system, therefore, requires proximity to figures or situations appropriate to the archetype's function. Moreover, it is necessary that these figures or situations should behave in archetypally anticipated ways.

In the course of development, complexes become, to varying degrees, conscious. Indeed, in the course of early childhood the most important of all complexes, the ego-complex, comes to function, as we have seen, as the vehicle of conscious awareness and personal identity. Some complexes, however, remain deeply unconscious, and the less conscious a complex is, the more complete its autonomy. Then it can develop great influence over us without our knowing it. Writing in 1921, after his 'experiment with the unconscious', Jung declared: 'Everyone knows nowadays that people "have complexes"; what is not so well known is that complexes can *have us*' (*CW* 6, para. 200). As a result, complexes can manipulate us into situations which may be disagreeable or even disastrous for our well-being. Certainly, complexes can exercise great restraint on our ability to live our lives as freely as we might wish.

Take, for example, the case of a woman whose childhood had been dominated by a tyrannical father, who insisted always on having his own way and made terrifying scenes whenever he was thwarted. The father archetype was activated in the girl's collective unconscious by this monster, but only *partially*: only the law-giving, authoritarian, commanding aspects of the father archetype were built into the father complex in her personal unconscious; the loving, protective aspects remaining in the collective unconscious as unactivated potential. The result was that throughout her life this woman seemed fated to be drawn into the orbit of bullying, self-righteous men, whom she felt she had no alternative but to placate, appease and obey. At the same time, there persisted in her an unfulfilled longing for the man who would do none of these things to her but, on the contrary, would give her love, support and protection. Unfortunately, she could never seem to find him, for she could never get into a relationship with such a man: he was too alien, too essentially unfamiliar to her, and she did not possess the emotional vocabulary necessary to share such love.

When she came into analysis with a male analyst, her father complex inevitably got into the transference: unconsciously she would project the *imago* of the tyrannical father on to the analyst, as became clear when she misinterpreted the analyst's words or gestures as signs that he was becoming furious with her for not being a better patient. At other times, her dreams, fantasies and behaviour revealed how much she longed for the analyst to activate in her the positive father potential that remained unlived in her unconscious.

As the analysis progressed, the woman was able to become conscious of the destructive influence of her father complex, to find the strength to stand up to the men who bullied and exploited her and to distance herself from them, integrating some of their authority in her own personality. Gradually, a warm, trusting relationship, freed of negative projections, developed between her and her analyst and this resulted in activation of enough positive father potential for a much healthier and more supportive father complex to form in her psyche. As a consequence, her capacity to relate to decent men, who were kindly disposed to her, began to improve.

As this case history would suggest, the more unconscious a complex and the more dissociated it is from the ego, the more readily it is *projected* out onto figures encountered in the environment who correspond in certain ways to essential characteristics of the complex. Thus, the woman just described projected her complex onto men possessing qualities reminiscent of her father's, and then became the victim of their sadistic power.

Alternatively, one may become *identified* with a complex, as was the case with another woman, who lost her mother in infancy. Brought up by a kind and solicitous father, whom she adored, she formed a powerful, positive father complex, with which, when she came into analysis, she was completely identified. At first, it was virtually impossible to speak with her as a woman in her own right. So identified was she with the father that she reproduced his opinions, attitudes and values with absolute conviction – as if they were her own. She could brook no argument with her analyst for if he disagreed with her over anything, he was quite simply 'wrong'.

We may believe we can master our complexes, but all too easily we become their slaves. If we wish to liberate ourselves from their influence, the only way is to make them conscious and confront them. This is not an easy matter, however. Complexes do not give up their secrets or their power very readily, and they can display tenacious *resistance* to the analytic process, particularly in people who have deep feelings of insecurity. Such people can be terrified of confronting their complexes, and will do anything to deny, project or rationalize them away rather than own them in consciousness. To find the courage to attempt conscious confrontation can require great trust in the analyst and can demand of him immense tact and skill. Success can bring enormous rewards. The ego develops greater awareness and wider latitude for action, and the archetype at the core of the complex becomes freed of its pathological accretions. The patient can then escape the constraints imposed by the complex and see the problem that previously ensnared him or her as one which has always been significant for humanity and, as a consequence, one that is capable of a more creative solution than it has hitherto been possible to attempt.

In this way, analysis can be instrumental in raising a major problem from the personal to the transpersonal plane. The youth who is locked in a desperate power struggle with his father, torn between feelings of guilt, fear and resentment, is immeasurably helped by the realization that his personal conflict is but a variant of the archetypal struggle that has occurred between fathers and sons through all the generations since our species began. The mother, despairing because her children have grown up and fled the nest, can come to terms with her situation when she recognizes that what she is suffering is the pain that all mothers have suffered as they go through the 'second parturition' of delivering their children to the world.

The important therapeutic truth is that whereas complexes *can* be pathological, archetypes cannot. Archetypes are entirely healthy expressions of nature. They contribute to pathology only when an unhealthy environment causes them to be built into pathological complexes. The treatment lies in confronting the complex, freeing the archetype and permitting the formation of healthier associations with the outside world.

ARCHETYPES AND THE COLLECTIVE UNCONSCIOUS

Jung's announcement of his collective unconscious hypothesis was one of the truly momentous events in twentieth-century psychology, yet it was not generally recognized as such, nor have its implications begun even now to be adequately appreciated. This is partly because of its timing and partly because of the manner in which it was proposed.

To begin with, the prevailing *Zeitgeist* held that all mental contents were determined by the environment, that the individual began life as a blank slate (a *tabula rasa*), and that the personality was assembled piecemeal out of experience and through learning. Jung, on the other hand, made it clear that he took the contrary view – that the whole personality is present, *in potentia*, from birth and that the environment does not *grant* personality, but merely *brings out* what is already there. Every infant is born with an intact blueprint for life, both physically and mentally, which has been granted not by the present environment but by a combination of selection pressure and heredity, operating in the context of the previous environments to which the species has been exposed. In the first half of this century, with behaviourism triumphant in the universities, this was a most unpopular position to adopt.

Second, because Jung initially described the contents of the collective unconscious as 'primordial images', derived from the past history of mankind, it was suspected that like Freud he subscribed to the discredited theory of the *inheritance of acquired characteristics*, originally proposed by Jean-Baptiste Lamarck (1744–1829). Lamarck believed that characteristics acquired by individual experience could be passed on genetically to subsequent generations. But this doctrine was completely supplanted by Darwin's theory of evolution by natural selection, together with Mendel's laws of inheritance.

Furthermore, when Jung formally proposed the idea of a collective unconscious, many thought that he was referring to something mystical like a 'group mind', or that he was attempting to resurrect von Schelling's concept of a 'World Soul', and this misconception has persisted in some quarters up to the present time.

In fact, the collective unconscious is a respectable scientific hypothesis, and one does not have to adopt a Lamarckian view of evolution to accept it. Indeed, it is entirely compatible with the theoretical approach adopted by biologists who study animal behaviour in natural environments. These scientists (ethologists, as they are called) hold that each animal species is uniquely equipped with a repertoire of behaviours adapted to the environment in which it evolved. This repertoire is dependent upon 'innate releasing mechanisms' which the animal inherits in its central nervous system and which are primed to become active when appropriate stimuli, called 'sign stimuli', are encountered in the environment. When these stimuli are met, the innate mechanism is released, and the animal responds with a 'pattern of behaviour' which is adapted to the situation. When due allowance is made for the greater adaptive flexibility of our species, the ethological position is very close to Jung's view of the nature of archetypes and their mode of activation.

Just as a male stickleback is moved to court a female whose belly is swollen with eggs, a mallard duck becomes amorous at the sight of the handsome green head of a mallard drake or a ewe becomes attached to her lamb as she licks the birth membranes free of its snout, so a human mother, presented with her newborn infant, perceives its helplessness, and its need for her, and is overwhelmed by feelings of love, the force of which may come as a complete surprise to her. All these patterns of response have been prepared for by nature and require no Lamarckian explanation to account for them. As Jung himself insisted, the term archetype 'is not meant to denote an inherited idea, but rather an inherited mode of functioning, corresponding to the inborn way in which the chick emerges from the egg, the bird builds its nest, a certain kind of wasp stings the motor ganglion of the caterpillar, and eels find their way to the Bermudas. In other words, it is a "pattern of behaviour". This aspect of the archetype, the purely biological one, is the proper concern of scientific psychology' (*CW* 18, para. 1228).

Statements such as this are biologically unimpeachable. Where the whiff of Lamarckism becomes perceptable is when Jung talks of archetypal experiences being 'engraved' upon the psyche by repetition through the millennia of human existence. For example, he observes: 'There are as many archetypes as there are typical situations in life. Endless repetition has engraved these experiences into our psychic constitution, not in the form of images filled with content, but at first only as *forms without content*, representing only the possibility of a certain type of perception or action' (*CW* 9, i, para. 99).

There is no problem about Jung's assertion that archetypes

represent only the *possibility* of certain types of perception or action, but no biologist would go along with the notion of archetypal experiences being *engraved* in the psychic constitution. While one must admit that Jung did himself a disservice by using such terms, he was, in fact, employing them figuratively and metaphorically rather than scientifically. Fortunately, they are easily dropped, since they are irrelevant to the archetypal hypothesis.

What becomes fixed in the genetic structure is the *predisposition* to these kinds of experience. Every organism evolves in its typical environment (which ethologists call its *Umwelt*) and, in the course of its life cycle, encounters 'typical situations'. As a result of genetic mutations, which occur spontaneously and at random, an individual will acquire a characteristic or a propensity which makes it better adapted than its fellows to respond appropriately to a certain typical situation – such as, for example, attack from a predator. This individual will tend to survive and pass its new genetic configuration to members of subsequent generations, who, possessing the desirable characteristic, will compete more effectively in the struggle for existence. As a result the new attribute eventually becomes established as a standard component in the genetic structure of the species.

In this manner, our archetypal propensities have become adapted to the typical situations encountered in human life. The repeated selection of fortuitous mutations, occurring through thousands of generations and over hundreds of thousands of years, has resulted in the present genotype or *archetypal structure* of the human species. And this expresses itself as surely in the structure of the psyche as it does in the anatomy of the human physique.

It was a long time before Jung would acquit himself of the charge of Lamarckism, but he eventually succeeded in 1946, when he announced a clear theoretical distinction between the deeply unconscious, and therefore unknowable, *archetype-as-such* (similar to Kant's *das Ding-an-sich*) and the archetypal images, ideas and behaviours that the archetype-as-such gives rise to. It is the archetype-as-such (the *predisposition* to have a certain experience) which is inherited, not the experience itself.

Thus, archetypes predispose us to approach life and to experience it in certain ways, according to patterns already laid down in the psyche. What is more, they also *organize* percepts and experiences so as to bring them into conformity with the pattern. This is what Jung means when he says that there are as many archetypes as there are typical situations in life. There are archetypal figures (e.g., mother, child, father, God, wise man), archetypal events (e.g., birth, death, separation from parents, courting, marriage, etc.) and archetypal objects (e.g., water, sun, moon, fish, predatory animals, snakes). Each is part of the total endowment granted us by evolution in order to equip us for life. Each finds expressions in the psyche, in behaviour and in myths. Again writing figuratively, Jung summed it up: 'The collective unconscious is an image of the world that has taken aeons to form. In this image certain features, the archetypes or dominants, have crystallized out in the course of time. They are the ruling powers' (*CW* 7, para. 151).

The collective unconscious, together with its archetypal components, is, therefore, a hypothesis possessing enormous significance, for it would bring dynamic psychology into the mainstream of biological science. It would establish the continuity between the human psyche and the rest of organic nature and would act as a bridge between the science of experience and the science of behaviour.

Like all great ideas, the archetypal hypothesis is not entirely original. It has a long and respectable pedigree, which goes back at least as far as Plato. Jung himself acknowledged his debt to Plato, describing archetypes as 'active living dispositions, *ideas in the Platonic sense*, that preform and continually influence our thoughts and feelings and actions' (*CW* 8, para. 154, my italics). For Plato, 'ideas' were mental forms which were supraordinate to the objective world of phenomena. They were *collective* in the sense that they embody the *general* characteristics of groups of individuals rather than the specific peculiarities of one. For instance, a particular dog has qualities in common with all dogs, which enable us to classify him as a dog, as well as peculiarities of his own, which enable his mistress to pick him out at a dog show. So it is with archetypes: they are common to all mankind, yet each person experiences them, and manifests them, in his or her own particular way. But there the similarity ends. Unlike Plato's *idea*, the Jungian archetype is no mere abstraction but a biological entity, a 'living organism, endowed with generative force' (*CW* 6, para. 6, n. 9), existing as a 'centre' in the central nervous system which actively seeks its own activation in the psyche and in the world.

With hindsight, it is clear that the archetypal hypothesis was the product of Jung's lifelong need to reconcile biology with the life of the spirit – the longing which became so apparent in him when he read Krafft-Ebing's textbook as a student and decided that the only course for him was to become a psychiatrist: 'Here alone the two currents of my interest could flow together and in a united stream dig their own bed. Here was the empirical field common to biological and spiritual facts, which I had everywhere sought and nowhere found. Here at last was the place where the collision of nature and spirit became a reality' (*MDR*, p. 111).

THE BIOLOGICAL FOUNDATIONS OF THE PSYCHE

With the theory of archetypes and the collective unconscious, Jung grounded his psychology in biology. The life of the individual is to be seen not only in the context of his culture but in the context of the species. Jung summed this up in a profound aphorism: 'Ultimately,' he wrote, 'every individual life is the same as the eternal life of the species' (*CW* 11, para. 146). As a consequence, Jung's model of the psyche is imbued with biological assumptions. Just as the structure of the psyche is determined by the essentially biological concept of the archetype, so psychic function proceeds in accordance with the biological principles of adaptation, homeostasis and growth. We will consider Jung's theories of psychic function – the 'physiology' as opposed to the 'anatomy' of his metapsychology – under each of these headings.

Adaptation

Adaptation is the process whereby an organism actively adjusts to its environment and to the changes which occur in it. Young animals of all species, our own included, start life with the innate equipment necessary for adaptation to occur, and the adaptation continues as the innate programme for life unfolds in the context of the *Umwelt* (the environment peculiar to each species). Learning plays an important role in this adaptation, the more important the more complex the organism.

Thus, in Jung's view, the human infant, far from being a *tabula rasa*, is a highly complex creature, endowed with a huge repertoire of built-in expectations, demands and patterns of response, whose fulfilment and expression depend on the presence of appropriate stimuli arising in the environment. As a result, the archetypal endowment with which each newborn infant is equipped enables it to adapt to reality in a manner indistinguishable from that of our remote ancestors. The sum total of this endowment Jung called the *Self*, which he often referred to as *the archetype of archetypes*.

The other psychic structures – the ego, the persona, the shadow, the animus or anima – all develop out of this matrix and remain under the guiding influence of the Self. All perform vital adaptive functions in the maturing psyche, and we shall examine each of them in turn. Since it is fundamental to the whole adaptive process, we shall begin with the Self.

The Self

The Self is the psychic organ of adaptation *par excellence*. As the organizing genius behind the total personality, it is responsible for implementing the blueprint of life through each stage of the life cycle and for bringing about the best adjustment that individual circumstances will allow. The Self, therefore, possesses a *teleological* function, in that it has the innate characteristic of seeking its own fulfilment in life. (*Teleo* is a combination word derived from *teleos*, meaning perfect, complete, and *telos*, meaning end; *teleology*, therefore, is about attaining the goal of completeness.)

The goal of the Self is wholeness. Jung called this lifelong process the quest for *individuation*, and individuation is the *raison d'être* of the Self: its inherent purpose is the attainment of the fullest possible Self-realization in the psyche and in the world.

Though the Self is rooted in biology, it carries us, nevertheless, into the ineffable mysteries of the soul. It gives intimations of ultimate matters of which the ego remains ignorant. The ego is privy purely to our conscious preoccupations, but the Self has access to an infinitely wider realm of experience. For this reason, the Self is commonly projected onto figures or institutions perceived as possessing pre-eminent power and prestige – either onto human figures like presidents, kings or queens or, more readily, onto suprapersonal entities such as the State, God, the sun, Nature or the universe. In most cultures, the phenomenology of the Self is identified with God or the pantheon of gods, with the result that both God and Self come to share the same symbolism. A typical example of this is the image known in Sanskrit as the mandala. Mandalas are found all over the world; they occur in most known periods of history and are age-old symbols of wholeness and totality. They are circular in form and incorporate some symbolic representation of quaternity, such as a cross or a square. The centre is emphasized and usually contains some reference to the deity.

The Self, therefore, provides the means of adaptation not only to the environment but also to God and the life of the spirit.

The persona

One's adaptation to society is accomplished through the development of a part of the personality which Jung called the *persona*, which was the name for the mask worn by actors in antiquity. The persona is 'a functional complex that comes into existence for reasons of adaptation or personal convenience, but is by no means identical with the individuality' (*CW* 6, para. 801). It is the role we characteristically play, the face we put on, when relating to others. The persona is the 'packaging' of the ego: it is the ego's PR man or woman, responsible for advertising to people how one wants to be seen and reacted to. It simplifies relationships, oils the wheels of social intercourse and avoids the need for lengthy explanations and introductions.

Social success depends on the quality of the persona. The best kind of persona to possess is one that adapts flexibly to different social situations while, at the same time, being a good reflection of the ego-qualities that stand behind it. Trouble occurs when, for neurotic reasons, one tries to assume a persona that does not fit or attempts to keep up some kind of posture which one does not possess the personal wherewithal to sustain. Then an already shaky sense of security is made shakier. Having put all the best things in the window, one fears customers may enter the shop and find nothing but the shoddiest of goods. Difficulty can also arise if one *identifies* with the persona, for this means sacrificing the rest of the personality and imposes a harmful degree of constraint on the realization of one's unutilized potential.

Initially, the persona grows out of a need to adapt to the expectations of parents, teachers and society in the course of growing up. Young children quickly learn that certain qualities are regarded as desirable, while others are not. There is a very understandable tendency, therefore, for desirable traits to be built into the persona, while qualities perceived as undesirable, unacceptable or reprehensible are repressed or hidden from view. These repressed dispositions come to form another complex or subpersonality, which Jung called the *shadow*.

The shadow

As can be predicted from its mode of development, the shadow complex possesses qualities opposite to those manifested in the persona. Consequently, these two aspects of the personality complement and counterbalance each other, the shadow compensating for the pretensions of the persona, the persona compensating for the antisocial propensities of the shadow. Should this compensatory relationship break down, it can result in the shallow, brittle, conformist kind of personality which is 'all persona', with its excessive concern for 'what people think', or, alternatively, it can result in the sort of criminal or psychopathic individual who has little time for social niceties or public opinion.

The coexistence of these two deeply contrasting personalities in the same subject is an endless source of fascination in life and has yielded some powerful literature – for example, Dostoevsky's *The Double*, E. T. A. Hoffmann's *The Devil's Elixirs*, Edgar Allan Poe's *William Wilson*, R. L. Stevenson's *The Strange Case of Dr Jekyll and Mr Hyde* and Oscar Wilde's *The Picture of Dorian Gray*.

Jung felt intuitively that the term 'shadow' was appropriate for this dissociated subpersonality because, denied the light of consciousness, it was relegated to a twilight zone in the personal unconscious. In effect, the shadow, which Jung regarded as only a part of the unconscious psyche, is roughly equivalent to the whole of the Freudian unconscious.

Although unconscious, the shadow does not cease to exist: it remains dynamically active. The rejected aspects of the developing ego continue to carry a sense of personal identity, and when, from time to time, they impinge on awareness, they are experienced as liabilities: they are tinged with feelings of guilt and unworthiness, and bring fears that one will suffer rejection should they be discovered or exposed.

To *own* one's shadow is, therefore, a painful, and potentially terrifying, experience – so much so that we usually protect ourselves from such disturbing awareness by making use of *ego-defence mechanisms*: we *deny* the existence of our shadow and *project* it onto others. This is done not as a conscious act of will but unconsciously as an act of ego-preservation. In this way we deny our own 'badness' and project it onto others, whom we hold responsible for it. This act of unconscious cunning explains the ancient practice of 'scapegoating': it underlies all kinds of prejudice against those belonging to identifiable groups other than our own and it is at the bottom of all massacres, pogroms and wars. Through shadow projection we are able to turn our enemies into 'devils' and convince ourselves that they are not men and women like 'us' but monsters unworthy of humane consideration. National leaders can make unscrupulous use of this propensity in order to achieve their own political purposes. The speeches of Adolf Hitler, for example, returned repeatedly to the theme of *Untermenschen* (subhumans), by which he meant people of Jewish and Slavic origin, declaring that there was only one thing to do with such 'vermin' and that was to exterminate them. By skilful use of the Nazi propaganda machine, he was able to induce a sizeable portion of the German population to project its shadow collectively onto these tragically unfortunate people. What makes such propaganda so devastating in its psychological consequences is that it can activate the archetype of evil, which may then be projected onto the 'enemy' in addition to the personal shadow. This combined projection then functions as a justification for the slaughter which ensues (Stevens, 1989).

In neurotic conditions some degree of split between persona and shadow is to be expected. An essential stage in Jungian treatment consists of bringing the shadow personality to consciousness in order to establish a *rapprochement* with the persona, thus promoting integration of both complexes within the personality as a whole. But this can be a long and arduous business because of the ease with which the shadow can unconsciously be denied and projected ('I didn't want to hit him; he *made* me do it!'). Often, as Jung says, 'both insight and goodwill are unavailing because the cause of the emotion appears to lie, beyond all possibility of doubt, in the *other person*' (*CW* 9, ii, para. 16, Jung's italics). We much prefer to entertain idealized images of ourselves rather than acknowledge our personal deficiencies. It is much easier to blame others for our own shortcomings, particularly if we can persuade ourselves that the blame is justified. But, as Jung observes, 'One does not become enlightened by imagining figures of light, but by making the darkness conscious. The latter procedure, however, is disagreeable and therefore not popular' (*CW* 13, para. 335).

There are, however, two relatively simple ways in which you may discover the main features of a person's shadow complex, if you should so wish. If he happens to possess overt racial prejudices, it is sufficient to ask him what it is about people of different colour that he dislikes. Common responses are that they are untrustworthy, sexually promiscuous or perverse, morally delinquent, dirty in their personal habits and so on. Should he deny all racial prejudice, then it is usually sufficient to persuade him to talk about the sort of person that he cannot stand. Once he gets going, he will give you a fairly good picture of his shadow. But it is wise to refrain from interpreting to him what he has just revealed about himself, for he will not like you for it and, indeed, could become aggrieved or deeply upset. A more likely outcome is that he will deny the validity of your suggestion and put it down to your obtuseness.

Like every other major complex, the shadow has its archetypal core – the archetype of the enemy, the treacherous stranger, the evil intruder. This, too, is part of our adaptive equipment. The shadow archetype becomes active early in life, since it is a matter of survival for all young animals to possess a programmed wariness of anything strange which may be potentially hostile, predatory or destructive. As time goes by, the archetypal nucleus becomes fleshed out with the personality qualities which are rejected by the parents as bad and unacceptable. This personal, intrapsychic manifestation of the shadow archetype is, therefore, an adaptive compromise between society and the developing Self. It is a form of licensed hypocrisy through which one goes on being what one is prohibited from being while not putting the fact on public display. Only when this charade becomes too costly in terms of energy, guilt or anxiety may it give rise to neurotic misery and require therapeutic intervention. Indeed, this is one of the commonest causes bringing people into analysis. It behoves analysts, therefore, to create a situation and an atmosphere in which the patient will feel secure enough to examine the dangerous contents of his shadow, and to free the psychic energy tied up in them (as well as in their repression), in the hope of bringing about a better balance within the personality and a better adaptation to society. However one may choose to set about it, assimilation of the shadow is a crucial step on the way to individuation.

The anima and animus

Of all the archetypal systems with which individuals are equipped in order to adapt to the typical events of human life, one of the most crucial is that involved in relating to the opposite sex. Through careful examination of thousands of dreams, Jung detected the presence of figures carrying the physical and psychological characteristics of members of the opposite sex to the dreamer. These figures possessed the power and influence of autonomous complexes. Jung called the female complex in man the *anima* and the male complex in woman the *animus*.

> Every man carries within him the eternal image of the woman, not the image of this or that woman, but a definite feminine image. This image is fundamentally unconscious, an hereditary factor of primordial origin engraved in the living organic system of the man, an imprint or archetype of all the ancestral experiences of the female, a deposit, as it were, of all the impressions ever made by woman ... Since this image is unconscious, it is always unconsciously projected upon the person of the beloved, and is one of the chief reasons for passionate attraction or aversion. (*CW* 17, para. 338.)

If the reader will again make allowance for Jung's figurative use of language when he writes of a primordial image 'engraved' in the living organic system, or of a 'deposit' of ancestral experiences, then it becomes possible to appreciate the value of the anima, and the corresponding male image in woman's unconscious, the animus, as parts of the innate system, bequeathed us by our evolutionary history, which is responsible for initiating and maintaining the heterosexual bond. Seen in this light, both animus and anima are indispensable to the survival of the species. Together they represent a supreme pair of opposites, the *syzygy*, 'giving the promise of union and actually making it possible'.

Within the psyche, these contrasexual complexes can be contaminated with the shadow. When this occurs, feminine qualities which, in themselves, are morally neutral are, nevertheless, experienced as 'bad' and are repressed in the male, and masculine qualities similarly repressed in the female, with the consequent experience of guilt if the contrasexual qualities are detected. This was more prone to happen in the patriarchal climate in which Jung was working, when there existed a more powerful social imperative for 'men to be men' and 'women to be women'. Happily, we now live in times of greater cultural freedom, but, as in all cultures, stereotypes still prevail, and men and women continue to experience guilt in contravening them, albeit to a less crippling extent than in the past.

Jung also found that both anima and animus act as mediators of the unconscious to the ego in dreams and in the imagination. The animus and anima thus provide the means for inner as well as outer adaptation.

That the psyche is so efficient an organ of adaptation Jung attributed to the fact that it evolved in the context of the world. The laws which prevail in the cosmos also prevail in the psyche because the psyche is 'pure nature'. In other words, the psyche is a microcosmic part of the macrocosmos. For this reason Jung referred to the collective unconscious as the *objective psyche*, so as to stress its conaturality with all existence: it is as *real* and as *existent* as anything in nature. This is why fundamental natural laws, like the principles of adaptation, homeostasis and growth, apply to the psyche just as surely as to any other biological phenomenon.

Homeostasis

Since the psyche is a dynamic system functioning in accordance with natural laws, psychology has to develop working hypotheses about how the system operates. Jung, like the early psychologists, borrowed hypotheses from physics and held the questionable view that psychic energy obeyed the first and second laws of thermodynamics. More appropriate principles are to be found in biology, and, fortunately, Jung made good use of them, one of the most important being the principle of homeostasis.

Homeostasis is the principle of self-regulation. It is the means by which biological systems keep themselves in a state of balance in the interests of survival. Natural environments on our planet are constantly changing, and no living organisms could have evolved had they not possessed within themselves the capacity to maintain a 'steady state'. To sustain such a state in a changing world requires the constant application of homeostatic controls.

Appreciation of the importance of homeostasis goes back to the ancient Greeks and the Chinese Taoists. Hippocrates identified health as a state of harmony existing between man, his vital forces and his environment; while the Taoists taught that all reality is permeated by two great opposing, yet complementary, masculine and feminine principles, Yang and Yin, and that all changes and all transformations are due to alterations in the balance between them. Homeostatic regulation can, indeed, be observed at all levels of existence, from molecules to communities, in living as well as non-living systems, and our whole planet is conceivable as a vast homeostatic system of infinite complexity.

The principle of self-regulation was first applied by modern science in the field of mechanics: examples are the 'governor' used to keep the speed of steam engines constant and the themostat used to maintain room temperatures steady by switching heating systems on and off. The same principle was then applied to physiological systems by Claude Bernard (1813–78) and Walter B. Cannon (1871–1945). Bernard demonstrated the physiological processes by which a state of dynamic equilibrium is maintained in the 'internal environment' of an organism despite fluctuations in the state of the 'external environment'. Thus, despite wide fluctuations in external environmental temperatures, the body temperature of a human being remains at a remarkably steady 98.4°F (37°C). Cannon showed that the centre responsible for this regulation is located in a region at the base of the brain called the hypothalamus. If the external temperature rises, the hypothalamus compensates for this by arranging for body heat to be lost through such means as increased blood flow through the skin, sweating, panting and a reduction of the basal metabolic rate. Falls in external temperature result in increased muscle tone and shivering.

It is now understood that all the essential functions of the body operate in accordance with this principle of dynamic opposition: they are arranged in opposing systems which, in health, are kept in balance through a process of positive and negative feedback.

Not only body temperature but blood-sugar levels, blood-oxygen levels and so on are all regulated in this way. Thus, hunger is balanced against satiation, sexual desire against gratification, thirst against fluid retention, sleep against wakefulness. In addition to being one of the most important concepts in biology, homeostasis is the basis of the new science of cybernetics, with its wide application of the principles of positive and negative feedback.

For his part, Jung was convinced that the psyche, like the body, was a self-regulating system. It strives perpetually to maintain a balance between opposing propensities, while, at the same time, actively seeking its own individuation. A dynamic polarity exists between the ego and the Self, between the persona and the shadow, between masculine consciousness and the anima, between feminine consciousness and the animus, between extraverted and introverted attitudes, between thinking and feeling functions, between sensation and intuition and between the forces of Good and Evil.

Just as the body possesses control mechanisms to keep its vital functions in balance, so the psyche has a control mechanism in the compensatory activity of *dreams*.

Dreams

In the Jungian view, the function of dreams is to promote a better adaptation to life by compensating the one-sided limitations of consciousness.

> The psyche is a self-regulating system that maintains its equilibrium just as the body does. Every process that goes too far immediately and inevitably calls forth compensations, and without these there would be neither a normal metabolism nor a normal psyche. In this sense we can take the theory of compensation as a basic law of psychic behaviour. Too little on one side results in too much on the other. Similarly, the relation between conscious and unconscious is compensatory. This is one of the best-proven rules of dream interpretation. When we set out to interpret a dream, it is always helpful to ask: what conscious attitude does it compensate? (*CW* 16, para. 330.)

While Jung agreed with Freud that dreams were the 'royal road to the unconscious', his understanding of their meaning and purpose differed very radically from Freud's. As we have seen, Freud considered the 'manifest content' of dreams to be the disguised fulfilment of a repressed wish which had its origins in infantile sexuality. Jung believed dreams had much wider and deeper implications than that. He rejected the idea that the dream is a façade concealing the true meaning: 'the so-called façade of most houses is by no means a fake or a deceptive distortion; on the contrary, it follows the plan of the building and often betrays the interior arrangement' (*CW* 7, para. 319). No sleight of hand is involved: 'dreams are the direct expression of unconscious psychic activity' (*CW* 7, para. 295). They provide a view of the dreamer's situation and mobilize the potential of the personality to meet it. The compensatory function of dreams is derived from the rich capacity of the unconscious to create symbols, to 'think' laterally and to derive information from a pool of data far more extensive than that directly available to ego-consciousness.

Since dreams can introduce new and unexpected factors into the total situation, they enable us to view things differently and in a more spacious perspective. Moreover, through their compensatory action, dreams can support and strengthen the ego and promote the development of the personality. An example will illustrate this process.

An introverted man, somewhat intimidated by his business colleagues and his formidable wife, was very apprehensive about having to address a difficult shareholders' meeting. Objectively, he need not have worried because he was extremely bright and industrious, a man of rare integrity with a strong flair for business. But although he was conscious of his good qualities, this awareness did little to calm his fears.

During the night before the dreaded meeting, he dreamed that he was entering the hall in which he was due to make his speech. A woman approached him, whom he did not recognize, yet who struck him as attractively familiar. She pressed a ring into his hand and, closing his fingers over it, said conspiratorially, 'Hold on to it, and don't lose it.' He passed on into the hall, aware that his apprehension had gone.

Before he left home the next morning, he telephoned his analyst to report the dream. It seemed the anima had come to his assistance and wished to lend him the support that his wife was incapable of giving. The ring was a magic gift, a symbol of union, a talisman with protective power. The analyst suggested that when the man rose to address the meeting, he should forget his audience and not give a moment's concern to the content of his address (which he could have delivered standing on his head) but should think only of the golden ring the anima had given him: 'Hold on to it, and don't lose it.'

This seems to have been a great help to him. After his speech, his colleagues and shareholders gave him virtually unanimous backing, and he even received congratulations from his wife. With this dream, and the subsequent success, something changed in him, and he began to feel more assured in all his dealings with people. Other powerful anima dreams followed, and the marriage, which had been a mistake from the beginning, broke down. By the end of the analysis, he was living happily with a lady who was far closer in spirit to his anima. Experiences like this are in accord with Jung's dictum that: 'dreams are our most effective aid in building up the personality' (*CW* 7, para. 332).

As an efficient homeostatic system, the psyche possesses the capacity to heal itself, and it is in the compensatory function of the unconscious that this power for self-healing resides. A vital expression of this propensity is the way in which the unconscious gives rise to symbols capable of reuniting conflicting tendencies which seem irreconcilable at the conscious level. This phenomenal capacity never ceased to fascinate and move Jung, and he called it the *transcendent function.* He came to see that we are never able to *solve* the most crucial problems in life, but we can, if we are patient, transcend them. Describing this, Jung wrote:

> Here and there it happened in my practice that a patient grew beyond the dark possibilities within himself, and the observation of the fact was an experience of foremost importance to me. In the meantime, I had learned to see that the greatest and most important problems of life are all fundamentally insoluble. They must be so, because they express the necessary polarity inherent in every self-regulating system. They can never be solved, but only outgrown . . . Everyone must possess that higher level, at least in embryonic form, and, in favourable circumstances, must be able to develop the possibility. When I examined the way of development of those persons who, quietly, and as if unconsciously, grew beyond

> themselves, I saw that their fates had something in common. Whether arising from without or within, the new thing came to all those persons from a dark field of possibilities; they accepted it and developed further by means of it ... but it was never something that came exclusively either from within or without. If it came from outside the individual, it became an inner experience; if it came from within, it was changed into an outer event. But in no case was it conjured into existence through purpose and conscious willing, but rather seemed to flow out of the stream of time. (Jung, 1962, pp. 91–2.)

In this passage, Jung makes his meaning clear: one has to become aware of both *poles* of every conflict and endure, in full consciousness, the tension created between them; then, some radical shift occurs which leads to their transcendence. This comes about through the power of the unconscious to create a new symbolical synthesis out of the conflicting propensities.

The practical importance of this realization is enormous, for it means that the *possibility* of reconciliation between apparently irreconcilable forces is forever present. Living from day to day in the light of this insight brings with it a gift of inestimable value: wisdom.

Growth

The theme that runs through the whole corpus of Jungian theory is the principle of growth, development, individuation, Self-realization. Jung saw the whole life cycle as a continuing process of metamorphosis which was commissioned and homeostatically regulated by the Self. He understood that the stages through which each human life proceeds are but an evolutionary extension of those observable in non-human species. 'Individuation,' he declared, 'is an expression of that biological process – simple or complicated as the case may be – by which every living thing becomes what it was destined to become from the very beginning' (*CW* 11, para. 144).

While conducting us through the life cycle, the Self causes us to experience the images, ideas, symbols and emotions that human beings have always experienced since our species began and wherever on this planet we have taken up our abode. That is why art, when it expresses archetypal reality, moves us wherever and whenever it is or was created. It speaks to the universal principles of human existence: it transcends nation, race and creed.

As the life cycle unfolds, so we accept and incorporate into our personalities our personal experience of living. But what you and I experience as the whole process is only the end result.

> We are a psychic process which we do not control, or only partly direct [wrote Jung]. The story of life begins somewhere, at some particular point we happen to remember; and even then it was already highly complex ... Life has always seemed to me like a plant that lives on its rhizome. Its true life is invisible, hidden in the rhizome. The part that appears above ground lasts only a single summer. Then it withers away – an ephemeral apparition ... What we see is the blossom that passes. The rhizome remains. (*MDR*, p. 18.)

We are aware of our personal history only; we are unconscious of the evolutionary blueprint on whose basis our personal experience proceeds. This helps to explain how it is that some of the best minds of the twentieth century rejected Jung in favour of behaviourist theories of development which looked no further than the conditioning to which each individual had been subjected in his or her own lifetime. By ignoring the archetypal dimension, they neglected the biological bedrock on which each human personality is built.

SUGGESTIONS FOR FURTHER READING

Jolande Jacobi, *The Psychology of C. G. Jung*

C. G. Jung, *Analytical Psychology: Its Theory and Practice* (The Tavistock Lectures)

—— *Two Essays in Analytical Psychology* (*CW* 7)

—— *The Structure and Dynamics of the Psyche* (*CW* 8)

—— *The Archetypes and the Collective Unconscious* (*CW* 9,i)

—— *Aion* (*CW* 9,ii, Chapters 1–4)

Edward Whitmont, *The Symbolic Quest*

Chapter Four

PERSONAL DEVELOPMENT AND THE STAGES OF LIFE

Few really important things happen to us through choice. 'Chance,' wrote Seneca, 'makes a plaything of man's life.' We are in a lottery whose outcome is decided by a capricious, rotating mandala, the wheel of fortune. At birth a hand of cards is dealt us which fixes the extent to which we are in the grip of determinism. We are free only inasmuch as we acquire skill in playing the hand we have been dealt. We cannot choose our parents, any more than we can select the cultural, social or economic circumstances into which we shall be born; and the most chancy aspect of the whole game is the particular shuffling of parental genes dealt out to us at the moment of conception.

At birth, you were just like any other baby, yet at the same time you were unique: no one with your genetic make-up had ever existed before or will ever be born again. Such is the impressive paradox inherent in all archetypal structures: they are at once *universal* in their basic forms and *unique* in their individual manifestations. As a consequence, all life is a balancing act between the personal and the collective, through which each one of us sustains his or her unique version of those universal regulators which govern all humanity.

The Self is commissioned at the instant of conception. This auspicious event proceeds in obedience to the archetypal imperatives of Yang and Yin – Yang the penetrating and assertive, Yin the receptive and containing. In virtually all species which procreate by copulation, sperms are introduced into the female, not ova into the male. It is the Yang nature of the sperm to be active and to seek, the Yin nature of the ovum to be passive and to wait. Feminine nurturance is provided from the very beginning, for it is the ovum and not the sperm which stores the nutrients necessary for embryonic growth and development. For this reason the ovum is 85,000 times bigger than the sperm.

Appropriately, the sex of the new individual is determined at the same moment by the presence or absence of a Y chromosome: if this tiny structure is present, the embryo will follow a distinctively male, as opposed to female, ground plan. While genetic males have an X as well as a Y chromosome, genetic females have two X chromosomes; this determines whether the embryo's gonadal cells become testes or ovaries.

If a Y chromosome is present, testes are formed about six weeks after fertilization. This is a critical moment in the destiny of the individual, as henceforth the foetus *manufactures its own male sex hormones* (the androgens). These have a radical effect on later development because the testes become productive before the formation of the external genital organs and the brain. If the embryo carries two X chromosomes, on the other hand, differentiation of the gonads occurs later, and the two ovaries are not formed until the sixth month. This means that for the first six weeks of life the Self is *hermaphroditic*, in the sense that the foetus has the same physical structure whether it is male or female. The presence of a Y chromosome, leading to the production of androgens, then results in development as a male.

In the absence of a Y chromosome and androgens the foetus continues its development along a pattern which eventually emerges as female. Thus it appears that when the conditions necessary for active masculine differentiation are lacking, development proceeds more passively along feminine lines. Here again the Taoist division is evident: females *are*; males have to be *made*.

The physical consequences of this early gender distinction are so obvious that there can be little dispute about them. Male foetuses grow faster than females, and at birth male infants are both heavier and longer. Thenceforth, from infancy to old age, males have larger and more powerful muscles; their hearts are bigger and stronger; their lungs have greater vital capacity; and their basal metabolic rate is higher. They make better athletes in that they can run faster, jump higher and put shots further; their pectoral girdle makes overarm throwing stronger and more accurate; and their hand grip is, on average, twice as strong as women's. The cardiovascular system of men is better able to adapt to stress and physical exertion, and one function of the male hormone, testosterone, is to promote the formation of red blood cells, with the result that, after puberty, male blood has more haemoglobin than female blood and can carry more oxygen. Males are also more efficient at eliminating metabolites like lactic acid, which are the by-products of muscular activity. The most striking female differences, on the other hand, become apparent after puberty, with the development of a larger pelvis, wider hips and capacious breasts.

It is necessary to stress these basic facts of sexual differentiation, for it is clear that in the course of evolution males have adapted more than females to a mode of existence which is physically demanding. This is evidently the biological basis of the division of labour between the sexes that is characteristic of the great majority of societies known to anthropology, where child-rearing is almost invariably the responsibility of women and hunting and warfare the responsibility of men. These differences have less to do with cultural 'stereotypes' than some fashionable contemporary notions would have us believe.

How curious it would be if such profound biological differences as exist between males and females had no psychological or behavioural consequences for the lives of men and women in all societies! When one reviews the evidence, it is apparent that they have, as we shall see in due course. The probability is that the Self with which we are born is already structured in a number of important ways as a masculine or feminine Self, and this provides the substrate on which the masculine and feminine stereotypes of the culture into which we are born begin to do their work. These bring out and develop the masculine or feminine potential with which the Self is already endowed.

The outdated idea that gender differences are due entirely to culture and have nothing to do with biology still enjoys wide currency in our society, yet it rests on the discredited *tabula rasa* theory of human ontogeny (Greek, *ont* = being, *genesis* = birth – i.e., the origin and development of individual being). Research in child development over the last thirty years has corroborated Jung's assertion that the human infant is no blank slate, passively submitting to the inscription of life's lessons, but an active participant in the developmental process. While he readily accepted that environmental factors exert an enormous influence over an individual's psychological development, Jung nevertheless insisted that what these factors influence are the predispositions and 'subjective aptitudes' with which all children are born.

Jung's understanding that these predispositions are concerned, among many other things, with gender is apparent from the following crucial passage, which states the basic assumptions of his developmental psychology:

> There is no human experience, nor would experience be possible at all, without the intervention of a subjective aptitude. What is this subjective aptitude? Ultimately it consists of an innate psychic structure which allows men to have experiences of this kind. Thus the whole nature of man presupposes woman, both physically and spiritually. His system is tuned in to woman from the start, just as it is prepared for a quite definite world where there is water, light, air, salt, carbohydrate, etc. The form of the world into which he is born is already inborn in him as a virtual image. Likewise parents, wife, children, birth, and death are inborn in him as virtual images, as psychic aptitudes. These *a priori* categories have by nature a collective character; they are images of parents, wife, and children *in general*, and are not individual predestinations. We must therefore think of these images as lacking in solid content, hence as unconscious. They only acquire solidity, influence, and eventual consciousness in the encounter with empirical facts, which touch the unconscious aptitude and quicken it to life. They are, in a sense, the deposits of all our ancestral experiences, but they are not the experiences themselves. (*CW* 7, para. 300.)

This quotation reveals how far removed Jung was from the environmentalist, behaviourist and culturist theories which prevailed in academic institutions throughout his lifetime. Far from being a *tabula rasa*, Jung maintained that the child is born with all the necessary aptitudes for life. Moreover, he or she is endowed with an elaborate programme for life which will conduct him or her through its various stages in pursuit of an inherent goal – the fullest possible realization of the Self.

To describe this view as controversial at the time when Jung espoused it is to be guilty of understatement. While most authorities acknowledged the existence of inherent *physiological* sequences underlying the physical changes of growth, maturation and ageing, the idea that comparable *psychological* changes were genetically determined was too eccentric even to be considered. It was too shockingly at variance with behaviourist orthodoxy, which held that the human organism was a mere response system which reacted to outer stimuli to build up a repertoire of behaviours through the process of learning.

The view of human development adopted by Jung was, therefore, extremely unfashionable and is an added reason why he was regarded by many as a crank and why his archetypal hypothesis was coolly received. Moreover, Jung's was a particularly bold position to adopt in view of the fact that it was based largely on clinical intuition and lacked hard evidence to back it up. Science had not developed the sort of concepts necessary to permit an understanding of how the characteristic transformations of life could be systematically encoded within the Self or how these transformations might be manifested in social behaviour or personal experience. Ethology – the biological study of animal behaviour in the wild – had yet to demonstrate how elaborate sequences of behaviour were programmed by nature into the central nervous systems of insects, birds, and mammals, and computer technology was insufficiently advanced to provide a comprehensive analogy of how millions of bits of information could be stored and transmitted within tiny areas of space. But Jung possessed in full measure the stubbornness of his psychological type (as we shall see, he was an introverted intuitive). He was convinced enough of the truth of his insight to swim against the academic tides that engulfed him and buoyant enough not to sink beneath the torrent of invective that such courage usually brings.

Now that behaviourism has lost its pre-eminence, we can see that what Jung was proposing was not so incredible as it may have seemed at the time. It is a matter of simple observation, after all, that humans do pass through different psychological and behavioural stages in the course of their lifetime and that these stages are characteristic of the age at which they occur. If the age-related changes apparent in our bodies are biologically ordained, it does not seem altogether improbable that fundamental changes occurring in the human mind should be pre-ordained as well.

Indeed, the idea that life typically proceeds through a number of stages is so ancient and so widespread as to leave one in little doubt that both the notion and the facts are archetypally determined. Opinions vary between different traditions as to the number and duration of the stages involved, but that stages exist as a phenomenological reality is a notion common to them all.

The irony is that, unlike his detractors, who rejected his views as unscientific, Jung understood that developmental psychology could have no basis in fact or theory unless it were grounded in biology. In stark contrast to the sociologists and academic psychologists who advanced their ideas in a manner which might make one wonder if they knew that Darwin had ever existed, Jung did not forget that we are all, behaviourists included, members of *Homo sapiens* and that we evolved through a long and honourable line of animal ancestors. Archetypes, he said, are 'inherited instinctive impulses and forms that can be observed in all living creatures' (*CW* 3, para. 565). Archetypes are biological entities. They evolved through natural selection.

When it came to understanding the biological basis on which the life cycle unfolds, the problem was not only to determine what the stages of life might be, but also to discover the constant features characteristic of each stage. Quite independently of Jung, the ethologists Niko Tinbergen and Konrad Lorenz tackled this problem through their study of the *patterns of behaviour* typical of members of each animal species as they pass through life – e.g., territorial acquisition and defence, courtship, mating, hunting, reproduction, rearing the young, etc. To account for the predictable occurrence of these behaviour patterns, the ethologists postulated, as we have seen, the existence of *innate releasing mechanisms*, primed to become active as and when an animal encounters appropriate stimuli (*sign stimuli*) in the environment.

Applying these ethological concepts to their study of the life cycle of rhesus monkeys, a couple of American researchers, H. F. and M. K. Harlow, concluded that there are five distinct *affectional systems* which come into operation in sequence as the animal matures. These are the *infant–mother system*, which bonds the infant to its mother; the *peer system*, which promotes the development of social and motor skills, sexual reproductiveness and exploration of the environment among the young; the *heterosexual system*, which mediates courtship, mating and sexual bonding at maturity; the *maternal system*, which ensures survival by prompting the mother to provide her infant with nurturance and emotional security; and, finally, the *paternal system*, which ensures protection of the young from predators and aggressive members of the group.

It is not unlikely that the archetypal systems responsible for the development of similar behaviour patterns in humans operate in much the same way. It seems probable that, as the individual matures, so he or she passes through a programmed sequence of stages, each of which is mediated by a new set of archetypal imperatives which seek fulfilment in both personality and behavioural development. Each set of imperatives makes its own particular demands on the environment, and its activation depends on those demands being met. Should the environment, for any reason, be unable to meet them, then the individual's development suffers the consequences of what I have called the *frustration of archetypal intent*. This is probably as true of human development as it is of the development of non-human species. If, for example, the infant–mother affectional system, or the heterosexual affectional system, is to be activated and to achieve fulfilment, then it is essential that the environment should provide the maturing individual first with a mother figure and then with a potential mate. Should these indispensable figures not be available, the appropriate archetypal system remains dormant in the unconscious, and the individual's development is, as a consequence, either arrested or forced to pursue a distorted or aberrant course.

The existence of this archetypal blueprint for life could help to explain how it is that human beings, in different places at different times, have spoken of life as something predetermined or pre-ordained. 'It is written,' they say in their different tongues: 'It is all meant.' What happens to us is somehow experienced as intended, controlled by an unseen hand operating mysteriously behind the scenes. It is as if each of us were living out a script already written – not in ink, but in DNA – and encoded in the genetic structure of our kind.

The archetypal heritage with which each of us is born, therefore, presupposes the natural life cycle of humanity: being mothered and fathered, exploring the environment, playing in the peer group, meeting the challenges of puberty and adolescence, being initiated into the adult group, establishing a place in the social hierarchy, accomplishing courtship and marriage, child-rearing, hunting, gathering and fighting, participating in religious rituals and ceremonials, assuming the responsibilities of advanced maturity, old age and the preparations for death.

Life's purpose lies in the progressive realization of this archetypal programme which is so remarkably incorporated within the Self. As one passes from one stage of the life cycle to the next, new aspects of the Self become salient in the psychic economy and demand expression. 'Behind a man's actions,' wrote Jung, 'there stands neither public opinion nor the moral code, but the personality of which he is still unconscious. Just as a man still is what he always was, so he already is what he will become. The conscious mind does not embrace the totality of a man, for this totality consists only partly of his conscious contents ... In this totality the conscious mind is contained like a smaller circle within a larger one' (*CW* 11, para. 390).

Since no one individual can ever display every quality that lies dormant in human nature, the *undiscovered* Self is forever imminent. All those aspects of the Self which have yet to be lived provide a prospective dynamic which gives to human existence a purpose and meaning. From earliest infancy, the Self seeks to become manifest in our lives, and, from the standpoint of Jungian therapy, what matters is not so much what we are, or what we have been, but what we are in the process of becoming. This is the very essence of the individuation process.

In formulating his theory of human development, Jung acknowledged an enormous debt to Freud, who was the first clinician in modern times to offer a systematic account of how childhood events can influence the personality of the adult. However, so preoccupied was Freud with unravelling these early influences that he seems to have given little thought to the possibility that development might continue beyond the onset of maturity and late into adult life. Jung, on the other hand, was of the opinion that any coherent discipline of psychology must encompass the life cycle *as a whole*. He proposed, therefore, that autonomous psychological changes continue far into adult life, and that these are prompted by sets of inner directives issuing from the Self. Moreover, he believed that this inner programme imparted to the second half of life a quality quite different from the first.

To represent the parabola of life's course from cradle to the grave, Jung drew a metaphor from the diurnal course of the sun – albeit a sun endowed with feeling and consciousness.

> In the morning it rises from the nocturnal sea of unconsciousness and looks upon the wide, bright world which lies before it in an expanse that steadily widens the higher it climbs in the firmament. In this extension of its field of action caused by its own rising, the sun will discover its own significance; it will see the attainment of the greatest possible height, and the widest possible dissemination of its blessings, as its goal. In this conviction the sun pursues its course to the unforeseen zenith – unforeseen, because its career is unique and individual, and the culminating point could not be calculated in advance. At the stroke of noon the descent begins. And the descent means the reversal of all the ideals and values that were cherished in the morning. The sun falls into contradiction with itself. It is as though it should draw in its rays instead of emitting them. Light and warmth decline and are at last extinguished ... Fortunately, we are not rising and setting suns ... But there is something sunlike within us, and to speak of the morning and spring, of the evening and autumn of life is not mere sentimental jargon. (*CW* 8, paras. 778, 780.)

Jung's image of the life cycle can be summarized in Figure 2.

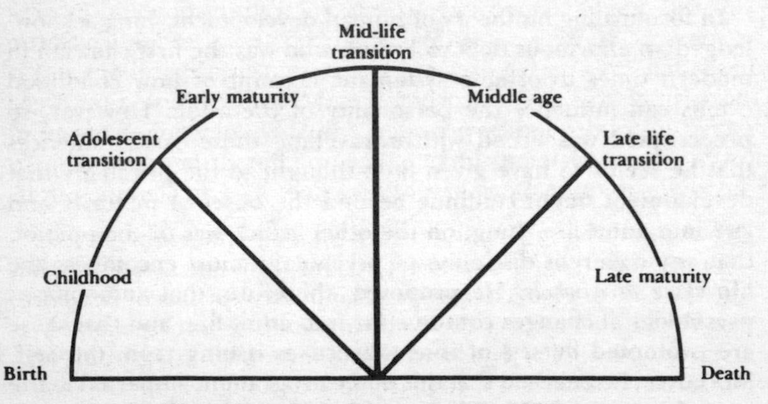

Figure 2 The life cycle (adapted from Staude, 1981)

> The one hundred and eighty degrees of the arc of life are divisible into four parts. The first quarter, lying to to the east, is childhood, that state in which we are a problem to others but are not yet conscious of any problems of our own. Conscious problems fill out the second and third quarters; while in the last, in extreme old age, we descend again into that condition where, regardless of our state of consciousness, we once more become something of a problem for others. Childhood and extreme old age are, of course, utterly different, and yet they have one thing in common: submersion in unconscious psychic happenings. (*CW* 8, para, 403.)

The 'problems' of the first and second quarters Jung saw as essentially biological and social, and those of the third and fourth quarters as essentially cultural and spiritual. 'Man has two aims,' he wrote. 'The first is the natural aim, the begetting of children and the business of protecting the brood; to this belongs the acquisition of money and social position.' Only when this aim has been achieved does the new aim – 'the cultural aim' (*CW* 7, para. 114) – become feasible.

Transition from one quarter to the next is a time of potential crisis for everyone. It was precisely in order to help the individual through these critical periods that *rites of passage* evolved in primitive societies. From his extensive analysis of these rites, the French ethnographer Arnold van Gennep (1873–1957) demonstrated in his book *Les Rites de Passage* (1909) that they themselves proceed through three stages: separation, transition and incorporation. Each rite is a death and rebirth ritual through which the individual 'dies' to his previous circumstances (separation) and is 'born into' the new (incorporation). Because these rites were sacred institutions, they provided a divinely sanctioned meaning for the life of each individual by relating him or her personally to the myths, totems and spirits of the tribe. As Van Gennep put it:

> to the semicivilized mind no act is entirely free of the sacred ... Transitions from group to group and from one social situation to the next are looked on as implicit in the very fact of existence, so that a man's life comes to be made up of a succession of stages with similar ends and beginnings: birth, social puberty, marriage, fatherhood, advancement to a higher class, occupational specialization, and death. For every one of these

> events there are ceremonies whose essential purpose is to enable the person to pass from one defined position to another which is equally well defined. (1960, p. 3.)

The inestimable value of these rituals was that they enabled both the individual and society to encounter each transition without undue disturbance, and they provided public confirmation of the fact that the transition had occurred. At the subjective level, a radical psychic transformation was ensured by the powerful symbolism of the ritual which activated archetypal components in the collective unconscious appropriate to the life stage that had been reached. These hitherto unencountered archetypal elements could then be incorporated in the personal psyche of the initiate on completion of the rite, promoting a sense of security and personal affirmation in the newly accomplished identity.

Of all the metaphors for life that the human imagination has conceived, perhaps the most evocative is that of the departure, the journey and the return: the departure, so full of the sadness of separation and excitement for the adventures to come; the journey, a series of hazards and transitions, of setbacks and triumphs; the return, marked by final transformation, fulfilment and completion. The longing for this adventure must underlie all journeys, both inner and outer, all ventures into science and literature, music and art, all self-imposed trials and ordeals. Even the contemporary package holiday must operate on the basis of this archetypal pattern, while leaving its goal essentially unfulfilled: flown effortlessly from one destination to the next, insulated from the indigenous culture within an anonymous 'tourist development', the modern pilgrim suffers no trial, experiences no adventure, encounters no unknown, undergoes no transformation; he may return more tanned than he departed, but, as far as individuation is concerned, he is no further on. The virtual disappearance of rites of passage from our culture, together with decline in the respect accorded to sacred ceremonial, has disconnected us from the archetypal imperatives which seek to transform our lives and has left us without a mythic context to give them meaning.

Yet, as in all previous ages, life's seasons still rule our destinies; and, as each spring moves on towards summer, the horizon exerts its primordial attraction. 'Than longen folk to goon on pilgrimages'

(Chaucer, Introduction to *The Canterbury Tales*). The journey was ever its own purpose and its own reward:

> Does the road wind up-hill all the way?
> Yes, to the very end.
> Will the journey take the whole long day?
> From morn to night, my friend.
>
> Christina Rossetti, 'Up-hill'

Which of us has never thought of life in this way? And who has not wondered, from the first moment of recognizing our own mortality, whether the day's journey will take the whole long day?

Fortunately, Jung's journey did take the whole long day, and his creative daimon remained active to the very end. Although there were times when he seemed to lose his way, he was for most of his life quite certain that his journey had a goal and a purpose. His was a journey into wholeness; his destination Self-completion. No act of choice caused him to take this path; rather, he felt the path had chosen him. 'From the beginning I had a sense of destiny, as though my life was assigned to me by fate and had to be fulfilled. This gave me an inner security, and, though I could not prove it to myself, it proved itself to me. *I* did not have this certainty, *it* had me' (*MDR* p. 57).

The journey on which he was embarked was essentially a journey taken by the ego, guided by the Self over terrain already mapped out for it. Early in boyhood Jung became aware of the existence of these dual aspects of himself, and he called them 'No. 1' and 'No. 2' respectively.

> Somewhere deep in the background I always knew that I was two persons. One was the son of my parents, who went to school and was less intelligent, attentive, hard-working, decent, and clean than many other boys. The other was grown up – old, in fact – skeptical, mistrustful, remote from the world of men, but close to nature, the earth, the sun, the moon, the weather, all living creatures, and above all close to the night, to dreams, and to whatever 'God' worked directly in him.

Besides the mundane life of the No. 1 personality there existed another realm,

> like a temple in which anyone who entered was transformed and suddenly overpowered by a vision of the whole cosmos, so

> that he could only marvel and admire, forgetful of himself. Here lived the 'Other', who knew God as a hidden, personal, and at the same time suprapersonal secret. Here nothing separated man from God; indeed, it was as though the human mind looked down upon creation simultaneously with God. (*MDR*, p. 55.)

The No. 2 personality, the Self, which is there in each of us from the very beginning, all the way through, and at the very end of life, is both the origin and the goal of its own realization through the intermediary of the travelling ego (No. 1). Jung referred to his No. 2 as 'having no definable character at all – born, living, dead, everything in one, a total vision of life' (*MDR*, p. 92). From earliest infancy the Self seeks to become manifest in our lives through working in unequal partnership with the ego. Thus, although they are unequal, they are mutually dependent: the ego cannot survive without the Self; the Self cannot achieve consciousness without the ego. '[The Self] is, so to speak, an unconscious prefiguration of the ego. It is not I who create myself, rather I happen to myself' (*CW* 11, para. 391).

To assert that there exist two mutually dependent aspects of the human personality may sound pathological to those who prefer to think of themselves as a stable unity, but Jung denied that the phenomena of ego–Self interaction were aberrant.

> The play and counter-play between personalities No. 1 and No. 2, which has run through my whole life, has nothing to do with a 'split' or dissociation in the ordinary medical sense. On the contrary, it is played out in every individual. In my life No. 2 has been of prime importance, and I have always tried to make room for anything that wanted to come from within. (*MDR*, p. 55.)

Jung's primary emphasis on the Self, as opposed to the ego, has been referred to as psychology's Copernican revolution. While all other theories of developmental psychology conceive of a strong and competent ego as the peak of psychic achievement, Jung maintained that the goal of all personality growth was a full realization of the Self. Since all those attributes which will later make up the psychology of the unique individual are prefigured in the Self, the ego – the necessary precondition for perception of one's own personal identity – is no exception. 'The ego,' wrote Jung, 'stands to the Self as the moved to the mover' (*CW* 11, para. 391). Gradually, the ego develops a sense of independence from the Self, while in fact remaining intimately related to it – a relationship which Jung's Israeli colleague, Erich Neumann, called the *ego–Self axis*. In a way, the Self is to the ego what the parent is to the child, or, in the great world religions, what God is to man, for the ego is, in a manner of speaking, the Self's representative 'on earth' (i.e. in physical reality).

Individual development of the ego–Self axis is represented diagrammatically in Figure 3. At first the ego exists only in *potentia* as a component of the Self. Then, as maturation proceeds, the ego gradually differentiates itself out from the Self. The perpendicular line connecting them represents the ego–Self axis, the vital link which sustains the integrity of the personality. The shaded areas of the ego represent the relative degree of ego-Self identity persisting at stages of the developmental process.

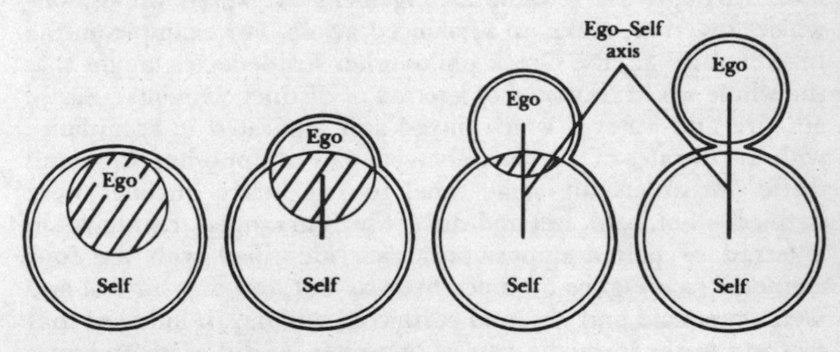

Figure 3 Diagrammatic representation of the development of the ego–Self axis (adapted from Edinger, 1972)

Extensive mythological and ethnographic research led Neumann to conclude that the archetypal image most evocative of the pre-ego stage of infantile development was the *uroborus* – the circular snake biting its tail (see Figure 4). As the ego gropes its way out of the uroborus, the opposites are constellated, and the homeostatic dialogue begins between conscious and unconscious parts of the psyche.

Jung's discovery that the Self finds expression in adults through the spontaneous production of circular and tetradic forms was

Figure 4 The Codex Marcianus Uroborus

but a modern rediscovery of an ancient phenomenon. The human mind, it seems, possesses a natural propensity to orientate itself through the tetradic arrangement of paired oppositions which, together, make up a balanced whole. For example, in the fifth century BC, the Greek philosopher Empedocles taught that the whole world consisted of a tetrad of distinct elements – earth, air, fire and water – which mixed and separated in accordance with the dictates of a great archetypal pair of opposites, Love and Strife. At about the same time, four primary qualities were defined – hot, cold, wet and dry – which arranged themselves in a tetrad of paired oppositions, each identified with the four elements (see Figure 5). Since fire was hot and dry, air hot and wet, water cold and wet, and earth cold and dry, it followed that fire and water formed a pair of opposites, as did earth and air.

The four humours of Hippocrates – blood, phlegm, dark bile and light bile – fitted in well with this scheme of things, it being affirmed by Galen in the second century AD that when the four elements were ingested into the body in the form of food and drink, they were transformed into the four humours by the heat of digestion.

Already by Graeco-Roman times many other tetradic concepts had developed, including the four points of the compass, the four winds, the zodiacal signs arranged in four groups of three and so on. Christian cosmology added other tetrads – the four living creatures before the throne of God, the four Gospels, the four rivers of Paradise, the four generations of peoples (Adam to Noah, Noah to Abraham, Abraham to Moses, Moses to Christ). The notion that there were four ages of man was but a logical extension of this cosmological system.

Throughout the Middle Ages, many diagrams were devised to illustrate the tenets of tetradic cosmology, and these often incorporated the four ages of man. Some of the most popular of these appeared in the seventh century AD in Isadore of Seville's *Liber de Natura Rerum*. This work contains seven cosmological diagrams, six of which are circular, and on their account the book came to be known as the 'Book of Wheels' (*Liber Rotarum*).

Isadore's diagrams are interesting for two reasons. In the first place he used them to illustrate a concept he borrowed from a Church Father, Ambrose, namely that of the *syzygy*, which referred to the pairing and interconnection of the four elements – a concept which Jung was in turn to use in his treatment of masculine and feminine psychology. In the second place, Isadore's diagrams linked *macrocosmic* quaternities (the elements and seasons) with *microcosmic* quaternities (the humours and ages of man), thus expressing the medieval conviction that man was a small

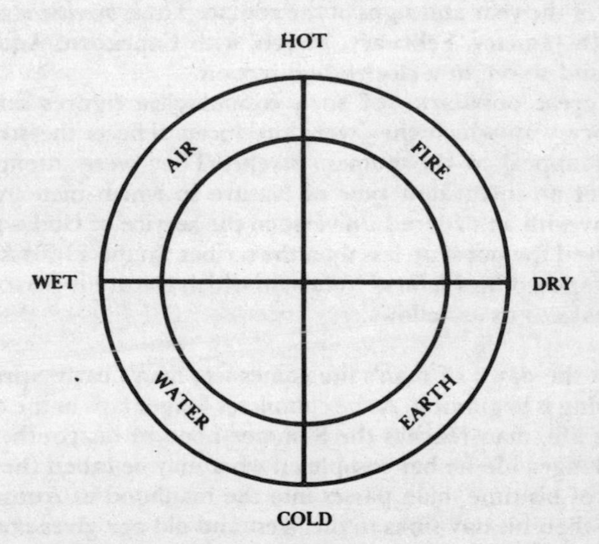

Figure 5 The four primary qualities

world and the world a great man. Plato was the authority behind this idea, and there are many references to man in Greek as *microcosmos* and in Latin as *minor mundus*. One commentator, Remigius of Auxerre, who died in AD 908, summed it up by declaring: 'For just as the world is composed of four elements and four seasons, so man is composed of four humours and four seasons.'

Early in the eleventh century a monk at Ramsey Abbey in East Anglia, called Byrhtferth, composed a widely influential work, *Enchiridion*, in which a mandala appears (see Figure 6). The cardinal points are marked by the equinoxes and solstices, which divide the figure into four quadrants. At the centre of the mandala the letters of God's name, DEUS, are arranged in a cross. This is circled by the name ADAM, together with the four directions in Greek. In this instance, ANATHOLE (East) is not correlated with spring, but is given place of honour at the top of the diagram. Beyond this are inscribed the four ages of man: *pueritia* (childhood, when, Byrhtferth tells us, blood predominates), *adolescentia* (adolescence, when red bile is strong), *iuventus* (prime, ruled by black bile) and *senectus* (old age, dominated by phlegm). Finally, each age is correlated with its appropriate months of the year and signs of the zodiac. Thus, *pueritia* is associated with January, February, March, with Capricorn, Aquarius, Pisces, and so on, in a clockwise direction.

The great popularity of such cosmological figures and the frequency with which they were produced reflects the strength of their appeal to the human psyche. They were attempts to represent an integrated view of Nature in which man lived in harmony with an ordered universe in the service of God – a view that moved the poets no less than the scribes. In the 1160s Alan of Lille composed his *Plaint of Nature*, in which Nature is personified and speaks to us as follows:

> When the dawn of man's life comes up, man's early Spring morning is beginning. As he completes longer laps in the course of his life, man reaches the Summer-noon of his youth; when with longer life he has completed what may be called the ninth hour of his time, man passes into the manhood of Autumn. And when his day sinks to the West and old age gives notice of life's evening, the Winter's cold forces man's head to turn white

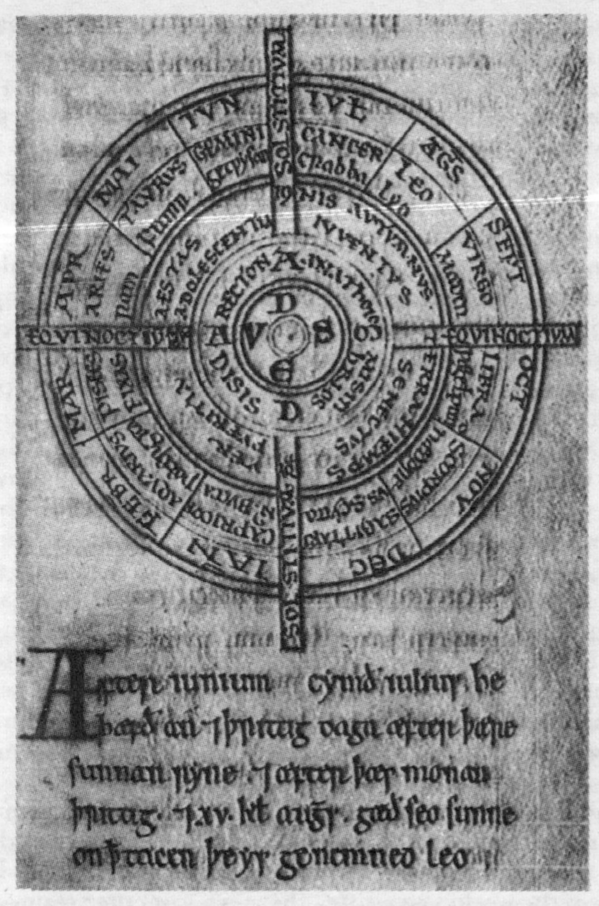

Figure 6 Tetradic diagram in 'Byrhtferth's Manual' (Ms Ashmole 328, page 85, Bodleian Library, Oxford)

> with the hoar frost of old age. In all these things the effects of my power shine forth to an extent greater than words can express (Sears, 1986.)

Jung's view of human life was entirely in tune with this tradition. His psychology was also a cosmology, for he saw all human endeavour as proceeding within the context of eternity. For him, the psyche existed in its own right as an *objective* part of nature.

It was subject to the same laws that governed the universe and was itself a supreme expression of those laws. While he conceived the whole process of life as unfolding in accordance with an inner blueprint, he was nevertheless convinced that the ultimate goal of this lifelong progress – namely, self-realization through individuation – had a divine or cosmic significance, so that, as he put it, 'the creator may become conscious of His creation, and man conscious of himself.'

Nature formed the collective unconscious. And since the collective unconscious exerts a direct influence over the development of our ideas, it follows that Nature conditions the hypotheses we formulate to account for natural phenomena just as she gives rise to the phenomena themselves. In this way, the human psyche, through the intervention of *consciousness*, acts as the mirror in which Nature sees herself reflected. Consciousness is indispensable to the perception of *meaning* and the appreciation of *value*; it carries with it a degree of autonomy and freedom of will, through which we can attain a measure of objectivity about Nature and a mite of independence from her decrees. For 'if man were merely a creature that came into being as a result of something already existing unconsciously, he would have no freedom and there would be no point in consciousness ... An absolutely preformed consciousness and a totally dependent ego would be a pointless farce, since everything would proceed just as well or even better unconsciously. The existence of ego consciousness has meaning only if it is free and autonomous' (*CW* 11, para. 391).

As Jung demonstrated, it is possible for the conscious ego, itself a product of Nature, to turn round upon its creatrix and study her in her psychic as well as her material manifestations. 'In my picture of the world,' he wrote, 'there is a vast outer realm and an equally vast inner realm; between these two stands man, facing now one way and now the other' (*CW* 4, para. 777). As an introvert he found the inner realm infinitely more appealing, and into that dark continent he carried the torch of consciousness further, perhaps, than any man before him.

This completes the first part of the book: we have reached the end of the general outline of Jung's psychology and its antecedents.

In what follows we shall apply the concepts, introduced in Part I, to each stage of the life cycle, following the schema presented in

Figure 2. Part II will take us from birth to the mid-life crisis, and Part III from middle age to the moment of death.

Each chapter will follow broadly the same pattern: first it will sketch the archetypal programme characteristic of the stage in question; then it will examine Jung's own experience of having lived through this stage; finally it will consider the significance of this experience for Jungian theory.

The final chapter will present an overview of Jung's contribution and attempt an assessment of its value.

SUGGESTIONS FOR FURTHER READING

Irenäus Eibl-Eibesfeldt, *Love and Hate*
C. G. Jung, *The Stages of Life* (in *CW* 8)
D. J. Levinson *et al.*, *The Seasons of a Man's Life*
J. E. Parsons, *The Psychobiology of Sex Differences and Sex Roles*
Elizabeth Sears, *The Ages of Man: Medieval Interpretations of the Life Cycle*
John-Raphael Staude, *The Adult Development of C. G. Jung*
Arnold van Gennep, *The Rites of Passage*

Part II

FROM BIRTH TO MATURITY

Chapter Five

CHILDHOOD

THE ARCHETYPAL PROGRAMME

The first five years are the busiest time for the Self. In this brief segment of the life span, the foundations which will determine the future structure of the personality are laid. Of all the archetypal programmes activated at this time, that mediating attachment to the mother is the most critical. Whether or not this *primal relationship* goes well will affect all later relationships with people, with society and with the world. Relationships with other significant figures – father, siblings, grandparents, family friends, etc. – are also of crucial importance at this stage, for they, together with the mother, release and influence the activity of archetypal systems concerned with play, exploration of the environment, discrimination against strangers, the development of gender consciousness and sexuality, the acquisition of language, formation of the moral complex, the persona and the shadow, and the animus or anima. All these are essential features of the archetypal prescription for the first years of life.

Since the bedrock on which the foundations of the personal psyche are built is the mother, we will begin with her, and with the archetypal quality she is best able to constellate – Eros, the principle of love.

Maternal Eros

The first and most urgent requirement of the Self is for survival. At birth, the human baby is one of the most helpless creatures in the world, and, in comparison with the young of other mammals, it appears unmistakably premature. If it is to stand any chance of survival, it will need constant care and attention from someone powerfully motivated to provide it. Who could this be? Nature's answer is – as it always has been throughout the aeons of mammalian evolution – the mother.

It is a demanding and, in many ways, a thankless task that a mother has to perform, and it is legitimate to wonder why any female, in her right senses, should be willing to take it on – especially when one takes into account the gross unfairness of the arrangement in terms of sexual economics. The relative cost to the mother, in time, effort, calories, libido and pain, is so much greater than to the father that it makes one wonder if nature can have any sense of justice at all. Yet the father's genes benefit equally with those of the mother. How has she been persuaded to put up with it all these hundreds and thousands of years?

The answer is *love*. And the loyal devotion that love brings. This love is not just a matter of willpower or social conditioning: a woman does not choose to love her child. It is something that happens to her. She has been well prepared by the months of waiting. Then, within moments of delivery – provided she has not been rendered medically insensible by well-meaning attendants – she perceives its helplessness and need for her, and is moved by feelings of pride, possessiveness and joy.

The infant, too, is archetypally prepared for this moment and at once begins to root for the breast. Here is one woman's description of these wonderful events:

> When the nurse took my first child and put him to my breast his tiny mouth opened and reached for me as if he had known forever what to do. He began to suck with such force it took my breath away. It was like being attached to a vacuum cleaner. I began to laugh. I couldn't help myself. It seemed incredible that such a tiny creature could have such force and determination. He too had a purpose. He was raw, insistent and real. With every fibre of his being, this child was drawing his life. And he would not be denied.
>
> Tears of joy ran shamelessly down my cheeks while he sucked. I thought back to my past conviction that only when I had a baby would I *know* whatever it was I had to know. Now I

did know. It is the only important thing I have ever learned, and so ridiculously simple: love exists. It's real and honest and unbelievably solid in a world where far too much is complex or confusing or false.

There, in the midst of all that clinical green and white, I had discovered what love was all about. It was a meeting of two beings. The age, the sex, the relationship didn't matter. That day, two creatures – he and I – had met. We touched each other, in utter honesty and simplicity. There was nothing romantic or solemn about it. No obligations, no duties, no fancy games. We'd met. Just that. Somewhere in spirit we were friends. I knew beyond all doubt that I'd found something *real*. And real it has remained. (Leslie Kenton, from 'All I Ever Wanted Was a Baby'.)

Since the beginning of mammalian time, mothers and infants have experienced their intimacy as something transcendent and transpersonal, something coming from beyond themselves. The strange idea that each mother–infant relationship should be anything less than a re-enactment of an ancient biological theme could have occurred only to an academic male, such as J. B. Watson, the founder of behaviourism. Yet right up to the late 1960s academic psychologists insisted that attachment between mothers and infants was simply a form of behaviour which was acquired through 'operant conditioning': according to this idea, infants became attached to their mother because she rewarded them repeatedly with food. Appropriately enough, it came to be known as the 'cupboard love' theory, and it remained virtually unchallenged until it was attacked by the British psychiatrist Dr John Bowlby, in a now famous paper published in 1958. Bowlby argued convincingly that attachment occurred not so much through learning as by *instinct*. Mothers and infants had no need to learn to love one another because they were innately programmed to do it from birth. The formation of attachment bonds is, Bowlby proposed, a direct expression of the genetic heritage of our species.

Bowlby's theory thus accorded well with Jung's view that the mother–child bond is formed on the basis of archetypal systems operating unconsciously in the psyches of both participants: each constitutes the perceptual field responsible for *evoking the archetype* in the other. That the process is permeated by the experience of love makes it rich in significance for both parties. To the mother it grants the energy and determination to provide her helpless charge with its life-support system in a hostile or indifferent world. To the infant this love is the basis of its entire future security. 'It is as if,' wrote Bowlby (1951), 'maternal care were as necessary for the proper development of personality as vitamin D for the proper development of bones.'

The sad truth is that just as children suffering from vitamin D deficiency grow up with bowed and distorted limbs, so children deprived of a mother's love are prone to develop rickets of the soul. This was recognized both by Freud and Jung long before Bowlby expressed it so graphically. Freud described the infant–mother bond as 'unique, without parallel ... the prototype of all other love relationships – for both sexes', and of all relationships Jung called this 'the deepest and most poignant one we know'. Jung also emphasized its biological basis, designating it 'the absolute experience of our species, an organic truth as unequivocal as the relation of the sexes to one another' (*CW* 8, para. 723). Indeed, our capacity to form a durable bond with a member of the opposite sex in later life is largely dependent upon the success (or failure) of this 'primal relationship' with mother.

Consistent experience of appropriate mothering confers upon the child a priceless gift which Erik Erikson termed *basic trust* – the secure feeling that mother, world and life can be trusted and relied upon. This is also sometimes referred to as the *mirror phase* of development, since, through her empathic sensibility, the mother is able to reflect back the emotions which seize hold of the child and make them intelligible to him. These earliest experiences are, therefore, crucial for healthy development and, when they proceed satisfactorily, act as a natural inoculation against the development of neurosis in later life.

The relationship which a mother provides is thus the most fateful of all relationships, and any woman who adopts the maternal role is taking on a huge and lasting responsibility. It is for this reason that nature has equipped woman so abundantly with *Eros* – the principle of love and psychic relatedness – for how else could she carry the burden of all that is required of her to bring her child to maturity? The moment the mother–child dyad is formed, Eros is constellated, and out of this nurturing matrix conscious identity is born. Awareness of the world, and security in the world, are thus created out of loving relatedness. We love life inasmuch as love was present in this our first great affair.

Paternal Logos

After the mother, the first person to whom an infant becomes powerfully attached is usually the father – assuming, of course, that he is there. The child's differentiation between these two parental figures probably begins very early on, since from the outset the father must feel, sound and smell different from the mother, as well as looking different. Moreover, the child was never physically united with him, or dependent on his body for nutrition: the father is thus the first person whom the child loves on a spiritual, as opposed to a physical, basis. As the relationship matures, there is also a growing awareness on the part of the child that father-love differs in quality from mother-love: it is less all-embracing, less uncritical. For the mother, it is usually sufficient that her child *exists*: her love is absolute and largely *unconditional*. A father's love, on the other hand, is somewhat more demanding: it is *contingent* love, conditional upon the adoption of certain values, standards and modes of conduct which are acceptable to him.

This accords with the phenomenological differences between the mother and father archetypes. While the mother archetype finds universal expression as Mother Nature, womb of life, goddess of fertility, dispenser of nourishment, the father archetype is personified in myth, dream and legend as Ruler, Elder, King. As Lawgiver he speaks with the voice of collective authority and is the living embodiment of the *Logos principle*: his word is law. As Father in Heaven, he symbolizes the spiritual aspirations of the masculine principle, and he sits upon a throne from which he passes judgement, rewarding with boons and punishing with thunderbolts.

'The archetype of the mother,' wrote Jung, 'is the most immediate one for the child. But with the development of consciousness the father also enters the field of vision, and activates an archetype whose nature is in many respects opposed to that of the mother. Just as the mother archetype corresponds to the Chinese *yin*, so the father archetype corresponds to the *yang*. It determines our relation to man, to the law and the state, to reason and the spirit and the dynamism of nature' (*CW* 10, para. 65).

The archetypal association of Logos (Greek, 'word', 'reason') with spirit and the masculine principle is exemplified in creation myths like Genesis. 'In the beginning was the Word,' says St John, 'and the Word was with God, and the Word was God.' Logos is the embodiment of divine intelligence: it brings order out of chaos and illuminates all creation with the light of consciousness. 'And the Spirit of God moved upon the face of the waters. And God said, Let there be light: and there was light' (Genesis 1:2). The development of consciousness and differentiation between the parents goes along with the emergence of gender identity in the first half of the second year and the beginnings of the use of language.

Language

The establishment of consciousness is immeasurably furthered when the child starts to use words – as, indeed, it was in the evolution of our species. With words we begin to create order in the world. This, too, is recognized in Genesis: 'And out of the ground the Lord God formed every beast of the field, and every fowl of the air; and brought them unto Adam to see what he would call them; and whatsoever Adam called every living creature, that *was* the name thereof.'

That the acquisition of speech is archetypally determined as part of the sequential blueprint for childhood development is supported by the researches of specialists in linguistics like Noam Chomsky and E. H. Lenneberg, who decisively reject traditional academic assumptions that language develops through imitation and learning, reinforced by rewards and punishments. In their view, every child comes into the world fully equipped with the capacity for speech: his brain contains a *language-acquisition device* which enables him rapidly to acquire the knack of using words and building sentences in a way that those around him will readily understand. This would help to explain why children everywhere begin to make rapid progress in the use of language between their eighteenth and twenty-eighth month and why the sequence of acquisition of linguistic functions is similar in all cultures.

Although individual languages differ with respect to their

grammar, Chomsky believes that their basic forms – what he calls their *deep structures* – are universal. Languages all perform the same functions in finite ways, and once their 'deep structures' have been defined, all languages should, he thinks, prove reducible to the universal (or 'archetypal') grammar on which all individual grammars are based.

Morality

As Lawgiver, the father is deeply implicated in passing on to his children the values, beliefs and attitudes of society. All societies codify themselves; and their continuity depends upon the ability of new members to assimilate the code. Were this not so, the aternative would lead to anarchy and a collective incapacity for competition or defence. Because of its fundamental importance for the survival of any human community, the *moral code* has everywhere been accorded the dignity of divine sanction. For this reason, Jung concluded that 'the idea of the moral order and of God belong to the ineradicable substrate of the human soul' (*CW* 8, para. 528).

Under the tutelage of his parents, the child acquires their version of the moral code and builds it into his own *moral complex*. Freud called this complex the *superego*, and thought that it developed during the *Oedipal phase* in response to a fear of being castrated as a punishment for forbidden incestuous desires. Jung, as we have seen, did not accept the universality of the *Oedipus complex* and insisted that there must exist an innate substrate for the superego in the brain, since the universally apparent phenomenon of *guilt* would otherwise be incomprehensible. Like anxiety, depression, hunger and sexual desire, guilt is an emotional characteristic of our species and, as a consequence, some innate structure must be responsible for its release.

If the child is under any coercion to learn the moral code, it arises not so much from fears of castration as from the fear of *abandonment* by the parents. The dread prospect of being cast beyond the pale on account of some unacceptable revelation of the Self is at the core of all feelings of guilt and all longings for punishment, reconciliation and atonement.

Acquisition of an effective superego is, therefore, a condition of the child's developing social autonomy as well as a guarantee of his continued acceptance as a member of the family group. As an inner policeman, the superego monitors both his behaviour and his thoughts so as to ensure some measure of conformity to group mores. In this way it functions as the keeper of the social contract and is the custodian of both character and culture: it is the *introjected parent* making society possible. Without it, we should live in a state of Hobbesian brutishness, aggressive psychopaths all, incapable of mutual toleration, polity or trust. Had the superego no foundation in phylogeny, our species could never have come into existence in the first place, let alone survived.

The shadow

Possession of a superego, however, imposes constraints upon the development of the Self. As parental quisling, it bugs communications passing along the ego–Self axis. When it gleans information about intentions which it judges incompatible with parental values, the superego intervenes to induce anxiety or guilt, and, not infrequently, it firmly cuts the wires, making further consideration of the subject impossible. So it is that those very persons in the environment who make actualization of the Self possible also require that some aspects of the Self must be *repressed* or otherwise hidden from view. As we saw in Chapter Four, these unacceptable components of the Self make up what Jung called the shadow personality, which is synonymous with the Freudian unconscious. It follows that the more rigid the cultural mores and the more coercive the parents, the more powerful and capacious the shadow.

Every time that superego censorship occurs it results in some degree of what Dr Edward Edinger has called *ego–Self alienation*. As development of the ego–Self axis proceeds, ego–Self *separation* alternates with ego–Self *reunion* in a rhythmic systolic/diastolic cycle. Ego–Self *alienation* is a painful disruption of this cycle, unavoidable from time to time but which, if too frequently sustained, can cause lasting damage to the growing personality. Criticism, blame, mockery and condemnation can be lethal weapons in the hands of a captious teacher or parent, as we shall see when we examine Jung's childhood.

Birth of the hero and the compulsion to explore

In mythology the dawning of consciousness is symbolized by the *separation of the world parents* (Father Heaven from Mother Earth) and the creation of light out of darkness. Sir James Frazer describes this in *The Worship of Nature* (1926): 'It is a common belief of primitive peoples that sky and earth were originally joined together, the sky either lying flat on the earth or being raised so little above it that there was not room between them for people to walk upright. Where such beliefs prevail, the present elevation of the sky above the earth is often ascribed to the might of some god or hero, who gave the firmament such a shove that it shot up and has remained up above ever since.' This separation of the parents is followed by the coming of light – the quintessential symbol of consciousness and 'illumination'.

Hero myths, in the Jungian view, reflect on the transpersonal plane the normal development of ego-consciousness and personality from infancy to adulthood. In addition to developing consciousness and differentiating between and from the parents, the *hero archetype* is about leaving home, overcoming fear and establishing personal autonomy in the world. It begins to operate as soon as the infant can crawl and is at the bottom of that intense curiosity which impels all young creatures to explore their environment. Hence, it is a primary expression of the individuation principle – the inherent determination of the Self to seek dialogue with the environment and through dialogue to achieve living actualization of the archetypal endowment of the collective unconscious.

So strong is this imperative that it manages to override the need for maintaining physical proximity to the mother, and, by responding to it, the infant displays the first signs of *autonomy* – his ability to function as an independent unit.

To begin with, the infant appears to make little distinction between his mother and the world. For him she *is* the world. Only later, with differentiating consciousness, does he begin to make a distinction between the two. But even then, it is as if he experiences the world as an extension of his mother, and, as a result, he extends his investment of libido in the mother to an investment in the world. In this way, the child's first perceptions of the world are permeated with Eros and verified through feeling and personal relatedness: gradually the world begins to rival the mother as a source of numinous enticement.

So exploration begins, with the mother functioning as a *secure base* to and from which the infant crawls in his heroic excursions. Repeatedly, he turns his back on her to go off on a brief adventure, only to return to reassure himself that she is still there. This recurrent to-ing and fro-ing is a paradigm of all subsequent development – a rhythmic cycle of separation and reunion, progress and regression, two steps forward and, with luck, only one step back.

The use of symbols

It is at this stage that the child begins to reveal one of the most interesting features of human psychology – the capacity to be passionate about *things* as well as people. For example, a child may become strongly attached to a soft toy, a piece of blanket or a rag, almost anything that can be sucked or cuddled. Dr D. W. Winnicott, who made a study of this phenomenon, called these precious things *transitional objects*, maintaining that their use represents the beginning of the capacity to use *symbols*. Transitional objects are symbols of the mother. They are of special value to a child on going to bed at night, or when feeling lonely or anxious, for the very good reason that they possess the magical power of rendering the absent mother symbolically present. Winnicott points out that by using symbolism in this way 'the infant is already distinguishing between fantasy and fact, between inner objects and external objects, between primary creativity and perception.' For it is true that transitional objects are *not* internal objects, since they exist outside the child. They are equally *not* the mother or the breast for which they stand as symbols. They are *intermediary* between the inner subjective world of the imagination and the outer objective world which is shared with everyone else. They also become invested with those emotions which are normally associated with the presence of the mother and with physical contact with her. They are thus the first indications of the individual's emerging capacity to live what Jung called *the symbolic life*.

Play

Exploration and the use of symbols are both indispensable to the most serious business of childhood, which is *play*. Play is nature's mode of education. Through play we acquire those basic skills which guarantee our autonomy. For this reason, the hero archetype is implicated in all games, however free and spontaneous they may appear: *au fond*, they are all about the struggle to break free from infantile dependence and achieve ever greater competence. They are also intensely enjoyable – a fact that demonstrates just how important play must be, for activity which is essential to the survival of the species is made intrinsically rewarding by nature. Hence, for example, the amazing delights of sex.

Most learned discussions of the function of play overlook this point. They forget that play is its own reward. Its biological importance may be inferred from its ubiquitousness: play not only transcends culture, it is much older than culture, older than humanity itself. All mammals do it, especially young mammals. In his great work on the subject, *Homo Ludens*, Johan Huizinga comments that if you watch young puppies, kittens or chimpanzees you discover that all the essentials of human play are present. 'They invite one another to play by a certain ceremoniousness of attitude and gesture. They keep to the rule that you shall not bite, or not bite hard, your brother's ear. They pretend to get terribly angry. And – what is most important – in all these doings they plainly experience tremendous fun and enjoyment.' He adds that 'In play there is something "at play" which transcends the immediate needs of life.' The truth is that all the archetypal activities of human life are filled with possibilities for play. Hence Schiller's famous aphorism, 'Man is only truly himself when he is at play.'

By ensuring that children play, nature provides the means of activating the unconscious potential and training the behavioural systems which are vital to life: social co-operation and conflict, intimacy with peers, sexuality, physical combat, the control of aggression, hunting, ritual, marital relations, child-rearing and creativity. Childhood is a period of immense vitality and inventiveness, when imagination is given free rein to complement the realities or compensate for the deficiencies of everyday existence. This is why all children are artists, actors and showmen, and why most of us experience nostalgia from time to time for this period of our lives.

It is one of the misfortunes of growing up that we readily lose touch with this rich land of childhood, becoming too set in our ways to delight in the spontaneous inventiveness of play. Yet nothing is lost to the Self, and play, like the child who sponsors it, lives on as a propensity of the psyche to its dying day. As Pablo Picasso observed, 'Every child is an artist. The problem is how to remain an artist once he grows up.' Perhaps one of the functions of art is to keep the child alive in us. As an archetypal symbol the child-hero evokes creative potential, future life and new possibilities, and, as Jung demonstrated in his own life, it is always possible for the adult ego to experience its influence in play or in spontaneous, uncritical use of the arts. When as a grown man Jung felt stuck in his life or work, he confessed that he would go and play in his garden, building model villages, dams and water works, so as to bring himself back into touch with the creative resources of childhood. And as we shall see, his use of *active imagination* and spontaneous drawing and painting after his break with Freud provided him with the material on which his psychological discipline was based.

Fantasy

Above all, childhood is the period of *fantasy* – that primary autonomous activity of the psyche which Jung called 'the mother of all possibilities'. Fantasy is itself a form of play – *introverted* play – and it is every bit as crucial for development as *extraverted* play. All children naturally indulge in both forms of play, often at the same time, since many games involve unfettered use of the imagination. Should a child indulge in one form in preference to the other it is usually, as we shall see, a consequence of his psychological type and the influence of his family. For example, Jung's extraordinarily rich fantasy life was probably due to the fact that he was an introverted intuitive who grew up in an environment which induced in him feelings of loneliness and isolation.

Fantasy is vital to development because it forms a natural link between conscious and unconscious processes and between inner and outer worlds. Fantasy is the product of play between the archetypes of the collective unconscious and the living circumstances of the individual. In creating fantasies the unconscious draws on material from personal life (e.g., memories of people and events) but in a way that expresses the teleological intention of the Self. In the Jungian view, fantasy is not a regressive means of escape from reality, as Freud maintained, but the *modus operandi* of psychological growth: it is the stuff of life, leading us on into the future. 'Life is teleology par excellence,' wrote Jung; 'it is the intrinsic striving towards a goal, and the living organism is a system of directed aims which seek to fulfil themselves' (*CW* 8, para. 798). These aims are first tested out in fantasy, dreams and games.

Stories

They are also tested out in *stories*. Because of their vivid fantasy life, children love stories and are particularly susceptible to their influence. Human societies have made ingenious use of this childhood delight, creating fairy tales, myths and legends whose unconscious intention is unmistakably educational: when listened to with rapt attention, as they usually are, stories have the effect of weaving the child, through imagination, into the traditional fabric of the culture and, at the same time, activating in his psyche those archetypes which will determine his advance into the next stage of life. Jung was not alone in stressing the importance of stories: Melanie Klein, for example, stated her belief that *inner stories* (fantasies, myths and tales) were the dominant forces controlling development throughout childhood. The social implications of stories for children are as profound, therefore, as the personal implications – a truth which modern television producers would do well to ponder.

Ritual

A fascinating characteristic of this stage is the capacity children reveal for turning fantasy into *ritual*, the religious intention of which is often clearly discernible. The religious orientation of the parents (or lack of it) seems not to matter, for the rituals are of a kind that antedates Judaeo-Christianity and which points to much more ancient, frankly 'pagan', origins. For example, one little girl, strictly brought up in an exclusive Protestant sect, 'kept a god' in the family backyard in a secret space between the garden wall and the back of a coke shed. 'I didn't seek to placate him', she recalled, many years later, 'but I dropped loving gifts down to him, especially sticks spotted with coral fungus.' Her parents would have been horrified by such heathen practices had they known about them.

Sex and gender

Like every other major component of the Self, sexuality is present *a priori* as an archetypal component which manifests itself in the course of development. Freud drew attention to certain 'component instincts' of adult sexuality, such as clasping and pelvic thrust, as being present from a surprisingly early age and provided striking behavioural evidence for the existence of what he called, to the horror of his contemporaries, *infantile sexuality*. On the subjective plane, sexuality reveals itself in the dreams and fantasies of children, however naïve or sexually uninstructed they may be. Examples of this are frequently encountered in the recollections of patients undergoing analysis. For instance, the lady who as a child kept a god behind the family coke shed also whiled away the tedious hours of chapel meetings with spontaneously produced fantasies possessing unmistakable sexual and initiatory symbolism – though at the time of their occurrence she had absolutely no conscious knowledge of such matters. Here, with her kind permission, is one of her fantasies which recurred frequently between her fifth and twelfth years:

> There is a special building in the town which all girls proudly attend when the time comes for them to *Go Through the Pike*. Inside there is a wall from which will protrude long tapering pikes. One is assigned to each girl. At first only the tip, not more than half an inch in diameter, appears. This is introduced into a girl's vagina and passes out through her anus. The pike is yards long and, as it slowly emerges from the wall, it gradually increases in girth.
>
> To start with it runs through easily, but as it gets thicker it becomes very hard work. Eventually it is about nine inches thick and difficult to push through. But it is cleverly made so that it can be broken off at any point. This is necessary because it will

take weeks for the procedure to be completed. When she has done as much as she can, the child is allowed to go away, retaining the portion of the pike which is lodged between the front and back of her body. She will return next day to join up with the remaining pike and work to achieve another inch or two.

The child in the fantasy is doing very well. She has gone in unusually young, and she surpasses the efforts of the other girls who get stuck when the pike grows wide. Each day she walks home with her mother. Kind people stop to inquire how she is getting on, and say 'well *done*' in admiration when they are given a discrete glimpse of the great wooden round in her vulva, ready to be connected up the next day. This child achieves the whole pike, while the other girls cannot manage so much.

Boys' fantasies are, if anything, even more physically explicit and, more frequently than with girls, accompanied by masturbation. This is a necessary preparation for adult sexuality. It is also a form of *play* which, when not hedged round with puritanical horror or Victorian prohibitions, is a source of measureless delight. As with other forms of play, 'playing with oneself' is an expression of the individuation principle: it is a prospective activity preparing the child for a vital adult role – in this instance, physical bonding with a mate.

Differences of *gender*, already apparent at birth, become more evident as the child grows towards puberty. A child's awareness of its gender is established by as early as eighteen months of age, and the bond to the father is important if this is to be satisfactorily achieved. Studies of children reared without fathers have indicated that they are more likely to experience difficulty in defining their gender identity than children whose fathers are present during the first years of life.

Recent evidence is compatible with Jung's assertion that the existence of a strong and lasting bond to a reliable father-figure is particularly important if a boy is to actualize, in consciousness and behaviour, his own masculine potential. Many studies confirm the relatively high incidence of sex-role confusion in boys who grow up without fathers, and the relative absence of such confusion in fatherless girls.

Initially, the mother functions as 'carrier of the Self' (i.e., the child's Self is unconsciously *projected* onto the mother in their original *participation mystique*) for both her sons and her daughters, and this means that they become intimately identified with her, irrespective of their sex. Gender awareness is superimposed on this sense of oneness with the mother, and, as a consequence, boys have to make a revolutionary transformation from mother-identity to identification-with-father. Girls, on the other hand, are required to make no such radical readjustment. Thus, as gender-consciousness emerges, the boy comes to recognize that his bond to his father is based on shared *identity*, while the girl comes to appreciate that it is based on *difference* (i.e., the father presents her with her first profound experience, spiritually, physically and sexually, of the essential 'otherness' of the male).

Although a father is not crucial to the development of a girl's gender-identity, he can nevertheless significantly influence the way in which she *experiences* her femininity in relation to a man. Happy adjustment to her female role is greatly assisted if she enjoys her father's loving affirmation, while his rejection or mockery can cause deep wounds which may never heal. Girls who grow up without fathers may have little doubt that they are women, but when it comes to living with a man as his partner they can feel badly confused and unprepared. They lack the necessary psychic vocabulary.

Fathers and mothers are important, therefore, in enabling their children not only to establish a sense of gender but also in assuring their capacity to make good relationships with members of the opposite sex. This they achieve through their day-to-day influence over the developing *contrasexual complex* in the child's psyche, the father presiding over the differentiation of the *animus* (the male complex) in his daughters, the mother mediating the development of the *anima* (the female complex) in her sons.

Gender and contrasexual awareness, having been stabilized in relation to the parents, are refined through interaction with the peer-group – especially in play. Many of the gender roles and attitudes adopted by children in play are, of course, culturally related, based on mimicry of the parents and other significant adults in the community. But, as has already been noted, these cultural influences proceed on the basis of an archetypal design, determined by the evolutionary history of our species. Sexual dimorphism has resulted in females being responsible for bearing embryos and rearing young, and in males being responsible for driving off intruders, maintaining the protein supply and dispersing populations over the available terrain. This holds true of virtually all mammalian species and is reflected in the play patterns of their young. It has been particularly well documented in rhesus monkeys, for example, whose young males characteristically indulge in rowdy forms of rough-and-tumble play and whose females prefer to pass their time in more sociable activities such as mutual grooming. The archetypal basis for this difference has been demonstrated experimentally: deprived of all opportunity to learn through imitation, infants reared in isolation from birth will nevertheless manifest the behaviours typical of their sex when given the chance to do so on introduction to their peers.

Similar differences are apparent in the play patterns of human young, not only in our culture but in many others. Throughout childhood, girls tend to be more *affiliative* than boys in that they are more prone to seek the proximity of others and to display pleasure in doing so. Boys, on the other hand, are less interested in social interaction for its own sake and prefer to spend their time in some form of physical activity, such as running, chasing and playing with large, movable toys. They are also rather less amenable to control by adults and their peers.

As a consequence of the common contemporary assumption that all gender differences are mere *stereotypes* induced by society, some of Jung's assertions concerning the archetypal foundations of masculine and feminine psychology have come under attack in recent years. It should not be overlooked, however, that a number of basic gender differences exist which are unlikely to be stereotypical, since their occurrence seems to be largely independent of the type of society in which individuals are reared. For example, one study (Whiting, 1963) investigated the behaviour of boys and girls in six cultures – India, Okinowa, the Philippines, Mexico, Kenya and New England – and found essentially similar patterns of male and female behaviour in all of them. In all cases, girls were found to be more nurturant and affiliative, boys more physically active and aggressive.

It is not possible, of course, to make a clear distinction between the role of constitutional and cultural influences in the development of any form of human behaviour, since both factors are undoubtedly involved. However, those who wish to attribute all gender differences to cultural stereotypes, and who deny any archetypal or biological basis for them, have to explain why it is that such stereotypes should have arisen in the first place. Why have different cultures in widely differing parts of the world chosen to adopt similar stereotypes? Why should human parents universally encourage aggressiveness in their sons and nurturance in their daughters? Is it possible that these universal 'stereotypes' could have come into being did they not reflect some deeper biological origin?

Certainly, it is true that in all cultures stereotypes exist: they are part of the social code which one generation passes on to the next; but it seems unlikely that they are pure cultural inventions. Cultures are, after all, expressions of the archetypal nature of the men and women who make them up. It is more possible, as the ethological and cross-cultural evidence would indicate, that human societies tend to encourage or condone aggression in boys and reward nurturance in girls because boys are inherently inclined to greater aggressiveness and girls to greater nurturance. In some instances stereotype reflects archetype.

School tends to facilitate the emergence of these gender-related components of the Self: sexually segregated schools strengthen the identity of children with their own sex, while sexually mixed schools enable their pupils to fill out their *a priori* assumptions about the qualities and characteristics of the opposite sex. Whatever the academic environment, however, peer play between the sexes is an important preliminary to later success in courtship and marriage.

Ideally, the school years are a time of expanding social horizons and of ethical, spiritual, intellectual and economic preparation for life. The success of the exercise depends on the quality and conviction of the teachers, as well as the underlying pedagogic assumptions of the culture. Much depends on the child's *psychological type* and the stimulation it has received at home.

The psychological type

The distinction between introverted and extraverted children becomes apparent when they begin to explore the environment using the mother as a *secure base*. Parents and nurses report that some children are clearly introverts or extraverts from birth. Extraverted infants are said to be more active, more attentive and responsive to external stimuli, more prone to smile and babble at their parents than their introverted brothers and sisters.

> Type differentiation begins very early, so early that in some cases one must speak of it as innate. The earliest sign of extraversion in a child is his quick adaptation to the environment, and the extraordinary attention he gives to objects and especially to the effect he has on them. Fear of objects is minimal; he lives and moves among them with confidence. His appreciation is quick but imprecise. He appears to develop more rapidly than the introverted child, since he is less reflective and usually without fear. He feels no barrier between himself and objects, and can therefore play with them freely and learn through them. He likes to carry his enterprises to the extreme and exposes himself to risks. Everything unknown is alluring. (*CW* 6, para. 896.)

The archetypal fear of the strange is less apparent, it seems, in extraverted children. Jung goes on:

> To reverse the picture, one of the earliest signs of introversion in a child is a reflective, thoughtful manner, marked shyness and even fear of unknown objects ... Everything unknown is regarded with mistrust; outside influences are usually met with violent resistance. The child wants his own way, and under no circumstances will he submit to an alien rule he cannot understand. When he asks questions, it is not from curiosity or a desire to create a sensation, but because he wants names, meanings, explanations to give him subjective protection against the object. (*CW* 6, para. 897.)

Since extraverted and introverted potential are inherent within the structure of the Self, along with the four functions thinking, feeling, intuition and sensation, it is legitimate to ask what may determine the particular typological suit that a given child grows into. Three main factors would seem to be involved. First, *heredity*. Genetic factors may predispose an individual to be introverted or extraverted and to develop one or two of the four functions rather than others. Second, *parental typology*. Parents of a certain type may evoke development of the same type in their children through identification and mimicry, or, on the contrary, they may evoke development of the opposite type through rebelliousness or the child's need to live out unlived components in the parents' shadow. Third, *developmental perseveration*. There is a natural tendency for children (and adults) to play their strongest cards in life – that is to say, one comes to rely increasingly on one's prevailing attitude and superior function as, through trial and success, one discovers that it achieves the best results.

The probability is that all three factors are involved in the personality development of each individual. Of the three, the one which must be of primary concern to the psychologist is the influence of parental typology. Parents are not only embodiments of the parental archetypes but, as carriers of the Self, they become figures of childhood idolatry. An idolized figure is one on whom we project our as yet unrealized potential. The idolized person, having received the projection, then *mirrors* this unrealized potential, enabling us to 'see' it, recognize it and integrate it. The unconscious mechanism of projection is thus an indispensable contributor to psychic growth.

From the typological standpoint, all is relatively plain sailing as long as the particular shuffling of the parental genes dealt to the child at conception predisposes him to develop the same typology as one or both parents. Should the child's genetic endowment incline him to develop a different typology, however, difficulties can arise. Trouble is particularly prone to occur if, for neurotic reasons, parents attempt to coerce the child into being a type other than that which nature intended. It can be an excruciating experience, for example, for an intuitive introverted child to be forced into a thinking extraverted mould by a compulsive parent who has an inflexible belief that thinking and extraverted is what one *has* to be. Such treatment can result in the formation of *pathological complexes* which may seriously hamper development through the rest of life.

On the other hand, 'good enough' parents who respect typological differences in the child will further his individuation by carrying for him the neglected attitude and functions in his inherent psychic constitution. For as the individual matures, undeveloped, 'inferior' components in the Self are, through projection, delegated to others in the environment – parents, peers, older relations, teachers, and so on. This results in the other person assuming magical importance. The occurrence of crushes and the phenomenon of falling in love are often sexual, of course, but they are also a common form of unconscious expression whereby the loved person becomes the custodian of underdeveloped aspects of the Self. By attaching oneself to this beloved figure one enters a state of relative *participation mystique* through which, by repetition of the projection–reintegration cycle, these neglected aspects gradually become integrated in the personal psyche and available to consciousness. In this manner, loving attachment advances individuation.

Family matters

To sum up, then, maturation proceeds through a sequence of innate archetypal *expectations* which the environment either succeeds or fails to meet. The most important of these expectations are that the environment will provide adequate *warmth and nourishment* for survival; a *family* consisting of mother, father and peers; sufficient *space for exploration and play*; *security* from enemies and predators; a *community* to supply language, myth, religion, ritual, codes of behaviour, stories, values, initiation and, eventually, a *mate*; and an *economic* role and/or *vocational status.*

Of all these archetypal anticipations, the most crucial is that the environment will provide a family. That families exist as an archetypal characteristic of our species can be deduced from the fact that all societies have them. Whether monogamy, polygamy or polyandry is practised does not matter: the universal finding is that, whatever marital arrangements a society may favour, families are formed in which at least one man and at least one woman accept a commitment to one another for the purpose of rearing children. So stable is this family configuration that it has withstood deliberate attempts to dismantle it on ideological grounds – as, for example, in post-revolutionary Russia and in the early kibbutzim of Israel.

The family has always been with us, and it formed the basis of what we might call the *archetypal society* – the extended kinship group in which our species lived for 99 per cent of its existence. In discussing family matters, we should not forget that the archetypal components of the human psyche evolved hundreds of thousands of years ago, and that they have not changed much in the past half million years. These ancient archetypes not only determine our contemporary expectations of what the environment should provide but they influence our *experience* of what it *does* provide: what we feel about our personal parents, therefore, is conditioned by our archetypal expectations of them.

Clearly, the actual qualities and behaviour of the personal parents are of great importance for development, but ultimately what matters most are *the archetypal experiences activated by them* in their child's maturing psyche. The critical factors are not what the mother and father actually do or say but the *mother and father complexes* – whether they be healthy or pathological – which the parents are instrumental in forming. These complexes, which are the foundation of later personality development, are never simple internalized reproductions, or 'video-recordings', of the parents-out-there, but the elaborate products of continuous interaction between the personal parents in the environment and the primordial parents dwelling in the collective unconscious.

Having reviewed the main features of the archetypal programme for the first stage of life, we are now in a position to examine Jung's own childhood experiences in the light of these facts, and to consider their implications for the development of analytical psychology.

JUNG'S CHILDHOOD

The first dream that one can remember may be one of the most important dreams of one's life. This was true of Jung's first dream, and we shall begin by analysing it because it reveals much about his family, his culture, his psychology, and his fate.

> In the dream I was in this meadow. Suddenly I discovered a dark, rectangular, stone-lined hole in the ground. I had never seen it before. I ran forward curiously and peered down into it. Then I saw a stone stairway leading down. Hesitantly and fearfully, I descended. At the bottom was a doorway with a round arch, closed off by a green curtain. It was a big, heavy curtain of worked stuff like brocade, and it looked very sumptuous. Curious to see what might be hidden behind, I pushed it aside. I saw before me in the dim light a rectangular

> chamber about thirty feet long. The ceiling was arched and of hewn stone. The floor was laid with flagstones, and in the centre a red carpet ran from the entrance to a low platform. On this platform stood a wonderfully rich golden throne. I am not certain, but perhaps a red cushion lay on the seat. It was a magnificent throne, a real king's throne in a fairy tale. Something was standing on it which I thought at first was a tree trunk twelve to fifteen feet high and about one and a half to two feet thick. It was a huge thing, reaching almost to the ceiling. But it was of a curious composition: it was made of skin and naked flesh, and on top there was something like a rounded head with no face and no hair. On the very top of the head was a single eye, gazing motionlessly upwards.
>
> It was fairly light in the room, although there were no windows and no apparent source of light. Above the head, however, was an aura of brightness. The thing did not move, yet I had the feeling that it might at any moment crawl off the throne like a worm and creep toward me. I was paralysed with terror. At that moment I heard from outside and above me my mother's voice. She called out, 'Yes, just look at him. That is the man-eater!' That intensified my terror still more, and I awoke sweating and scared to death. For many nights afterward I was afraid to go to sleep, because I feared I might have another dream like that. (*MDR*, pp. 25–6.)

In practice, dreams usually yield something of their meaning if one approaches them in three stages. First, it is important to establish the context of the dream in the life of the dreamer: this will reveal something of its purely personal significance. Second, the cultural context of the dream needs to be defined, since it invariably relates to the spirit of the times. Third, one must explore the archetypal content of the dream so as to set its context in the life of mankind, for dreams link us in the most profound way with the age-old experience of our species.

We will apply this three-stage approach to the dream of the man-eater.

The personal context

Jung says that he was between three and four years old when he had this dream. He lived with his parents in the vicarage at

Laufen, which stood on its own, close to the Falls of the Rhine. Although his earliest memories were happy ones – the agreeable taste and smell of warm milk, the sun glittering through leaves, the Alps glowing sunset-red in the distance – he was, at the same time, oppressed by 'dim intimations of trouble' in his parents' marriage, and by a pervasive atmosphere of death, melancholy and unease. In his autobiography, Jung tells us that his nights were troubled with vague fears.

> The muted roar of the Rhine Falls was audible, and all around lay a danger zone. People drowned, bodies were swept over the rocks. In the cemetery nearby, the sexton would dig a hole – heaps of brown, upturned earth. Black, solemn men in long frock coats with unusually tall hats and shiny black boots would bring a black box. My father would be there in his clerical gown, speaking in a resounding voice. Women wept. I was told that someone was being buried in this hole in the ground. Certain persons who had been around previously would suddenly no longer be there. Then I would hear that they had been buried, and that Lord Jesus had taken them to himself. (*MDR*, p. 24.)

His mother attempted to comfort the boy's fears with a prayer she taught him to say every night:

> Spread out thy wings, Lord Jesus mild,
> And take to thee thy chick, thy child.

This did not have the desired effect. Children wonder about things, particularly when they are bright, and Carl was disturbed by the thought that he was a chick whom Jesus 'took', presumably as he 'took' other people when they were put in a hole in the ground. As a result, Carl began to distrust Lord Jesus and to associate him with 'the gloomy black men in frock coats, top hats, and shiny black boots who busied themselves with the black box' (*MDR*, p. 25).

Then there was a traumatic incident. 'One hot summer day I was sitting alone, as usual,' he reports, 'on the road in front of the house, playing in the sand ... Looking up, I saw a figure in a strangely broad hat and a long black garment coming ... It looked like a man wearing woman's clothes ... At the sight of him I was overcome with fear, which rapidly grew into a deadly terror as the frightful recognition shot through my mind: "That is a Jesuit"'

(*MDR*, p. 25). From something he heard his father say, Carl gathered that Jesuits were specially dangerous. He had no clear idea what Jesuits were, but he was sure that they must have something to do with Jesus. 'Terrified, I ran helter-skelter into the house, rushed upstairs, and hid under a beam in the darkest corner of the attic ... For days afterward the hellish fright clung to my limbs and kept me in the house' (*MDR*, p. 25). As this episode demonstrates, the stranger archetype was active in him and, with his Protestant family background, had become fleshed out, so to speak, by the alien and sinister image of 'the Jesuit'.

It was about this time that he dreamed of the man-eater, and already we know enough to make some important connections. In his dream, the little boy had dared very bravely, though 'hesitantly and fearfully', to enter the hole in the ground where Lord Jesus 'took' people. The underground chamber was a tomb, the lair of the subterranean Jesus. And his mother's chilling words, 'That is the man-eater,' are an echo of the dreadful realization, 'That is a Jesuit.'

Jung tells us that this dream haunted him for years, and that only much later did he recognize that the terrifying object he had seen on the rich golden throne was a huge erect phallus – 'a ritual phallus'. He says he could never discover whether his mother meant, '*That* is the man-eater' (i.e., that it was the phallus which devoured people) or 'That is the *man-eater*' (i.e., that the phallus merely 'stood for', or belonged in some way to, Lord Jesus and the Jesuit). But, evidently, the phallus was of the utmost importance, for there it stood, huge, erect and inexpressibly frightening, on a throne beneath the earth.

Instead of God and Lord Jesus sitting in all their glory on more magnificent thrones high up in the blue heavens, there lurked something very different in the subterranean depths, 'something non-human and underworldly, which gazed fixedly upward and fed on human flesh ... a subterranean God "not to be named", and such it remained throughout my youth, reappearing whenever anyone spoke too emphatically about Lord Jesus. Lord Jesus never became quite real for me, never quite acceptable, never quite lovable, for again and again I would think of his underground counterpart, a frightful revelation which had been accorded me without my seeking it' (*MDR*, p. 27).

There is another detail in the dream that requires examination, and that concerns the role played by Carl's mother. She is not close to him in this place of horror. She does not reassure or protect him, nor is she there to comfort him. On the contrary, she heightens his terror when her disembodied voice says, 'That is the man-eater.' How are we to understand this?

We know from the work of Bowlby and his colleagues that one of the most distressing and disruptive things that can happen to a young child is loss of, or separation from, its mother. As Bowlby amply demonstrated, the protest and despair which forced separation induces are *primary responses* which are not reducible to other causes: they are due to the *a priori* nature of the attachment bond – that is to say, to the frustration of the child's absolute need for the maternal presence. The extent of the child's suffering and the damage caused is related to the duration of the separation: brief separations are bad enough; long ones can be devastating. Children predictably pass through three stages, which Bowlby described as protest, despair and detachment, and he showed how the experience of separation can affect the personality for life. In particular, the development of *basic trust* tends to be impaired, the child becoming a prey to neurotic anxiety and to doubts about its capacity to elicit care and affection – a state which Bowlby termed 'anxious attachment'. The result can be the adoption of a defensive posture of *detachment* from others, the child becoming self-absorbed and self-reliant to an unusual extent. Such individuals appear 'odd' to their fellows, who may be disconcerted by their remote, somewhat aloof manner, and they commonly experience difficulty in achieving social integration at school and within their local community.

This fate seems to have befallen Jung as a result of his mother's depressive illness during his early childhood and his prolonged separation from her on this account at the age of three, at about the time of this dream. 'My mother spent several months in a hospital in Basel, and presumably her illness had something to do with the difficulty in the marriage.' In her absence he was cared for by an aunt and by the family maid, but he was 'deeply troubled' by his mother's being away and developed a form of nervous eczema. 'From then on, I always felt mistrustful when the word "love" was spoken. The feeling I associated with "woman" was for a long time that of innate unreliability. "Father", on the other hand, meant reliability and – powerlessness' (*MDR*, p. 23).

We shall be returning to these circumstances and examining their consequences further.

Certainly, Emilie Jung's withdrawal from her son into depressive illness may help to explain the lack of maternal protectiveness and reassurance in his dream; but it does not enable us to understand why such an alarmingly obscene image of 'Lord Jesus mild' should erupt from the unconscious of a little boy living in a Swiss parsonage in 1879. To do this we must move on to consider the cultural context of the dream.

The cultural context

Sexual puritanism, so prevalent in Europe during the second half of the nineteenth century (until Freud discovered that it was making people ill), was nowhere more oppressive than in Switzerland. It is not surprising that young Carl felt quite unable to share his dream with anyone and guarded it for most of his life as a deadly secret. In those days there would have been no phallic talk in the home of a country parson. Sex was the unmentionable subject: it was suppressed and (as Freud revealed) *repressed* 'underground'. In portraying this state of affairs so dramatically the dream would almost seem to be trying to compensate for it in some way by bringing it to the attention of the dreamer. Somehow, unbidden and without his seeking it, a parson's small son was granted a vision of the great phallus of Lord Jesus, whom nineteenth-century pietism had castrated. 'I do not know where the anatomically correct phallus can have come from,' commented Jung. 'The interpretation of the *orificium urethrae* as an eye, with the source of light apparently above it, points to the etymology of the word phallus (φαλός, shining, bright)' (*MDR*, p. 27). It is as if the ritual phallus were carrying the light of consciousness to illuminate the shadowy nether regions of the religious culture into which the child had been born.

Such is the power of the sexual archetype that it will not be denied, however puritanical the culture. As children, we do not invent our sexual desires or fantasies; they happen to us. Parental attitudes may make them unwelcome, and even frightening, but they do not stop them from occurring. In Carl Jung, sexuality manifested itself not only in the overpowering symbol of the underground phallic god, but also in later anxiety dreams which, he says, occurred as a prelude to puberty, the sexual significance of which he understood only in adulthood: 'I had anxiety dreams of things that were now small, now large. For instance, I saw a tiny ball at a great distance; gradually it approached, growing steadily into a monstrous and suffocating object. Or I saw telegraph wires with birds sitting on them, and the wires grew thicker and thicker and my fear greater until the terror awoke me' (*MDR*, p. 31).

That phallic tumescence should be experienced by him as a threat is a subject that Jung does not examine. Unlike Freud, sexuality is something about which he was curiously reticent. We do not know how seriously affected he may have been by horror stories predicting the consequences of masturbation, but he cannot have escaped altogether from the repressive taboo which rendered all sexual experience unspeakable. We cannot know how fearful Emilie Jung may have been of her husband's penis, or how much Carl may have identified unconsciously with her fears, if she had them. But we do know that all was not well with the marriage.

At a time when large families were the rule, Pastor Jung and his wife had only three children. The first of these, Paul, was born in 1873 and survived only a few days. Then, after Carl's birth in 1875, there was a nine-year gap before his sister, Gertrud, was born in 1884. She never married. Since no clergyman in those times would have countenanced the use of contraception, it seems unlikely that conjugal relations between the couple were very passionate. Indeed, Jung tells us that his parents slept in separate rooms, that he slept in his father's room (is it possible that Carl glimpsed his father's erect penis when thought to be asleep?) and that, as a result of the strained relations between his parents, he suffered from psychosomatic attacks of choking, during which he feared he would suffocate: 'the atmosphere in the house was becoming unbreathable' (*MDR*, p. 32). Clearly, there was a deal of sexual tension in the air, and Carl felt himself to be its victim.

The Jung parsonage was not the only household to be afflicted with gloom and despondency at that time. Religious conviction as a potent source of spiritual vitality was departing from the world of everyday existence. Pastor Jung struggled, so his son tells us, through daily repetition of his offices, to keep his faith alive, but, to his private grief, he knew the battle to be lost. Later in childhood Carl was to feel compassion for him, when he began to realize what ailed his father as he worked so conscientiously among his flock. In the pulpit, everything he said sounded stale and hollow, 'like a tale told by someone who knows it only by hearsay and cannot quite believe it himself. I wanted to help him but I did not know how' (*MDR*, p. 53).

It is not impossible that the pastor's feelings of spiritual impotence extended from the religious to the sexual sphere of his life, in which case Carl's dream would have served to compensate for both inadequacies on the masculine side of the family. Whether or not this is so, the pastor's private struggle, like his son's secret dream, was a response to the spiritual malaise of the times. God was not only emasculated, but, as Nietszche diagnosed, he was dead. The Gothic cathedrals of Europe were but his tombs and monuments. The life cycle of a great religion was following its inexorable course. For all gods 'die' eventually and return to the soil from which they sprang, there to undergo a transformation ending in their rebirth in another form. Such a fate was preordained in the Christian myth at the moment of its inception – in the passion and death of Christ, his deposition from the cross, his sojourn in the tomb and his resurrection. The cycle was now repeating in microcosm in the inner myth of this family: what was dying in the father was reincarnating in the son – as the phallic god 'not to be named'.

The archetypal context

We begin to see that this dream of a young child reaches beyond the confines of his personal history to touch on themes which have universally been the concern of humanity – life, death, sex, religion and even cannibalism. Jung confesses that it was not until fifty years after the dream that 'a passage in a study of religious ritual burned into my eyes, concerning the motif of cannibalism that underlies the symbolism of the Mass. Only then did it become clear to me how exceedingly unchildlike, how sophisticated and oversophisticated, was the thought that had begun to break through into consciousness' (*MDR*, p. 28).

Even as a little boy he experienced an urgent curiosity to know where such dreams came from: 'Who was it speaking in me? . . . Who talked of problems far beyond my knowledge?' (*MDR*, p. 28). As a result of the man-eater dream, and others which followed it, the realization grew on him that he had access to a source of knowledge which was independent of anything he had experienced in the Laufen parsonage. Where could this have come from, were it not directly from God? This thought ensured that this and all subsequent dreams carried a religious connotation for him. When he contemplated his phallic dream, it was its religious rather than its sexual implications that interested him and continued to interest him for the rest of his life. When he mentioned the phallus in his writings it was usually in connection with its ancient religious symbolism, e.g., 'The phallus is the source of life and libido, the creator and worker of miracles, and as such it was worshipped everywhere' (*CW* 5, para. 146). That phallic worship was ever as universal as Jung suggests is open to doubt, but it is still extant in the Shivaite cult of Hinduism, the world's oldest religion, which originated about ten thousand years ago. Shiva is worshipped in the form of the *lingam*, which appears as an upright stone, an ithyphallic (Greek, *ithys* = upright) image of the god, or as a wooden pillar.

Already, in discussing the archetypal context of this dream, we have begun to use a procedure of which Jung was an enthusiastic advocate and which he called *amplification* – the comparison of dream images with homologues derived from myth, religion, ethnography, cultural history and art.

One of the most gifted of practitioners in the art of dream amplification is Dr Marie-Louise von Franz of Zürich, and she has linked the man-eater phallus with the grave-phallus which ancient Etruscans, Greeks and Romans used to erect over a man's tomb as a symbol of the after-life of the spirit. In discussing his dream, Jung agreed that the hole through which he descended in the meadow represented a grave: 'The grave itself was an underground temple whose green curtain symbolized the *meadow*, in other words the mystery of Earth with her covering vegetation' (*MDR*, pp. 26–7). In ancient Egypt the spirit of vegetation was embodied in the person of Osiris, god of the underworld, who underwent a ceaselessly recurring cycle of death and rebirth. When an Egyptian king died, his spirit was identified with that of Osiris, who was represented by a phallic 'Djed' pillar (the trunk of a fir tree), erected in the burial chamber in order to guarantee the resurrection of the king.

In ancient Greece, the equivalent of Osiris was Hermes, the

messenger of the gods. Hermes means 'he of the stones', and stone heaps were used to mark roads and boundaries. From cross-cultural evidence we know that stone heaps are archetypal images of gods. Later representations revealed him as ithyphallic, and, as with Shiva, the images were of wood or stone. Hermes also appears as a *herm* – a rectangular pillar with bearded head and erect phallus, placed as guardian at the entrance to houses. Like Shiva and Osiris, Hermes was a phallic god. All three stand proudly erect as sacred manifestations of the masculine spirit, its generative life-force and creative energy.

This excursion into archetypal symbolism widens the basis for an understanding of Jung's dream. It also affords an opportunity to demonstrate a crucial feature of Jungian dream interpretation. A symbol is a psychic statement, complete in itself. It comes into existence as the best possible expression of meaning that the psyche can achieve at the moment of symbol-creation. Because every symbol encompasses more than can be said about it, it is important not to 'reduce' it to its archetypal origins, but to *amplify its meaning* by examining it in an archetypal light. When working with a dream symbol, one must not rationalize it or smother it with categories but *circumambulate* it (literally, walk round about it), so to speak, reflecting its different facets in consciousness. Amplification is, therefore, essentially a *circumbendibus*, a round-about method, by which one gives due honour to the symbol.

To circumambulate the symbolism of Jung's dream is to see that it is related not just to the marital problem of his parents, his mother's withdrawal or the spiritual crisis of his culture, but to the eternal human themes of life, death, rebirth, renewal and masculine generativity. More important still, it permits us to participate in a *felt* awareness of the profundity of the dream's implications.

Only the most striking dreams contain clear reference to archetypal themes, but, when these occur, they are experienced as awe-inspiring and 'numinous'. (*Numinosity* is a term which Jung borrowed from the German theologian Rudolf Otto, who used it to describe what he regarded as the fundamental experience common to all religions – namely, the sense of awe and exaltation generated by the feeling of being in the presence of the Creator, an experience which Otto designated the *mysterium tremendum et fascinans*).

Viewed in the context of the transcultural history of humanity, it is not at all surprising that sexual and religious themes should be combined in the mind of a Christian child – though it would doubtless have proved as shocking to his contemporaries as Carl feared. Different archetypal components can be activated in association with one another, and it is unremarkable that, in cultures other than our own, a conjunction between the sexual and sacred has occurred, and that this conjunction, when it is encountered, should still be experienced as *numinous*. It was Judaeo-Christianity which forced them apart, extolling the sacred and despising the sexual, while it could be said that Freudian psychoanalysis made the opposite mistake. Since any archetypal symbol is an opening to the *numinosum*, itself identical with awe of the gods, it is understandable that the phallus, symbol of a primal generative power, should be experienced as holy.

Jung regarded this first dream as one of the major experiences of his life. He never forgot it. It was his first encounter with the primordial ground on which all psychic life is based. Already a deeply introverted and solitary child, it emphasized for him the supreme importance of inner events, a conviction which grew ever richer with time, so that in old age he could still be moved by Sir Thomas Browne's dictum, 'We carry within us the wonders we seek without us: there is all Africa and her prodigies in us' (van der Post, 1975, p. 50).

This inner Africa compensated for a lifetime sense of solitude and isolation, and it meant that the fantasies and rituals common to childhood had for him a particularly vivid intensity. They were precious secrets, and he felt that his life depended on them. So important were they to him that he had no difficulty in remembering them in detail when he began work on his autobiography at the age of eight-two. One of them referred to his tenth year:

> I had in those days a yellow, varnished pencil case of the kind commonly used by primary-school pupils, with a little lock and the customary ruler. At the end of this ruler I now carved a little manikin, about two inches long, with frock coat, top hat, and shiny black boots. I coloured him black with ink, sawed him off the ruler, and put him in the pencil case, where I made him a little bed. I even made a coat for him out of a bit of wool. In

> the case I also placed a smooth, oblong blackish stone from the Rhine, which I had painted with water colours to look as though it were divided into an upper and lower half, and had long carried around in my trouser pocket. This was *his* stone. All this was a great secret. Secretly I took the case to the forbidden attic at the top of the house (forbidden because the floorboards were worm-eaten and rotten) and hid it with great satisfaction on one of the beams under the roof – for no one must ever see it! I knew that not a soul would ever find it there. No one could discover my secret and destroy it. (*MDR*, p. 34.)

This gave him a feeling of safety and protection.

> In all difficult situations, whenever I had done something wrong or my feelings had been hurt, or when my father's irritability or my mother's invalidism oppressed me, I thought of my carefully bedded-down and wrapped-up manikin and his smooth, prettily coloured stone. From time to time – often at intervals of weeks – I secretly stole up to the attic when I could be certain that no one would see me. Then I clambered up on the beam, opened the case, and looked at my manikin and his stone. Each time I did this I placed in the case a little scroll of paper on which I had previously written something during school hours in a secret language of my own invention. The addition of a new scroll always had the character of a solemn ceremonial act ... my 'letters' constituted a kind of library for him. (*MDR*, p. 34.)

At the time he had no idea why this ritual carried such significance for him. He was satisfied to possess something that no one else knew about. It was an inviolable secret which must never be betrayed:

> This possession of a secret had a very powerful formative influence on my character; I consider it the essential factor of my boyhood. Similarly, I never told anyone about the dream of the phallus; and the Jesuit, too, belonged to that mysterious realm which I knew I must not talk about. The little wooden figure with the stone was a first attempt, still unconscious and childish, to give shape to the secret. (*MDR*, p. 35.)

As a child he never thought of a connection between Lord Jesus, the Jesuit in a black robe, the men in frock coats standing at the graveside, the underground temple of the phallus, and his little man in the pencil case. 'The dream of the ithyphallic god was my first great secret; the manikin was the second ... They are the individual shoots of a single rhizome, like stations on a road of unconscious development' (*MDR*, p. 39).

Throughout his childhood he was interested in all the things that delight boys, who always and everywhere, it seems, love to play at building things (and then destroying them), at battles and other variations of group conflict, usually requiring the use of weapons. But, characteristically, he preferred, on the whole, to play them on his own: 'I played alone, and in my own way ... I was passionately fond of playing with bricks, and built towers which I then rapturously destroyed by an "earthquake". Between my eighth and eleventh years I drew endlessly – battle pictures, sieges, bombardments, naval engagements' (*MDR*, p. 31).

He did not mix well with other children and had few friends, for he was a vulnerable, timid child. 'This timidity was ... linked with a distrust of the world and its potentialities. To be sure, the world seemed to me beautiful and desirable, but it was also filled with vague and incomprehensible perils. Therefore I always wanted to know at the start to what and to whom I was entrusting myself. Was this perhaps connected with my mother who had abandoned me for several months?' (*MDR*, p. 42). In the light of what we now know about the consequences of maternal separation in early childhood, it probably was. It appears to have impaired his development of 'basic trust', and this made for difficulties when he went to school, where his schoolfellows and schoolmasters caused him to feel alienated from himself and compounded the lack of basic trust induced by his mother's depressions and absence. He felt that his teachers thought him stupid and crafty and his schoolmates were hostile to him. His sense of personal singularity was heightened on a traumatic occasion when a master accused him of copying an essay which was entirely his own work and of which he was justly proud. He protested his innocence in vain. 'My classmates threw odd glances at me and I realized with horror that they were thinking, "A-ha, so that's the way it is"' (*MDR*, p. 72). Henceforth he felt branded and completely isolated: 'all the paths which might have led me out of unusualness had been cut off' (*MDR*, pp. 72–3).

These experiences accentuated his introverted disposition and increased his investment in his 'secret' inner life, which was more exciting and more trustworthy than the life proceeding round him. 'I remained alone with my thoughts. On the whole I liked that best. I played alone, daydreamed or strolled in the woods alone, and had a secret world of my own' (*MDR*, p. 58).

CONSEQUENCES FOR JUNG'S PSYCHOLOGY

Although he could not have known it at the time, this reclusiveness was to have profound consequences for twentieth-century psychology: Jung's introspective concentration, which started in childhood and increased in intensity over the years, caused him to become vividly aware of psychological events which most of us ignore – for good reason. We ignore them precisely because we are *too successfully related to the outer world.*

Some degree of dissonance between inner and outer worlds is common to all human beings, and the need to correct this can be a powerful source of creative endeavour. However, if the dissonance becomes too great, then sanity is threatened, and it requires the mobilization of much psychic energy to prevent the two worlds from splitting apart. Jung gives several intimations of this split occurring in his own life: 'I had a premonition of an inescapable world of shadows ... I sensed a splitting of myself, and I feared it. My inner security was threatened' (*MDR*, pp. 32–3).

It is, alas, always possible for the compensatory functions of the psyche to break down completely; but they can also work to heal the split through the symbolic power of the imagination, and this psychodynamic was at the heart of Jung's achievement.

In this he resembled other intellectual pioneers who, deprived of their mothers in early childhood, abandoned hope of achieving emotional fulfilment in the outer world of human relationships, and turned inwards to create a symbolical world which was for them of equal validity. Two such men were Isaac Newton and René Descartes: both suffered maternal deprivation in infancy; both lived reclusive lives; and both constructed intellectual worlds of such ingenuity that they made the scientific age possible.

As Dr Anthony Storr has suggested in his fine book *The Dynamics of Creation* (1972), it is likely that, had Newton and Descartes received all the maternal love they required, they would have felt too emotionally at home in the world to become intellectually objective about it. For them, as for Jung, scientific hypotheses carried a value similar in quality to a child's transitional object: hypotheses were the symbols through which they found meaning and fulfilment in life.

Jung's discovery of the collective unconscious, his theory of archetypes, his psychological typology and his description of the structure and function of the psyche were at once consequences of his emotional isolation and brilliant attempts to compensate for it. It was no accident that the *principle of compensation* between inner and outer realms of experience became the cornerstone of analytical psychology.

The childhood insight that did most to sustain him was that the inner symbolical life possesses an absolute *primal* validity, which we share with all the human beings that have ever lived. When, in his early thirties, he began to prepare the book on *Symbols of Transformation* which was to be the final cause of his rupture with Freud, he read about a cache of 'soul-stones' near Arlesheim, and about the *churinga* stones of the Australian Aborigines, and realized that they were derived from the same source as the painted stone he had placed in his pencil case with the manikin long before as a child. *Churinga* was a term used for sacred ritual objects, especially decorated oval stones of any size from a few inches to several feet in length, which came from the mythical 'dreaming' time. They were caressed by hunters before the chase, rubbed over the body as a cure for sickness and, most important, they were used in initiation rites, which culminated in the revelation of the *churinga* stone to the initiate. Through the *churinga* the life force of the ancestors was shared with the initiate, and continuity was established between the present and the past, between individual, tribe and ancestor. Further research enabled him to make other connections, too: 'The manikin was a little cloaked god of the ancient world, a Telesphorus such as stands on the monuments of Aesculapius and reads to him from a scroll' (*MDR*, p. 35). With these realizations, he tells us, came his first clear intimation that there must exist 'archaic psychic components which have entered the individual psyche without any direct line of tradition'.

> Ultimately, the manikin was a *kabir*, wrapped in his little cloak, hidden in the *kista*, and provided with a supply of life-force, the

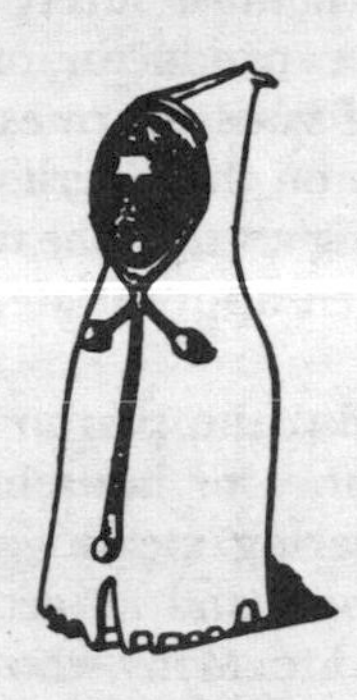

Figure 7 Telesphorus, one of the Kabiri, the *familiaris* of Aesculapius: (a) bronze figure in St Germain-en-Laye; (b) marble statuette in Avignon

> oblong black stone. But these are connections which became clear to me only much later in life. When I was a child I performed the ritual just as I have seen it done by the natives of Africa; they act first and do not know what they are doing. Only long afterward do they reflect on what they have done. (*MDR*, p. 36.)

Discoveries like that led Jung to the conclusion that 'the unconscious psyche of the child is truly limitless in extent and of incalculable age' (*CW* 17, para. 94). Moreover, he realized that symbols must possess implications which extend far beyond Freud's notion that they were symptomatic of latent sexual desires. To Jung symbols were living things, spontaneous creations which arose from the unconscious because 'God' had put them there – that is, the *means* for their production had evolved over the millennia – and this explained the human capacity for producing parallel symbols at different places at different times in history.

Freud could not have begun to give him a satisfactory interpretation of his childhood phallic dream, for he would have reduced it to a concern with mere genitality. To Jung a phallic symbol inferred much more than the penis; indeed, the penis is, he said, *itself* a phallic symbol!

The spirit which inspired Jung's life and the psychology that bears his name was already apparent in him as a child – a spirit essentially *hermetic*. And if, with hindsight, we are to give Carl's unnamed phallic god a name, then it must surely be Hermes, messenger of Zeus, god of travellers, conductor of souls. The friendliest and most approachable of gods, Hermes was a great benefactor of mankind, guiding men on their perilous journeys, presiding over their affairs, conveying to their hearts the sentiments which Zeus inspired and, when appropriate, conducting their souls to the underworld.

Curiously enough, Hermes was also the patron of servants, granting them skill in the performance of household duties – chopping wood, lighting fires, preparing meals – all crafts he learned as a servant of the Olympians, and all activities which were to delight Jung to the end of his life. Many who knew him in later life have testified to his ready hospitality, his irrepressible sense of humour and fun, his love of life and good fellowship and the Olympian quality of his laugh. After the great change that came over him in mid-life, he had what his friend Laurens van der Post called 'a genius for propinquity'.

However, it was as *Hermes Psychopompus* (conductor of souls) that the god most touched him: the guide and companion of heroes – Orpheus and Hercules – on their underworldly quests. As god of inner journeys Hermes turned Jung into a great explorer of the soul, granting him the insight that everything unconscious aspires to the condition of consciousness, and that this aspiration possesses a fundamentally *religious* intention.

So it was that a dream at the age of four set the stage for his life. His phallic tree trunk linked him directly to the ancient symbol of the *axis mundi*, a motif dating from the fourth millennium BC, which conceived the axis about which the whole cosmos rotates to be a phallic *tree of life*, its roots deep in the underworld, its trunk bearing rich foliage up to the heavens. The *axis mundi* was also central to the life of the shaman, whose initiation required repeated ascents of the world tree to parley with the gods and repeated descents to commune with the spirits of the dead. Jung's own brave descent into the underworld, initially accomplished at so tender an age, was to be repeated many times in the course of his long life, sometimes with almost disastrous consequences for his sanity, but he seldom returned from these perilous excursions empty-handed. It is to these shamanistic descents that we owe our understanding of the archetypal foundations of the human mind.

That first dream determined his fate. Henceforth the main focus of his interest would be underground, his destiny being a lifelong struggle to redeem the *numen* interred in this subterranean vault. His was to be the twelfth labour of Hercules, with Hermes as his guide. This extraordinary quest carried him into psychiatry, led to his association with Sigmund Freud, drove him into the study of Gnosticism, alchemy, mythology and religion, and culminated in the establishment of his own psychological discipline. Most important of all, the sperm generated by the dream phallus resulted, after thirty years' gestation, in the birth of one tremendous idea: *the hypothesis of the collective unconscious.* For psychology, it was possibly the twentieth century's most momentous epiphany. And it all started with a little boy's dream: 'Through this childhood dream I was initiated into the secrets of the earth,' he wrote at the end of his life. 'What happened then was a kind of burial in the earth, and many years were to pass before I came out again. Today I know that it happened in order to bring the greatest possible amount of light into the darkness. It was an initiation into the realm of darkness. My intellectual life had its unconscious beginnings at that time' (*MDR*, p. 28).

Figure 8 Hermes: Greek vase painting in the Hamilton collection

SUGGESTIONS FOR FURTHER READING

Pat Berry (ed.), *Fathers and Mothers: Five Papers on the Archetypal Background of Family Psychology*
John Bowlby, *The Making and Breaking of Affectional Bonds*
Michael Fordham, *Children as Individuals*
M. Esther Harding, *The Parental Image*
Corinne Hutt, *Males and Females*
C. G. Jung, *The Development of the Personality* (*CW* 17)
—— *Psychological Aspects of the Mother Archetype* (in *CW* 9, i)
—— *The Psychology of the Child Archetype* (in *CW* 9, i)
—— *The Significance of the Father in the Destiny of the Individual* (in *CW* 4)
Erich Neumann, *The Child*
Anthony Storr, *The Dynamics of Creation*
Frances G. Wickes, *The Inner World of Childhood*

Chapter Six

ADOLESCENT TRANSITION

THE ARCHETYPAL PROGRAMME

The tasks we all face as adolescents are formidable indeed: if one is to leave home, support oneself in the world, attract (and keep) a sexual partner and eventually start a family of one's own, then the bonds to the parents must be loosened, a job prepared for and found, sexual development completed, an appropriate persona acquired and enough confidence and self-esteem achieved to be able to hold one's head up in society.

The archetypal programme responsible for this elaborate transformation of the child into the adult can be summarized under four headings: (1) the attenuation of the parental bond, (2) the war of the generations, (3) the activation of the sexual affectional system and (4) initiation into the adult role.

Successful passage through each of these archetypal stages depends largely on the personal characteristics of the parents and the quality of the parenting they have provided throughout childhood. We will examine each of these factors in turn.

The attenuation of the parental bond

Just as nature is absolute in her decree that children must become bonded to their parents in the first year of life, so she is adamant that these bonds must be loosened soon after the onset of puberty. Evidence from human and animal studies shows that a lasting bond to a sexual partner is hard to achieve in adult life unless there were close and enduring bonds to parent figures throughout childhood. However, full sexual autonomy only occurs when these bonds have been sufficiently loosened. Then courtship and mating can proceed.

Within the adolescent psyche what seems to happen is that the parental archetypes lose their pre-eminence, young people becoming much more objective about their personal parents than hitherto. Moreover, as the parental archetypes lose their ascendancy, so other archetypal programmes scheduled to become active later in the ontogenetic sequence are alerted, and this is probably assisted by rapidly rising levels of sex hormones in the blood. The most apparent of these are the *hero* and *anima* archetypes in the boy and the *haitera* and *animus* archetypes in the girl, all of which promote awareness of identity with one's own sex and susceptibility to the compelling attractiveness of the other.

Just as the child withdraws the projection of the parental archetypes from his or her father and mother, so the parents now have to relinquish their *identification* with these archetypes in themselves and to withdraw their own projection of the child archetype from the adolescent.

Clearly, the most desirable outcome for all concerned is that both parties should withdraw their projections at the same time. Unfortunately, this is unlikely to occur, since it is improbable that powerful archetypal constellations could undergo such radical change at precisely the same moment – unless some dramatic event should arise which affected them all equally. It was this event that the initiation rite so effectively provided in pre-literate societies.

In our own culture this vital transition is less tidily arranged, the usual pattern being that the child withdraws the projections before the parents, or vice versa. In cases where parents persist in their projections after the children have begun to withdraw theirs, adolescents have little choice but to rebel and fight for their freedom. When, on the other hand, the parents withdraw their projections before the child is prepared to make any such withdrawal, the result can be the development of *anxious attachment* and the start of a quest for parental substitutes, the child remaining stuck meanwhile in adolescent psychology, unable to make any lasting commitment to a sexual partner or a job and doomed to live what Jung called 'the provisional life'. This is referred to in

Jungian circles as the problem of the *puer aeternus* (the eternal boy) or the *puella aeterna* (the eternal girl), and it can persist well into middle age.

For both sexes, therefore, the greatest danger at this stage is to be psychically devoured by the parental complexes and be incapable of breaking free. This is particularly liable to occur if the parents show reluctance to co-operate with their children in loosening the bonds which still tie them to the family. This peril is greater for boys than for girls, and its universality may be deduced from the ubiquitous mythical motif of the devouring monster that has to be slain if the hero is to win a damsel and inherit a kingdom. The monster may be a dragon that lives in a cave or a monster of the deep. It was these primordial matters that Jung dealt with in his *Symbols of Transformation.*

While the natural impetus of the Self is to take the individual onwards and outwards into life, this impetus is not so invincible that its goal can be achieved without assistance from the environment. Satisfactory accomplishment of the goals of adolescence depends primarily on whether or not the parents are, as D. W. Winnicott put it, 'good enough' – that is to say, whether they are capable of discharging the basic obligations of parenthood.

The father is particularly important at this time, for in our society, as in most others, he acts as the bridge between the family and the community at large. This is what the American sociologist Talcott Parsons (1955) called the father's *instrumental* role (as opposed to the mother's *expressive* role). Traditionally, the father's orientation is *centrifugal*, i.e., towards the outside world (in contrast to the mother's *centripetal* concern with home and the family), and his is the primary responsibility for facilitating the transition of his adolescent children from home to society. Through his *contingent* love he encourages the acquisition of those skills which will be necessary for adult life, while at the same time representing to the child the values and mores prevailing in the adult group to which he or she will have to adjust. In this guise the father is experienced as the embodiment of social authority and has a decisive influence on how the child will relate to authority throughout life. Inasmuch as he succeeds in his role, the father helps liberate the adolescent from involvement with the mother and fosters the autonomy needed for life as a full member of the adult community. In this sense his role is primarily *initiatory*. For her part, the mother, through her *expressive* role, provides the emotional support and the 'secure base' from which the adolescent will go out to meet the world's challenges.

Parsons's distinction corresponds closely, therefore, to Jung's differentiation between the father's *Logos* and mother's *Eros* functions. In contemporary society these differences between paternal and maternal roles are becoming less sharp, with more mothers developing instrumental capacities and fathers becoming more expressive in relating to their children.

However, the archetypal basis on which parenting proceeds does not change, for archetypes are as fixed as the genetic structure of our species, and, as has already been indicated, it is the degree to which the personal parents succeed in mediating the *archetypal* father and mother which determines whether they are *experienced* by their children as good enough. By the middle childhood years, children know whether their parents are up to the mark and are embarrassed for them when they are not, often to the extent of colluding with them to help conceal their deficiencies. Moreover, failure on the part of the parents to live up to the child's archetypal expectations of them will yield 'unfinished business' which will be carried on into adult life, where it will continue to exert a powerful influence.

What is of particular importance is the actual *quality* of the relationship which exists between the parents, for it is well established that later success or failure in relating to members of the opposite sex has much to do with experience gathered in childhood of repeated interactions between one's mother and father. The brutal husband who denigrates his wife will damage his daughters' self-concept and encourage equally chauvinistic attitudes in his sons. An ineffectual husband, on the other hand, who is patronized by his wife, will forfeit the respect of his children and fail to actualize in them those aspects of the father archetype which are concerned with the exercise of authority and the assertion of will. All schools of analysis are agreed that there can be no better start in life than to be born of parents who value and respect one another and who are consistently honest and loving in their personal dealings with each other and with their children.

So while it is true that the archetypal potential for heterosexual and parental behaviour is part of the constitutional endowment of us all, the degree to which any of us succeeds in actualizing that potential depends as much on how our parents treated each other as on how they treated us. Loving couples are the children of loving couples; loving parents the children of loving parents. A prime function of the family is to pass on the secrets of successful marriage and parenting to the next generation.

The contribution that happy, well-adjusted parents make to the lasting welfare of their children cannot be overestimated, therefore, and it is no cause for surprise to learn that the majority of people who consult psychiatrists with neurotic difficulties give a history of parental care which was deficient in some crucial way – deficient in the sense that the care provided was such as to frustrate the fulfilment of important archetypal expectations as they arose in the maturing Self, e.g., those concerned with the formation of attachment bonds, the development of basic trust, the emergence of a secure and competent ego, the integration of a moral complex adjusted to prevailing cultural values and so on.

In such cases, the commonest forms of parental deficiency noted are parental absence, loss or separation from the child, unresponsiveness to the child's attachment needs, the use of threats of abandonment and the induction of guilt as a means of discipline or coercion, and parental clinging on to the child so as to impair its autonomy. Of these, parental deprivation and loss are potentially the most disastrous.

On the whole, it is true to say that parents who provide adequate parenting tend to have children who deal satisfactorily with the tasks of adolescence and who become, in their turn, adults capable of being 'good enough' spouses and parents themselves. The outlook for children who have been inadequately parented is less promising, however. For them the tasks of adolescence may prove insurmountable, and, far from displaying eagerness to assume the responsibilities of marriage and parenthood, they are more likely to embark on an unconsciously motivated quest, like Flying Dutchmen seeking to redeem themselves from a bitter fate: they pass from one dependent relationship to another – employers, teachers, older companions and lovers – people perceived as being able to make good the deficiencies of the parents. The pangs of such *parent hunger* can be powerful indeed and may gnaw away in the unconscious for the rest of life.

There is, it seems, a critical period during which parents must be available, and a critical degree to which the parental archetypes must be activated, if normal development is to occur. It was Jung's most important contribution to the psychology of adolescence to realize that, from the viewpoint of the young adult, what the personal parents *succeed* in actualizing in the child's psyche is often not as significant as what they *fail* to actualize. Mothers and fathers are, after all, ordinary, fallible mortals, and ordinary women and men cannot hope to embody all the attributes of the mother and father archetypes: it is not reasonable to expect them to be more than good enough. Yet, as children we expect them to be gods, and it comes to all of us as a painful disappointment when we discover them to be fallible, like everyone else. As Oscar Wilde put it: 'Children begin by loving their parents; as they grow older they judge them; sometimes they forgive them.'

So good parents are those who actualize enough of the parental archetypes for us to complete the business of childhood and move on into the next stage of life; but what they leave unactualized persists as unconscious potential which will continue to seek fulfilment as individuation proceeds. The less adequate the parents, the greater unfulfilled potential, the more ravenous the parent hunger and the more obsessive the Flying Dutchman quest. 'Generally speaking,' wrote Jung, 'all the life that the parent could have lived, but of which they have thwarted themselves for artificial motives, is passed on to the children in substitute form. That is to say, the children are driven unconsciously in a direction that is intended to compensate for everything that was left unfulfilled in the lives of their parents. Hence it is that excessively moral-minded parents have what are called "unmoral" children, or an irresponsible wastrel of a father has a son with a positively morbid amount of ambition, and so on' (*CW* 17, para. 328).

It seems that the child is driven not only to make good the archetypal deficiencies of the parents but to live out powerful aspects of their shadows as well: 'To put it bluntly, it is that part of life that they have always shirked, probably by means of a pious lie. That sows the most virulent germs' (*CW* 17, para. 87). In all relations between parents and children, Jung argues, 'we seem to be dealing with some fate-like ethos beyond the reach of our conscious judgement. Such things as proletarian inclinations in the scions of noble families, outbursts of criminality in the offspring of the respectable or over-virtuous, a paralysing or impassioned laziness in the children of successful businessmen, are not just bits of life that have been left deliberately unlived, but compensations wrought by fate, functions of a natural ethos which casts down the high and mighty and exalts the humble' (*CW* 17, para. 90).

Families may be conceived, therefore, as homeostatic systems in which parents and children act as opposing poles which correct and compensate one another. The family system is, however, but a part of the larger social system, the opposite poles of which are the younger and older generations, and the conflict between them has affected all societies since human society began.

The war of the generations

Like all wars, the war of the generations is an essentially masculine affair. While mothers and daughters can become caught up in it, it is primarily a battle which involves fathers and sons. For children of both sexes the father is initially experienced as all-powerful. As carrier of the paternal archetype, he is the personification of masculine authority, of *Logos* and wisdom. Then, with the onset of puberty, the father archetype begins to lose its salience and sinks back deeper into the unconscious. Divested of his archetypal magic, the personal father emerges in all his human fallibility. Then he is judged. Loved and appreciated though he may be, he is gradually seen to be outmoded, obsolescent and somewhat in the way. To his sons, he is not so much a sexual rival, as Freud insisted, but an obstructive bastion of the old order. To his daughters, he is a constraint upon their sexual and social liberty. The more rigid the law he lays down, the more imperative it is felt that he be overthrown and replaced with a new order appropriate to the times. Repeated generation after generation, it is a theme of ancient lineage, recurring again and again in the ubiquitous myths of Old Father Sky castrated by his sons and forced to yield his power.

The biological perspective on this is illuminating. Through evolution, culture has come to perform in human societies the same function as instinct in mammalian societies, for culture is the means by which adaptive wisdom is passed from one generation to the next. Survival depends on how each generation relates to its cultural inheritance. While culture is a gift which each generation acquires, it cannot be taken for granted; it has to be *earned*. This is another reason why initiation rites have been of world-wide importance: they are enabling rituals through which the dying past is reincarnated in the living present.

Now, while the accumulated treasury of tested experience can never become obsolete between one generation and the next, cultural traditions would, nevertheless, stultify if they were handed on automatically, as in societies of ants. In all human communities, therefore, some sort of balance has to be achieved between the traditional forces of conservation and the progressive forces of change. Progress and survival demand that in the recurring conflict between the generations there should be no outright winner. A homeostatic balance must be maintained between the two opposing systems: the youthful revolutionaries and the elderly traditionalists. A complete break with tradition brought about by a walkover of the youthful progressives would imperil the competitive efficiency of society as much as the triumph of conservative inflexibility through an implacable dictatorship of elders.

Freud considered that the older generation of males was wary of the rising generation because of the *sexual* threat that it posed; but this is only part of the story, and not the most significant part. Male adolescence is cued by a sudden dramatic increase in the amount of male hormone circulating in the blood: this fuels the sexual appetite, it is true; but it makes for much more aggressiveness as well. This is why young males challenge the status and authority of their elders and not merely their sexual prerogatives. More important still, they threaten the coherence and viability of the group which cannot hope to survive in the struggle for existence if torn apart by inner strife between the generations. For this reason, all successful societies in the history of our species have had to find means of disciplining their young men and of channelling their energies into the service of society.

The dangerous moment comes at puberty when, intoxicated with a huge shot of testosterone, youths seek to shake off the constraints imposed by tradition and cast about for new ideals to pursue, new causes to embrace and new goals to be won. Konrad Lorenz has called this time 'the moult' (*die Mauser*), declaring that 'it implies hazards quite as great as those threatening the newly moulted soft-shelled crab'! He sees the pubertal moult as 'the open door through which new ideas gain entrance'. But these new ideas have to be compatible with the old and have to achieve balance with them: the arrogance of youth has to be countered by the wisdom of collective experience, as the young themselves come to appreciate when they get older. Plato understood this very well: 'You are young, my son, and, as the years go by, time will change and even reverse many of your present opinions. Refrain therefore a while from setting yourself up as a judge of the highest matters' (*Laws*, 888).

The arrogance of youth is a necessary arrogance, however. A boy needs conviction to make good his lack of experience if he is to break out of the family circle. Somehow, the bond to mother has to be loosened and the father has to be 'slain'. This psychological parricide requires, of course, not the actual demise of the father but slaughter of his outmoded beliefs. The son is then free to go the way of the hero.

The activation of the sexual affectional system

As Joseph Campbell has shown in his classic work *The Hero With A Thousand Faces* (1949), hero myths all have a great deal in common. The hero receives a call to adventure and sets out from his home. After he has crossed some kind of threshold he is subjected to a series of trials and ordeals. Eventually, he undergoes the supreme ordeal, which is the fight with the monster. When, finally, he defeats the monster, he is rewarded with *the treasure hard to attain* – that is, the throne of the kingdom and the beautiful princess as his bride.

These myths express in symbolic form the experience of Everyman: to embark on the adventure of life, he must free himself from his parents, leave home and cross the threshold into manhood. If he is to win a bride, he must undergo a second birth from his mother – a final breaking of the psychic umbilical cord. Victory over the dragon-mother often involves entry into her. Then, after a period in her belly, he succeeds in cutting his way out or causes her to vomit him up. Failure to overcome the monster signifies failure to get free of the mother: the hero languishes in her belly for ever, and the princess (the *anima*) is never liberated from the monster's clutches. She remains trapped in the unconscious in the vigilant custody of the mother complex.

Where the bond between mother and son persists with undiminished intensity into adulthood, Jung spoke of a 'secret conspiracy' as existing between the two partners through which 'each helps the other to betray life' (*CW* 9, ii, para. 21). To break free would be a heroic feat far beyond the boy's capacity, especially in the absence of a strong and effective father. To leave her, 'he would need a faithless Eros, one capable of forgetting his mother and undergoing the pain of relinquishing the first love of his life' (ibid., para. 22).

The sexual consequences of this 'secret conspiracy' are usually either homosexuality or Don Juanism. If the son's adjustment is homosexual, it is because his heterosexual libido has remained wedded, so to speak, to the mother and is consequently not available for another woman. When this happens there is not infrequently a history of a defective relationship with the father and an associated difficulty for the boy in realizing his own masculine potential. Denied heterosexual love by the unloosened bond to mother, he now embarks on an erotic quest for the masculine.

When male homosexuals come into analysis it is often because they have been questing, unsuccessfully, for two things: the love partner and the actualizer of the masculine, both condensed in the same figure. Consciousness of the meaning of this quest can pave the way for an 'individuation relationship' with another man, in which each helps the other to find what he is questing for. Analysis is often necessary, in addition, to free the individual from his mother complex, but this is not invariably the case, since there is evidently a genetic factor at work in the production of homosexuality, and by no means all homosexuals have been locked in a 'secret conspiracy' with their mothers. Homosexual behaviour is common throughout the animal kingdom and occurs as an alternative to the heterosexual bond in the most intelligent primates, such as rhesus macaques, baboons and chimpanzees. Sociobiologists accept homosexuality as entirely normal in a biological sense and believe that homosexuals have always existed in socially well-adapted populations because they are genetic carriers of rare altruistic propensities which are of importance to the survival of the group. Moreover, studies have revealed a greater concordance for homosexuality between identical twins than between fraternal twins – even when the identical twins are reared apart.

Development of a homosexual orientation, therefore, depends on several factors. If a genetic predisposition to the condition exists, it is hard to know whether an unresolved bond to the mother is an added cause or a consequence of the predisposition.

In the case of Don Juanism, however, matters are more straightforward. Here the son dares a little faithlessness to the mother by searching for her idealized replacement. Now the quest is for the ideal woman who is really all-mother: he is looking for an incarnation of the Great Mother Goddess. Each time he becomes infatuated with a woman he believes he has found what he is looking for. But, alas, no mortal woman can ever begin to come up to his inflated expectations, and so the goddess develops feet of clay, and he is forced to acknowledge that she is a mere mortal after all. Sadly, he drops her, and moves on to the next encounter. The cycle is often repeated many times.

More usually, in the majority of boys, however, the sudden increase in male hormone heralds a passionate interest in female sexuality. Since this cannot be experienced with the mother on account of the *incest taboo*, the adolescent is consequently driven to look elsewhere. He thus has a further impetus to loosen the ties to his mother and to heed the increasingly insistent promptings of his anima. The quest for the soulmate then begins.

In the development of female sexual maturity, similar difficulties can beset the relationship between fathers and daughters as between mothers and sons. If a girl is to conceive of herself as loveworthy and desirable, then it is important that she should have experienced a lasting bond to her father (or to a father substitute) and that this bond should have possessed an erotic charge. The erotic nature of the bond guarantees the significance of the relationship. Deprived of this experience, it is hard for a girl to pass into the reproductive stage of her life with any confidence that she will find or keep a male partner.

Many fathers manage to perform this function for their daughters with ease and genuine delight, but others can get it seriously wrong. While mothers experience a physically erotic bond with their sons from the start, fathers are often inhibited in giving any overt expression of their feelings of attachment to their daughters. They may appear indifferent or, through *reaction formation* (i.e., manifesting the opposite of something one feels guilty about), become sexually censorious or rejecting. This can do terrible damage to the girl's concept of herself as a female. Alternatively, the father may betray his symbolic responsibilities, as a result of some personal inadequacy, and attempt actual physical incest. This can result in feelings of shame and disgust in the daughter which can, without psychotherapeutic help, grievously complicate her sexual adjustment for the rest of her life.

So the expression of erotic love between parents and children is a tricky business. It has to be present, but it has to be self-limiting in both duration and intensity. That so many parents and children manage to do roughly the appropriate thing speaks volumes for the power of the archetypal programme which works unconsciously to promote erotic attachment in the first phase of childhood and to encourage its gradual attenuation in the last.

However, it is by no means an easy passage for everyone, and the enormous demand on psychiatric services for adolescents (where they are available) reveals how many young people experience difficulty in achieving the adolescent transition. One reason for this great and growing problem could well be the abandonment by our culture of socially sanctioned rites of initiation.

Initiation into the adult role

The majority of cultures known to anthropology have developed initiation rites for boys at or about the time of puberty. Comparison of rites from all over the world suggests that these initiation rituals themselves possess an archetypal structure, for the same underlying patterns and procedures are universally apparent.

As a rule, when a boy is judged ready, he is removed by older males from his mother and told that he will 'die' to the maternal world and eventually, after a series of great trials and ordeals, be 'reborn' as a man. During the heightened suggestibility of this state, he is instructed in tribal lore, myths, secrets, traditions and the arcane wisdom of the ancestors. Finally, there is a sacred ceremony when he is ritually mutilated (e.g., a tooth is knocked out, or he is subjected to circumcision, subincision or scarification) in order to render him for ever identical with the adult members of his sex. The whole procedure is a form of brainwashing or shock treatment designed to transform children into men capable of being brave hunters and defenders of the tribe, and it is conducted within a sacred context, with the absolute approval of the gods, who send the dreams which may be required for the ritual's completion.

Where they are practised, the greatest importance is accorded to these rites. They can be protracted over a period of many months, and the ordeals can be so great as to result in the death of some initiates. That such practices should have evolved and become so widely distributed demonstrates that they possess survival value. They are, in a sense, public-health measures whose purpose is to guarantee that the largest possible number of individuals will be able to meet the demands imposed by adolescence – namely, attenuation of the bonds to parents, achievement of a sense of identity and confidence as an adult member of one's sex, development of competence in a socially useful role, attainment of sexual maturity, readiness to mate for the purpose of procreation, and so on.

Puberty is a time of upheaval for everyone – for girls no less than boys. For the girl, the loosening of the bond to her parents is associated with the transformation of her body and personal identity from girl to woman and, in many cultures, from daughter to wife. However, this feminine transformation is usually accomplished by less elaborate means than the transformation of boys into men. While the majority of cultures have initiation rites for boys, comparatively few deem it necessary to organize similar rituals for girls. In those cultures where female initiation does occur, it is customarily a less demanding and protracted process than that required for boys. (The appalling rite of female circumcision is, fortunately, practised by very few societies and must be regarded as a form of cultural aberration.)

There are probably two main reasons for this disparity: in the first place, feminine gender consciousness does not demand a radical shift of identification from mother to father as it does in boys; and, second, females do not usually constitute a threat to the male social hierarchy. As a result, female initiation, where it occurs, consists essentially of a ceremonial recognition that a young woman has now entered the reproductive phase of her life.

Sometimes the ritual is conducted in stages: it may begin with the first menstruation, be extended during the first pregnancy and be completed with the birth of the first child. Through initiation, the woman comes to a full realization that, unlike man, she is *creative on the plane of life* and she is granted access to a realm of sacred experience that man can never know. Initiation thus heightens her introverted awareness of herself as a woman.

However, in many cultures this new feminine consciousness is marked by no rites at all, and it falls to the initiated male to foster its development through his recognition and pursuit of the girl's newly acquired womanhood: it is not an impersonal ritual but the intimate presence of a man that awakens the woman out of the slumbering child. Hence the heroine who, in myth, legend and fairytale, lies sleeping until her prince comes to awaken her with a kiss. She is the Sleeping Beauty surrounded by a thicket, or the slumbering Brynhild awaiting the arrival of her Siegfried within a circle of fire placed round her by Wotan. She is the goal of the hero's quest. And in the male psyche she is the anima who dozes patiently in the unconscious waiting for the heroic ego to slay the dragon-mother and inherit the kingdom.

For both sexes, then, initiation is a cultural strategy designed to promote severing of the bond to the parents and a public awareness that reproductive status has been achieved. In this way initiation functions as a psychotherapeutic measure whose purpose is to overcome the child's regressive longings for the womb and to push him or her onwards into the next stage of life.

To the Jungian it is of particular interest that, although our culture no longer provides rites of initiation, there persists in all of us, regardless of gender, *an archetypal need to be initiated*. We can deduce this from the fact that patients in analysis frequently produce, at critical periods of their lives, dreams which are rich in initiatory symbolism – at puberty, betrothal, marriage, childbirth, at divorce or separation, at the death of a parent or spouse, and so on. Attainment of a new stage of life seems to demand that symbols of initiation, appropriate to that stage, must be experienced. If society fails to provide them, then the Self produces them *faute de mieux* in dreams. Examples of such dreams can be found in books by Campbell (1949), Henderson (1967) and myself (Stevens, 1982).

The masculine principle, in particular, seems to *demand* culturally sanctioned trials and ordeals if it is to achieve full actualization in maturity. It appears that initiation is anticipated by the male Self as a normal attribute of social existence. This is a phenomenon of which analysts are increasingly aware, for in the absence of culturally sanctioned procedures the mantle of grand initiatory master not infrequently falls on them inasmuch as they must point out the significance of initiatory symbols as they arise and must encourage the 'initiate' to press onwards when regressive longings and premonitory fears would prompt him to turn back. There is apparent in many people coming into analysis what one might call *initiation hunger* – the desire to become a disciple or an apprentice and to belong to an identifiable group. The same hunger is also apparent outside the consulting room, where it shows itself in the bravado, tattoos and dress of Hell's Angels, punk rockers, football hooligans and people 'into S/M'.

Since our elders – in accordance with the general crisis of confidence in our culture and our collective loss of respect for traditional symbols and beliefs – no longer initiate the young (for they have little idea what they would be initiating them for), adolescents are forced to turn elsewhere. If they are unable to undergo a 'Jungian' initiation through an inner relationship to the Self, they will seek initiation through the achievement of economic or intellectual status by joining a hierarchically structured organization like the Army (which still formally initiates its recruits) or through informal initiation into a less structured group, whether it be sporting team, 'drug culture' or delinquent gang. The problem with these less formal alternatives is that the aggressive masculine energies which were traditionally channelled through initiation into the service of society can now flow into forms of group behaviour which are socially disruptive; and instead of producing mature males inspired with the ideals of the community, we are in danger of fostering large populations of morally and sexually ambivalent men in whom the masculine principle is only imperfectly actualized.

Initiated or not, the young human being grows steadily out of the reassuringly familiar past and into the challenges of the strange and unknown future. If at some point these challenges seem overwhelming, the individual may remain fixated at the stage already reached or, if the challenges are too dreadful, regress to a previous stage of development. Such a tactical withdrawal usually leads back to the mother in her archetypal aspect of nurturer and container. This may represent a total cop-out, but it may be a *reculer pour mieux sauter*, a retreat to a secure place in order to recharge batteries and gather strength for a more concerted effort to overcome the challenge encountered. He who fights and runs away lives to fight another day.

In adolescence, then, a battle is fought on two fronts: on one front there is the struggle to establish a sense of identity and social competence as a personality in one's own right and, on the other, the fight to overcome regressive longings for mother and the past. This is a conflict that no one escapes. Nature has decreed that we must grow away from the mother and separate from her but, at the same time, hold on to the love and security that she represents. As Jung put it: 'Whoever sunders himself from the mother longs to get back to the mother. This longing can easily turn into a consuming passion which threatens all that has been won. The mother then appears on the one hand as the supreme goal and on the other as the most frightful danger' (*CW* 5, para. 352).

This brings us to a fundamental truth: a dual dynamic is at work in all development. One drives us outwards and onwards into the future; the other pulls us inwards and backwards to the past. Development of the personality is not a simple, linear progress but a spiral with progressive ascents and regressive descents. The important thing to remember, however, is that regression can act in the service of growth. Success or failure in life, like success or failure in analysis, can depend on how firmly this truth is grasped. In a culture devoid of rituals, we each have to assume some responsibility for our own initiation.

JUNG'S ADOLESCENT TRANSITION

In many ways, Jung was fortunate in his parents. Both kind, decent people, they were devoted to their only son and, although relatively poor, provided him with a good home, ensuring that he lacked none of the essentials of life. Both were certainly 'good enough' to activate the mother and father archetypes in Carl's psyche.

Emilie Jung's illness, apparently linked with the state of her marriage, may have compelled her to desert the family home for several months at a critical stage in her son's development, but Carl always thought of her as a positive force in his life. 'My mother was a very good mother to me,' he wrote. 'She had a hearty animal warmth, cooked wonderfully, and was most companionable and pleasant' (*MDR*, p. 58). As a boy he came to realize that she too possessed a 'No. 2' personality of uncanny originality and power: 'She held all the conventional opinions a person was obliged to have, but then her unconscious personality would put in an appearance. That personality was unexpectedly powerful: a sombre, imposing figure possessed of unassailable authority' (*MDR*, p. 58). This second personality was 'like a priestess in a bear's cave. Archaic and ruthless; ruthless as truth and nature' (*MDR*, p. 60). She became the embodiment at such times of what he later described as the *natural mind* (the 'mind that says absolutely straight and ruthless things ... it wells up from the earth like a natural spring, and brings with it the peculiar wisdom of nature' (*MDR*, p. 60, note).

Jung owed to his mother the earthiness, the 'hearty animal warmth' and the companionableness that were to become so apparent in him in later years. But, most important of all, it was her deeply intuitive 'natural mind' that provided him with the 'secure base' from which to make his own heroic explorations of the psyche.

Carl's father was more of a disappointment to him, but at least he was *there* and, as far as his personality permitted, made himself available to his son until his death in 1896, during Carl's first year as a student at Basel University. Jung wrote of him as 'my dear and generous father, who in so many ways left me to myself' and 'never tyrannized over me' (*MDR*, p. 64). He tells a touching story of how much his father wanted to take him to the top of the Rigi but, not having enough money for two, pressed the fare into the boy's hand and waited patiently below while Carl ascended this great mountain by the cogwheel railway and 'stood on the peak in the strange thin air, looking into unimaginable distances'. It was an experience he never forgot: 'This was the best and most precious gift my father had ever given me' (*MDR*, p. 84). There can be little doubt that the pastor was present and attentive enough to awaken the father archetype in the boy's soul.

However, it was precisely because the archetype was awakened that Carl was able to perceive his father's deficiencies and was later driven unconsciously to seek their compensation in intellectually forceful men like Sigmund Freud.

What distressed Jung most about his father was his inability to acknowledge his loss of faith and his refusal to face the spiritual consequences of his situation. Jung could feel little respect or admiration for him because he seemed powerless and weak, as if his own initiation into manhood had been arrested at the student stage. Emotionally and intellectually, Paul Jung's life seems to have reached a standstill on graduation from Göttingen University. 'As a country parson he lapsed into a sort of sentimental idealism and into reminiscences of his golden student days, continued to smoke a long student's pipe, and discovered that his marriage was not all that he imagined it to be' (*MDR*, p. 96).

Again and again, as an adolescent, Carl attempted to initiate real discussions with his father, but to no avail. All his arguments and questions were met with lifeless theological answers, based on rote learning and not on personal religious experience. Each time Carl tackled him, the pastor became irritable and defensive: 'You always want to *think*,' he would complain. 'One ought not to think, but *believe*.'

Carl reflected inwardly, 'No, one must *experience* and *know*!' But aloud he said, 'Give me this belief.' Whereupon his father would shrug and turn away (*MDR*, p. 53).

This behaviour was incomprehensible to the boy, for he believed that he personally had already experienced, in his twelfth year, a religious revelation of epoch-shattering importance. God Himself, so Carl believed, had on that occasion set up a decisive test for him. It began one fine summer day in Basel:

> I came out of school at noon and went to the cathedral square. The sky was gloriously blue, the day one of radiant sunshine. The roof of the cathedral glittered, the sun sparkling from the new, brightly glazed tiles. I was overwhelmed by the beauty of the site, and thought: 'The world is beautiful and the church is beautiful, and God made all this and sits above it far away in the blue sky on a golden throne and . . .' Here came a great hole in my thoughts, and a choking sensation. I felt numbed, and knew only: 'Don't go on thinking now! Something terrible is coming, something I do not want to think, something I dare not even approach.'

To continue the thought would be the most terrible sin:

> the sin against the Holy Ghost, which cannot be forgiven. Anyone who commits that sin is damned to hell for all eternity. That would be very sad for my parents, if their only son, to whom they are so attached, should be doomed to eternal damnation. I cannot do that to my parents. All I need do is not go on thinking. (*MDR*, p. 47.)

But that was easier said than done. The thought of God sitting on high above his beautiful cathedral kept returning with compulsive force, and he repeated to himself: 'Don't think of it, just don't think of it!' (*MDR*, p. 48.) For two days and three nights he lived in torment, and his mother began to fear he must be ill. But he resisted the temptation to confess what troubled him for fear of causing both parents intense sorrow. On the third night, the torment became so unbearable that he no longer knew what to do with himself:

> I awoke from a restless sleep just in time to catch myself thinking again about the cathedral and God. I had almost continued the thought! I felt my resistance weakening. Sweating with fear, I sat up in bed to shake off sleep. 'Now it is coming, now it's serious! *I must think.*' (*MDR*, p. 48.)

The conviction grew that God Himself was willing him to think the forbidden thought, but he wondered how on earth this could be. He sought a biblical precedent in his memory and reflected that Adam and Eve had committed the first sin by doing what God had forbidden them to do. Suddenly it occurred to him that *God must have intended them to sin* because he had given them the capacity to do so and had created the serpent to tempt them to it. This thought greatly relieved him, for he now felt certain that God had contrived this ordeal specially for him: God must be testing his courage and obedience by imposing on him the dread task of doing something so contrary to religious teaching that it could damn him for ever. He could now act.

> I gathered all my courage, as though I were about to leap forthwith into hell-fire, and let the thought come. I saw before me the cathedral, the blue sky. God sits on his golden throne, high above the world – and from under the throne an

> enormous turd falls upon the sparkling new roof, shatters it, and breaks the walls of the cathedral asunder. (*MDR*, p. 50.)

Immediately he felt enormous, indescribable relief. Instead of damnation he had found grace, and with it an 'unutterable bliss' such as he had never known. He had discovered that 'One must be utterly abandoned to God; nothing matters but fulfilling His will' (*MDR*, p. 51). But the experience also brought home to him the terrible side of God's nature:

> I had experienced a terrible secret. It overshadowed my whole life, and I became deeply pensive ... My entire youth can be understood in terms of this secret. It induced in me an almost unbearable loneliness. My one great achievement of those years was that I resisted the temptation to talk about it with anyone. Thus the pattern of my relationship to the world was already prefigured: today as then I am a solitary, because I know things and must hint at things which other people do not know, and usually do not want to know. (*MDR*, pp. 51–2.)

To the post-Freudian reader this whole account may sound suspiciously like that of an extremely bright, but sexually naïve, schoolboy battling to overcome moral scruples about having his first (non-productive) orgasm – the nights spent struggling with the irresistible urge, the eventual capitulation associated with the fantasy of allowing something obscene to happen, followed by a feeling of 'unutterable bliss'. But whether or not this is so, it was *experienced as a direct encounter and struggle with God.* The sexual element, if it were present, would merely serve to highlight the parallel with Adam and Eve and their divinely willed defiance of the Divine Will. It would also stress the symbolical continuity between this experience and that other awesome secret – the dream of the phallic god in his underground temple.

It was in the light of this extraordinary personal revelation that Jung tackled his father's religious doubts. But his well-intentioned efforts only increased the pastor's irascibility. Despite this, they both went through the charade of preparation for Carl's first Holy Communion – the rite of initiation into full membership of the Christian Church. Not surprisingly, it was a disaster. 'My father personally gave me my instruction for confirmation. It bored me to death.' Only one subject grabbed the boy's interest and that was the Trinity: how could the one simultaneously be three? But his father said: 'We'll skip that, for I really understand nothing about it myself' (*MDR*, p. 62). When his confirmation occurred, his hopes that it might yet reveal God in the context of His Church were irrevocably dashed: he experienced absolutely nothing.

> I had reached the pinnacle of religious initiation ... and nothing at all had happened ... I knew that I would never again be able to participate in this ceremony. 'Why, that is not religion at all,' I thought. 'It is an absence of God; the church is a place I should not go to. It is not life which is there, but death' (*MDR*, pp. 63–4).

After this experience, he says:

> I was seized with the most vehement pity for my father. All at once I understood the tragedy of his profession and his life. He was struggling with a death whose existence he could not admit. An abyss opened up between him and me, and I saw no possibility of ever bridging it, for it was infinite in extent ... I saw how hopelessly he was entrapped by the Church and its theological thinking ... Now I understood the deepest meaning of my early experience: God himself had disavowed theology and the church founded upon it.

The God who had absented Himself from Carl's confirmation had nevertheless revealed Himself shitting on His own cathedral: 'For God's sake I now found myself cut off from the Church and from my father's and everybody else's faith' (*MDR*, pp. 64–5).

Carl Jung's conflict with his father was an extreme variation on the archetypal theme of war between the generations, for in this instance the parricide was not purely symbolic. Destruction of the father's religion and authority was followed by his actual physical death, and the event seems to have occasioned in Carl little sadness or remorse: 'There was a rattling in his throat, and I could see that he was in his death agony. I stood by his bed, fascinated.' Later, his mother commented in her 'second' voice: 'He died in time for you,' by which Jung understood her to mean, 'You didn't understand each other and he might have become a hindrance to you.' Carl was made uncomfortable by these words but, at the same time, he felt suddenly grown up: 'a bit of manliness and freedom awoke in me. After my father's death I moved into his room, and took his place inside the family' (*MDR*, p. 100).

These events in the Jung household must be seen in the context of their time. Until then, the great majority of human cultures had been what the sociologist David Riesman (1952), called *tradition-directed* cultures: their values, attitudes and beliefs were held to be absolute and were passed on (usually through elaborate initiation rituals) in such a way as to permit only minimal changes in these values to occur. In modern times, however, practically all tradition-directed cultures, including our own, have moved rapidly towards *other-directedness*, their members showing intolerance of traditional values and seeking new meanings in 'revolutionary' ideas and fashionable movements. This shift is associated with three significant phenomena: (1) the 'centre of gravity' of the culture tends to move backwards along the lifespan from old age to youth, from *senex* to *puer*; (2) there is a decline in the power, importance and practice of initiation rites; (3) there is a growing emphasis on rebellion against the tradition of the fathers and on solidarity with peers. All three of these phenomena result in a widening of the generation gap.

In our culture these changes began over two hundred years ago with the Enlightenment, and their accelerating progress in the second half of the nineteenth century, together with the failure of the confirmation ritual, explains, in part, the width of the gulf which opened up between Jung and his father: an initiation that fails the initiate alienates him from all that the father stands for. Jung experienced his own alienation as due not merely to the cultural failure of the Church but also to the personal failure of his father.

In similar circumstances, most boys become 'other-directed', turning to each other to find security and a new ethos to live by. But being both introverted and solitary by nature, this more usual course was denied to Carl Jung. Instead of turning outwards to join his contemporaries, he turned inwards to embrace his 'No. 2'.

Not that this solution was peculiar to Jung; many others have adopted it. Riesman called it the *inner-directed* orientation. Often the most original, creative and outstanding men and women are of this type. They derive their sense of value not from tradition or from conformity to peer-group fashion but from the resources they find and develop in their own nature. For them the centre of gravity is neither in the younger nor the older generation, neither in the past nor in the community: it is in the Self.

But even the inner-directed life requires dialogue, and this too was denied Jung, except for dialogue with himself. Throughout adolescence he experienced the Self as God-like, and inner communion with this 'other' was the central commitment of his life, supplanting in importance all relationships with the people round him. 'I had the feeling that in all decisive matters I was no longer among men, but was alone with God ... These talks with the "Other" were my profoundest experiences: on the one hand a bloody struggle, on the other supreme ecstasy' (*MDR*, p. 58).

Vivid though these colloquies were, they increased his isolation until it grew hard to bear, and there were times when he longed to break out of his solitude. 'Other people all seemed to have totally different concerns. I felt completely alone in my certainties. More than ever I wanted someone to talk to, but nowhere did I find a point of contact ... Why has no one had experiences similar to mine? I wondered ... Why should I be the only one?' (*MDR*, p. 71).

Bereft of all communication with like-minded souls, he turned to literature, philosophy and the history of religion. He was struck by the Hegelian dogmatics of Aloys Emanuel Biedermann and in particular by Biedermann's definition of religion as 'a spiritual act consisting in man's establishing his own relationship to God', but, on reflection, he disagreed with it, for he had come to understand religion as something that God did to *him*. He realized that God's existence does not depend on our proofs. On the contrary, for him God was the most certain and immediate experience. 'After all,' he thought, 'I didn't invent that horrible image about the cathedral' (*MDR*, p. 70).

Among philosophers he was attracted by Pythagoras, Heraclitus, Empedocles and Plato, though he found them rather academic and remote. There was more life in Meister Eckhart. But his greatest find was Schopenhauer's *The World as Will and Idea*. 'Schopenhauer's sombre picture of the world had my undivided approval ... I felt sure that by "Will" he really meant God, the Creator, and that he was saying that God was blind' (*MDR*, p. 77). Far from being distressed by this view, the adolescent Jung considered it to be justified by the facts as he had experienced them. From Schopenhauer he proceeded to devour Kant's *Critique of Pure Reason*, which yielded even greater illumination and, he tells us, brought about a revolutionary alteration of his attitude to the world and to life. 'I now began to display a tremendous appetite on all fronts. I knew what I wanted and went after it. I also became noticeably more accessible and communicative' (*MDR*, p. 77).

Prompted by his mother, he also read Goethe's *Faust* and found in this legendary figure a dramatic equivalent of his own No. 2 personality. *Faust*, he says, poured into his soul 'like a miraculous balm' and it gave him 'an increased feeling of inner security and a sense of belonging to the human community'. He no longer saw himself as a sport of cruel nature: 'My godfather and authority was the great Goethe himself' (*MDR*, p. 93).

When Jung entered Basel University as a student in 1895, therefore, the tasks of adolescence were only partially accomplished. He continued to live at home with his mother and remained under the influence of her 'No. 2' personality. Although he had apparently won the generation war with his father, he was left with an as yet unfulfilled need for a powerful mentor to whom he could turn for guidance through all the spiritual and intellectual uncertainties that beset him. He had, nevertheless, established a sense of membership of the human race through feelings of kinship with outstanding figures in literature and philosophy, had formed an intense personal conviction in the supreme importance of his inner life and had begun to live in optimistic anticipation of the destiny which he felt was being prepared for him.

CONSEQUENCES FOR JUNG'S PSYCHOLOGY

A favourite word of Jung's was *enantiodromia*, a term he took from Heraclitus. It refers to the inherent tendency of all entities to go over to their opposites – an essential characteristic of all homeostatic systems. An expression of this tendency is the propensity shown by children to compensate in their own lives for the deficiencies of their parents – a tendency spectacularly present in the life of Jung himself. Whereas his father displayed spiritual timidity and intellectual inertia, Jung was both spiritually bold and intellectually athletic. While his father suffered from some degree of arrested development, Jung devoted his life to the fullest possible development of the personality. If his father was disposed to question nothing and to adhere to all dogmatic articles of faith, Jung was inclined to question everything and to resist dogma in whatever form it took. In all these examples of psychic *enantiodromia*, we can see the Self at work, performing its healing task of *compensation* for the deficiencies of Jung's upbringing and the failings of his father. As is so often the case, this compensatory process was to become a major influence persisting throughout the first half of his life. The laws of family homeostasis required Jung to make good the 'part of life that [his father had] always shirked' – namely, the pastor's inability to give up his passive acquiescence to ecclesiastical dogma and, instead, to accept the reality of his own experience. Where the father could only strive fruitlessly to believe, the son had to suffer and to know. Because Paul Jung ducked the major issues of his life, Carl had always to confront his head-on, whatever the cost to himself and however far he departed from the well-trodden paths of conventional opinion.

This compensatory drive turned him into a lifelong *gnostic* – one dedicated to knowing and experiencing the reality of the spirit. The early Christian sect of *Gnosticism* (Greek *gnostikos*, one who knows) held that *gnosis* (knowledge) must be distinguished from *sophia* (wisdom) and *epistēmē* (general knowledge), for *gnosis* differs from other kinds of knowledge: it is derived not from ordinary sources but directly from God through special revelation. *Gnosis* demanded that Jung grant central importance to his dreams, visions and fantasies and insisted that he try to understand them through the study of literature, philosophy and religion. *Gnosis* guided him into the choice of natural science as a university student (the only 'instrumental' guidance his father had provided was the gratuitous advice to eschew theology), prompted him to qualify as a doctor and then caused him, much to the disgust of his tutors, who foresaw a brilliant career ahead of him as a physician, to take up psychiatry as his profession.

Pastor Jung's powerlessness, his lack of valid authority acquired through confrontation with the truth, meant that those aspects of the father archetype implicated in the *Logos* functions of the masculine principle were only partially activated in the adolescent psyche of Jung. This was his 'unfinished business', and it set him off on a dual quest – for the intellectually courageous father that he lacked and for the initiatory experience that the pastor had failed to provide. This explains Jung's attraction to men who declared their insights with powerful conviction and his desire to sit at their feet – not only Freud and Eugen Bleuler (his superior at the Burghölzli Psychiatric Hospital in Zürich, where he went to work on completion of his medical studies) but also such intellectual giants as Nietzsche and Goethe, as well as Schopenhauer and Kant. His need to find archetypal compensation for his bitter disappointment with his father also helps to explain Jung's apparent enjoyment of the 'annoying legend' that Goethe was his great-grandfather and his feeling that in some mysterious way he belonged to the eighteenth century.

Jung's immense intellectual appetite, which first manifested itself during his adolescent years, was to continue unsated into old age. This, too, was evidently a compensation for his father's lack of intellectual curiosity and rigour. His mature investigations into the phenomenology of the Trinity and the Mass were consequences of his father's ignorance of such matters and his refusal to discuss them. By such strategies as these does the Self seek to amend the shortcomings of parents and their culture.

In the absence of any culturally sanctioned form of initiation, Jung was guided by the unconscious to achieve *inner* initiation – the type of initiation, had he known it at the time, undergone by those destined to become *shamans* in Siberian, Eskimo and American Indian tribes. In contrast to priests, shamans were not instructed in any formal body of knowledge but acquired their powers individually through personally imposed ordeals such as fasting and through trance-induced visions and encounters with spirits from realms unknown to ordinary men and women. Their initiation completed, shamans were attributed formidable powers of healing, rain-making, influence with the dead and access to divine revelation. The term 'shaman' comes from the Tunguso-Manchurian word *šaman*, meaning literally 'he who knows'.

In retrospect, one can see that Jung's initiation began with his phallic dream at the age of four. It was continued through his childhood rituals with stones, fire, the *kabir* in the *kista* and his vision of the Almighty defecating on Basel Cathedral, and it culminated in the five-year ordeal of his 'experiment with the unconscious' which began after he ended his association with Sigmund Freud. It was a painful, difficult path which entailed much suffering, but he felt he had no alternative than to go through with it. He did not choose the shamanic way; it chose him: and suffering is an inescapable part of the journey. As the Eskimo shaman Igjugarjuk told the explorer Knut Rasmussen early this century: 'The only true wisdom lives far from mankind, out of the great loneliness, and it can be reached only through suffering. Privation and suffering alone can open the mind of a man to all that is hidden to others.'

Jung's recognition of the crucial role of dreams in psychic development was to prove yet a further source of conflict with the conventions of his time and was a major factor in his attraction to Freud when he eventually read *The Interpretation of Dreams*. To many people it still seems strange that a boy could discover his vocational purpose through attending to his dreams and, through them, achieve initiation into the life of a healer. Yet numerous cultures other than our own have attributed particular importance to dreams in rites of initiation – not only those of shamans but of hunters and warriors as well – the timing and the form of the ritual being determined by the contents of the initiate's dreams. For Jung, a vital preparation for the life that lay ahead came in a dream shortly after he began his studies at Basel:

> It was night in some unknown place, and I was making slow and painful headway against a mighty wind. Dense fog was flying along everywhere. I had my hands cupped around a tiny light which threatened to go out at any moment. Everything depended on my keeping this little light alive. Suddenly I had the feeling that something was coming up behind me. I looked back, and saw a gigantic black figure following me. But at the same moment I was conscious, in spite of my terror, that I must keep my little light going through night and wind, regardless of all dangers. When I awoke I realized at once that the figure was a 'spectre of the Brocken', my own shadow on the swirling mists, brought into being by the little light I was carrying. I knew, too, that this little light was my consciousness, the only light I have. My own understanding is the sole treasure I possess, and the greatest. (*MDR*, p. 93.)

This dream brought him the realization that his No. 1 personality was the bearer of the light, and that No. 2 followed him like a shadow. 'In the role of No. 1, I had to go forward – into study, moneymaking, responsibilities, entanglements ... The storm pushing against me was time, ceaselessly flowing into the past ...' (*MDR*, p. 93). Until this time he had thought that dreams came directly from God, but now he understood that the key to the future lay deep in himself. He decided that the insight conveyed by the dream had been ripening within him for a long time. Something must, therefore, have been at work behind the scenes, something more intelligent than himself. There was no longer any doubt in his mind. No. 2 was his most precious asset, and from that source all future wisdom would flow. For the time being, however, as a student, with his way to make in the world, he must devote his energies to the advancement of No. 1.

SUGGESTIONS FOR FURTHER READING

Joseph Campbell, *The Hero with a Thousand Faces*
Mircea Eliade, *Birth and Rebirth (or Rites and Symbols of Initiation)*
M. Esther Harding, *The Way of All Women*
Joseph Henderson, *Thresholds of Initiation*
Talcott Parsons and R. F. Bales, *Family, Socialization and Interaction Process*
David Riesman, *The Lonely Crowd*
Andrew Samuels (ed.), *The Father*
Lionel Tiger, *Men in Groups*
Marie-Louise von Franz, *The Problem of the Puer Aeternus*
D. W. Winnicott, *The Maturational Process and the Facilitating Environment*

Chapter Seven

EARLY MATURITY

THE ARCHETYPAL PROGRAMME

Early maturity is the time when one is most highly motivated to look after No. 1 – a time when one has (and needs) much energy for self- (that is to say, ego-) advancement, a time to establish oneself economically, professionally and socially, and, for the majority, to marry, buy a home and rear a family. Freud, whose psychology was essentially a theory and a therapy for the first half of life, summed up the tasks of this stage as 'love and work'.

Psychological development proceeds apace at this stage, though it is, of necessity, one-sided in the sense that one has to live on one's wits and bring to high proficiency one's dominant attitude and function, polish up one's persona and generally put one's best foot forward. This is not a period when people have much time for their inner life, and Jung insisted that individuation was not an appropriate undertaking at this stage. Rather, one has to pay one's dues to society and purchase the right to individuate, which then becomes the task of the second half of life.

While early maturity can certainly coincide with spiritual growth, with maturation of the capacity to love and to relate and with the development of taste in music, literature and art, these are all accretions of talent already present in the adolescent, the fruition of what is already *known* and made actual on the plane of life. Much hidden potential remains undiscovered in the Self, and there it remains until one is well enough placed in the world to give it due attention.

[illegible]amme of this stage has to do with [illegible]. Normally, the capacity to relate to [illegible]uring adolescence to the point where [illegible]ecomes possible and immensely desir- [illegible] we have seen, on the activation and [illegible] contrasexual complexes, the animus or [illegible] anticipations which each sex has of the other. The [illegible] 'falling in love' occurs when one meets a woman [illegible] who, rightly or wrongly, appears to be the living embodimen[illegible] one's anima or animus. This experience is a vivid example of what it means to be 'taken over' by the power of an autonomous complex. One does not *choose* to fall in love – particularly if it is with someone unattainable, for such a catastrophe can cause deep unhappiness. Yet, as human disasters go, unrequited love is commoner than traffic accidents. The very use of the verb 'to fall' equates the phenomenon with the force of gravity, and the comparison is apt.

So susceptible is the young adult to anima/animus projection that the phenomenon of 'love at first sight' is no rarity. Originally attributed to the arrows of Cupid, this instant form of projection of the contrasexual complex recurs abundantly throughout the literature of Europe. The most poignant examples have arisen, as often as not, out of the author's own experience. For instance, the prototype for the ravishingly beautiful heroine of Alain-Fournier's *Le Grand Meaulnes* was Yvonne de Quièvrecourt, whom Alain-Fournier encountered at his *lycée* in Paris. She trapped his anima at first sight, and her image haunted him for the rest of his short life – with an intensity that rivalled that of Dante's obsession with Beatrice. Fournier worshipped her from afar, never achieving anything more intimate than a murmured 'You are beautiful' as he passed her by. Yet this obsession was to prove the great emotional experience of his life and, without it, *Le Grand Meaulnes* would never have been written. On the whole, it is true to say that a man is more likely to achieve full conscious awareness of the power and quality of his anima when he is unable to establish a relationship with her embodiment in real life.

Inherent in every archetype is the notion of unfulfilment: an inner awareness of need. Man needs woman, either as mother or mate, if he is to fulfil himself. The archetype seeks its own completion. 'Thus the whole nature of man presupposes woman, both physically and spiritually. His system is tuned to woman from the start' (see p. 57 above). For woman it is precisely the same story: her whole nature presupposes man. At its most basic, the contrasexual archetype represents the psychic equivalent of the physical characteristics of the other sex carried by all men and women – androgens and the clitoris in women, for example, and oestrogens and breasts in men. But, far from being a mere archaic vestige, it is a dynamic complex that plays a vital role in mediating life between the sexes and an equally crucial symbolic role in the psychic life of the individual.

Inextricably linked with the animus and anima is the archetype of sex. Sexuality is more than a mere 'drive' or amorphous 'instinct'; it is better conceived as an archetypal system because of its structure, its numinosity, its universality and its power. Its influence extends from infancy to old age and is manifested in all forms of erotic excitement, whether heterosexual or homosexual, fetishism, sado-masochism, voyeurism, exhibitionism or interest in pornography. Although reproduction is clearly the biological purpose of sexuality, it is usually not experienced as such, since people seldom mix sexual enjoyment with the intention to produce children. Sexuality is concerned as much with pleasure and with bonding as with procreation. But it is the energy which fuels both animus and anima in their quest for completion through discovery and acceptance by a soulmate.

Bonding with a sexual partner is, then, a question of sexual interest and mutual unconscious projection. But for the bond to last it has, of course, to be much more than this. It requires recognition by each partner of the other as a real person, possessing qualities, needs and expectations over and beyond what has been projected. Most couples experience difficulties in this area; but the success of their union depends on the degree to which each partner can forgive the other for those aspects of the animus or anima which he or she *does not* embody and on the extent to which each is capable of learning to love and accept the other for being the person he or she happens to be.

These are issues which Jung was very aware of because, as we shall see, he came up against them in his own marriage. His essay 'Marriage as a Psychological Relationship', published in 1925, clearly relates to his personal experience, but it contains a number of original observations which are, nevertheless, of general interest and apply to many marriages.

Jung argues that the degree to which a marriage can be regarded as a true relationship depends precisely on how *conscious* both partners are of each other's psychic reality. Traditionally, he says, marriage tended to be an instinctive, largely unconscious bond, regulated by custom and convention. This he calls the 'medieval marriage': it was an effective instrument for maintaining the species and sustaining social stability, but it was not a 'psychological relationship'.

He acknowledges, however, that marriages based on blind mutual anima/animus projections can succeed, both partners remaining cheerfully unconscious of them, sublimely unaware of the illusory nature of much of what they 'see' in one another. 'This state,' he says, 'is described as one of complete harmony, and is extolled as a great happiness ("one heart and one soul") – not without good reason, since the return to that original condition of unconscious oneness is like a return to childhood. Hence the childish gestures of all lovers' (*CW* 17, para. 330).

But in modern social conditions, it is difficult for such blissful unions to survive. Already, as Jung was writing in the mid-1920s, social changes following the First World War were rendering marriage a more conscious, less stereotyped institution, but at the cost of a growing incidence of marital breakdown and divorce. For a couple to become aware of the anima/animus-based assumptions they have been indulging does enable them to perceive one another as people in their own right, but it also brings with it a sense of let-down – for it entails some sacrifice of idealism, fantasy and hope. It is akin to the decline in the magical power of the parents which occurs when the adolescent ceases to experience them as embodiments of the parental archetypes. In both instances conflict and a modicum of disillusionment are to be expected. But marriage as a true 'psychological relationship' comes into existence only when mutual projection of the contrasexual archetypes is withdrawn and the original sense of unity and shared identity broken up. Unfortunately, this seldom, if ever, happens smoothly or without crisis: 'There is no birth of consciousness without pain' (*CW* 17, para. 331).

A measure of inequality is involved in all marriages with regard to the 'degree of spiritual development' attained by each partner, and this results in one partner being 'contained' by the other. By 'degree of spiritual development' Jung is referring not to 'holiness' or 'religious sanctity' but to 'a certain complexity of mind or nature, comparable to a gem of many facets'. A husband or wife possessing such a many-sided nature will 'contain' the partner of less complexity. This does not cause problems as long as both are in the grip of their anima/animus projections, but as consciousness grows it brings marital disharmony in its train. 'One could describe this as the problem of the "contained" and the "container"' (*CW* 17, para. 331c).

Trouble arises because the contained partner lives entirely within the confines of the marriage: 'Outside the marriage there exist no essential obligations and no binding interests.' The containing partner, on the other hand, begins to experience this as an irksome constraint on life. 'The simpler nature works on the more complicated like a room that is too small,' not granting enough space. 'The complicated nature, on the other hand, gives the simpler one too many rooms.' This causes frustration in the container and insecurity in the contained, with the result that the marriage becomes unstable. 'The more the contained clings, the more the container feels shut out of the relationship ... At this juncture things are apt to occur that bring the conflict to a head' (*CW* 17, para. 333).

Either, as often happens today, the marriage disintegrates and the container moves out to seek greater fulfilment with another partner elsewhere, or both partners choose the braver and more difficult alternative of confronting the reality of their situation in their relationship and in themselves. If they take the latter course, their union becomes what Adolf Guggenbühl-Craig (1977) calls an 'individuation marriage'. The container becomes aware of an unfulfilled personal need for containment in relationship and of an inner need for unity, simplicity and integration. The contained, on the other hand, deprived of outer security and outer complexity, is forced to turn inwards, to find the security, previously so desperately sought in the partner, residing in the Self and to develop those complex abilities existing as latent unconscious potential which were previously projected on to the spouse. This involves crisis and suffering for both parties and can bring one or other of them to the point of emotional collapse and psychological breakdown, but, if these issues can be confronted with insight and understanding, the marriage, and the individual partners, are profoundly enriched. Jung concludes: 'This is what happens very frequently about the midday of life, and in this wise our miraculous human nature enforces a transition that leads from the first half of life to the second. It is a metamorphosis from a state in which man is only a tool of instinctive nature to another in which he is no longer a tool, but himself: a transformation of nature into culture, of instinct into spirit' (*CW* 17, para. 335).

Towards the end of his essay he says, revealingly: 'One understands nothing psychological unless one has experienced it oneself' (*CW* 17, para. 343), and, as we shall now see, there is little doubt that his observations about the phenomenology of marriage were largely derived from his own experience of that venerable institution.

JUNG'S EARLY MATURITY

For the best part of two decades after his enrolment as a student at Basel University in 1895, Jung was true to his resolve and devoted immense energy to the advancement of his No. 1 personality. He proved to be an excellent student, completing his medical studies in the shortest possible time. Though not a great one for parties, he did share sufficiently in student life to become a member of the University Zofingia Society, where he delivered a number of papers on subjects close to his heart. Some of the ideas he developed on these occasions found mature expression much later in the principles of analytical psychology. For example, in one paper he argued that the primary task of scientific psychology must be to demonstrate the existence of the soul, which he conceived as a form of intelligence independent of time and space. He believed that the scientific study of somnambulism, hypnotism and spiritualism would yield data establishing the soul's phenomenological reality. On another occasion he argued that religious experiences are often accompanied by erotic emotions – an interesting reflection in the light of his phallic dream and his vision of the Almighty defecating on Basel Cathedral.

In his fourth year he began to apply his ideas concerning the scientific study of metaphysical phenomena by attending the séances of Hélène Preiswerk, a fifteen-year-old cousin. Evidently influenced by Flournoy's classic investigation of Helen Smith (see p. 15 above), he regularly attended these séances over a period of two years, systematically recording his observations for his medical dissertation, which he presented in 1902.

Two things particularly impressed Jung about this girl. One was how vivid and real her 'spirits' seemed to her when she was in the trance state. She told him: 'I do not know if what the spirits say and teach me is true, nor do I know if they really are the people they call themselves; but that my spirits exist is beyond question. I see them before me, I can touch them. I speak to them about everything I wish as naturally as I'm talking to you. They must be real' (*CW* 1, para. 43). The other thing that impressed him was the way in which Hélène spoke perfect High German in the course of her trances instead of her customary Basel dialect. When in a trance, her 'control' said her name was Ivenes, and she spoke in a quiet, dignified manner that was in marked contrast to her usual conscious personality, which was shy, embarrassed and gauche. Jung came to the conclusion that 'Ivenes' was the differentiated, adult personality that was in the process of developing within the medium's unconscious. Because her natural psychic growth had been impeded by psychological and social obstacles, she had unconsciously resorted to the stratagem of taking up a career as a spiritualistic medium in order to overcome the hurdles which were blocking her further development. In this interpretation we find the seed which was later to grow into the theory of individuation.

Towards the end of his time as a medical student, Jung's tutor in internal medicine, Friedrich von Müller, suggested that he should accompany him to Munich to work as his assistant. Jung was almost persuaded to accept this flattering invitation, but it was then that he read Krafft-Ebing's *Textbook of Psychiatry* and discovered his true vocation. 'The decision was taken. When I informed my teacher in internal medicine of my intention, I could read in his face his amazement and disappointment. My old wound, the feeling of being an outsider and of alienating others, began to ache again' (*MDR*, p. 111).

Having obtained his medical degree with distinction in 1900 and completed his first spell of national service in the Swiss Army, Jung left Basel in order to live and work in Zürich. The motives for this move were partly personal and partly professional. 'My friends could not understand my going away, and reckoned I would be back in no time. But that was out of the question, for in

Basel I was stamped for all time as the son of the Reverend Paul Jung and the grandson of Professor Carl Gustav Jung. I was an intellectual and belonged to a definite social set. I felt resistances against this, for I could not and would not let myself be classified' (*MDR*, p. 113).

The professional motive for moving to Zürich was no less powerful. There he had the good fortune to be taken on to the staff of the Burghölzli Psychiatric Hospital as an assistant to Eugen Bleuler (1857–1939), one of the outstanding psychiatrists of his time. Bleuler had been director of the Burghölzli for only two years when Jung took up residence there. A stickler for hard work and accurate clinical observation, Bleuler was for a time an influential father-figure for Jung, and Jung regarded his nine years at the Burghölzli as an invaluable period of apprenticeship. Bleuler was to become famous after the publication in 1911 of a now classic book in which he introduced the term 'schizophrenia' to replace the obsolete and inaccurate term 'dementia praecox'.

Bleuler created throughout the hospital a humane atmosphere based on his view that the mental processes of psychiatric patients are fundamentally similar to those of normal people – a view that Jung entirely endorsed: 'At bottom we discover nothing new or unknown in the mentally ill; rather, we encounter the substratum of our own natures' (*MDR*, p. 127). Bleuler also did much to reverse the therapeutic pessimism which was typical of psychiatrists at that time: he insisted that a positive approach on the part of the doctor could bring about improvements in even the most disturbed patient. These were all lessons which Jung learned well.

Initially Jung got on cordially with Bleuler, who was quick to recognize his brilliance and industry. As a result of Bleuler's support, Jung's professional advancement was rapid: in 1905 he became Bleuler's deputy at the Burghölzli, was appointed head of the Outpatient Department and made a lecturer in psychiatry and psychotherapy at the University of Zürich. It was also Bleuler who encouraged Jung to do the research on the word-association test which made his international reputation and brought him into contact with Freud.

In February 1903 Jung married Emma Rauschenbach, having fallen in love with her six years earlier, when she was a mere girl of fourteen. It was love at first sight. He caught a glimpse of her at the top of a staircase and instantly thought to himself: 'That girl is my wife.' This was a classic case of anima projection, since he knew nothing about the personal qualities of this girl but was, nevertheless, possessed by the feeling that he knew her, loved her and intended to marry her.

On Emma's side the animus was somewhat slower to stir, and on the first occasion that Jung proposed to her, she turned him down. This may have been due to the incompatibility of their circumstances. She was a rich industrialist's daughter, while he was without money of his own and a specialist in an unglamorous branch of his profession. He had no property to offer a wife, only an apartment in a large mental hospital. He was not an obvious catch. However, he was tall, well-made and charismatic and, in the opinion of those who knew him, destined for a brilliant future. His confidence in himself had grown immeasurably since his schooldays, and his desire for Emma was so strong that he would not allow himself to be rebuffed. He continued to court her, and when he asked her to marry him a second time, she accepted.

Apparently undeterred by the prospect, she moved in with Carl at the Burghölzli, where they lived in a flat above the Bleulers, while they built their own house beside the lake at Küsnacht. It was a spacious, dignified house, set in a beautiful garden with magnificent views of the lake. Over the front door Jung caused an inscription to be engraved: *Vocatus atque non vocatus, Deus aderit* ('Called or not called, God will be there'). They eventually took up residence in 1908, when Jung fell out with Bleuler (who felt his assistant was neglecting his hospital duties in favour of his private practice and personal research), and his services as resident psychiatrist at the Burghölzli were no longer required. Between 1904 and 1914 Emma gave birth to five children – four girls and a boy – and she proved an admirable wife and mother.

In the years up to his break with Freud, therefore, Jung had every reason to be content with the way in which he discharged the duties of the first half of his life. Rapidly achieving eminence in his profession, he had found a mentor in Freud capable of healing the wound left in his psyche by his poor father; he had married a rich, attractive wife who was as well-endowed with intelligence and social grace as a man could wish. He had created a home and founded a large and healthy family. Yet all was not as well as it seemed.

By 1908 trouble was brewing in two quarters: one concerned

the ambivalence of his relationship with Freud; the other arose from the divided nature of his own anima.

Jung's relationship with Freud

The relationship which developed between Freud and Jung after their meeting in Vienna in 1907 was one of the most creative influences in the lives of both men. Freud valued Jung deeply, regarding him as 'the ablest helper to have joined me thus far'; he rapidly became emotionally attached to Jung and perceived him as his probable successor as leader of the psychoanalytic movement. In addition, there were several practical reasons why Jung was important to him. In the first place, Jung was a successful psychiatrist, working at an internationally respected hospital and university, and his support was most welcome at a time when Freud was widely execrated for his views on infantile sexuality. Secondly, Jung was not Austrian and he was not Jewish, which meant that he might rescue psychoanalysis from seeming like some cabbalistic cult of a Viennese clique.

For his part, Jung was able to make a considerable contribution to psychoanalysis. Not only did he provide empirical proof of the existence and power of unconscious complexes through his use of the word-association test, but he was one of the first psychiatrists to apply psychoanalytic concepts to the study of schizophrenia, and he was responsible for stimulating Freud's interest in mythology.

But the main reason for Jung's adherence to Freud was clearly personal. For him, Freud was a distinguished elder colleague who represented the intellectually courageous father that his own father was not. In contrast to the spiritually inadequate pastor, Freud was a towering figure who spoke with total conviction out of his hard-won knowledge and experience. Soon after their first meeting, Jung wrote to Freud: 'Let me enjoy your friendship not as one between equals but as that of father and son.' In a letter to Jung, Freud spoke of his 'long years of honourable but painful solitude' and of 'the serene certainty which finally took possession of me and bade me wait until a voice from the unknown multitude should answer mine. That voice was yours.'

To begin with, each clearly fulfilled a powerful longing in the other. If Jung needed a father, Freud needed a son whom he considered worthy to inherit his kingdom and continue his rule. Unfortunately, this was not the sort of relationship that can be prolonged indefinitely. On his side, Freud was not particularly keen to see his son grow up. He would have preferred a devoted disciple willing to accept his doctrines and respect his authority without reservation. 'Don't deviate too far from me,' Freud warned Jung, 'when you are really so close to me, for if you do, we may one day be played off against one another.' Then a veiled threat: 'My inclination is to treat those colleagues who offer resistance exactly as we would treat patients in the same situation.'

For several years, Freud continued to make fulsome allusions to Jung's brilliance as a psychoanalyst and to his crucial importance for the future of the movement. But all this embarrassed Jung, as he knew he would never be able to uphold Freud's ideas *in toto*. The last thing Jung wanted was to become the leader of a party – it just wasn't in his nature, and he knew that he could never bring himself to sacrifice his intellectual independence as his father had done before him. Nevertheless, in accordance with Freud's wishes, he became the first president of the International Psychoanalytic Association and chief editor of the first psychoanalytic journal, the *Jahrbuch*.

But what Jung really needed was a father whom he could admire sufficiently to overcome his adolescent doubts and discover his own masculine authority. Because he had walked over his weak father as a teenager, the war of the generations was delayed for Jung into his thirties, when he was able to live out his 'moult' in relation to Bleuler and Freud. His relationship with Bleuler, which began with the utmost cordiality, was, after the initial years, to become acrimonious, and resulted in Jung's expulsion from the Burghölzli five years before he was to part from Freud. In both cases he was 'slaying the father' all over again. They had to 'die' so that he might come of age in his own work.

Freud was as much caught up in the father–son archetypal constellation as Jung, with the added fact that in Freud's personal myth the son was equated with thrusting ascendancy and the father with inexorable decline. As a consequence, Freud readily detected the parricide in Jung, and it deeply upset him – to the extent that he fainted on two separate occasions when Jung happened to mention the subject of death.

After the famous evening in 1909 when Freud 'annointed' Jung his 'eldest son', successor and 'crown prince', Jung greatly offended him by writing to say, 'That last evening with you has, most happily, freed me inwardly from the oppressive sense of your paternal authority.'

However, Jung continued to play an important role in the psychoanalytic movement right up to the publication of his *Symbols of Transformation* in two parts in 1911 and 1912. These, particularly the second part, made plain just how heretical his view had become, and at the meeting of the International Psychoanalytic Association held in Munich in September 1913 Jung found himself in conflict with many of the members. A few weeks later he decided that the time had come for him to sever his links with the Freudians. As a result, he resigned from the Association and from his editorship of the *Jahrbuch*. He also resigned his position as lecturer at the University of Zürich. Once more he found himself entirely on his own.

Up to the publication of *Symbols of Transformation* he was in something of a cleft stick: to stay in close relationship with Freud he would have to toe the party line and remain second in command: if, on the other hand, he asserted his personal views, he would lose Freud's friendship and his prestige in the International Psychoanalytic Association. But it was inevitable, given his character and disposition, that he would eventually go his own way. His individuation demanded it.

He began to prepare Freud for his defection early in 1911, writing to the effect that 'it is a risky business for an egg to be cleverer than the hen. Still, what is in the egg must eventually summon the courage to creep out.' A year later he was quoting *Zarathustra*: 'One repays a teacher badly if one remains only a pupil.'

Ultimately, the creative person must serve his own creative daimon. To have remained a Freudian would have been a negation of what Jung saw as life's highest purpose, namely, to become oneself. He was not going to preach individuation; he practised it. His whole life was an affirmation of that principle.

When the final break came it was, in a sense, fulfilling Freud's expectations and also, perhaps, gratifying some masochistic need in him, for such painful defections were a recurrent pattern in Freud's life.

Jung's situation was now summed up for him in a dream:

> I was with an unknown, brown-skinned man, a savage, in a lonely, rocky mountain landscape. It was before dawn; the eastern sky was already bright, and the stars fading. Then I heard Siegfried's horn sounding over the mountains and I knew that we had to kill him. We were armed with rifles and lay in wait for him on a narrow path over the rocks.
>
> Then Siegfried appeared high up on the crest of the mountain, in the first ray of the rising sun. On a chariot made of the bones of the dead he drove at furious speed down the precipitous slope. When he turned a corner, we shot at him, and he plunged down, struck dead.
>
> Filled with disgust and remorse for having destroyed something so great and beautiful, I turned to flee, impelled by the fear that the murder might be discovered. But a tremendous downfall of rain began, and I knew that it would wipe out all traces of the deed. I had escaped the danger of discovery; life could go on, but an unbearable feeling of guilt remained. (*MDR*, p. 173.)

Jung tells us that this dream filled him with compassion, as though he himself had been shot. He took this as 'a sign of my secret identity with Siegfried, as well as of the grief a man feels when he is forced to sacrifice his ideal and his conscious attitudes' (*MDR*, p. 174).

When he reflected on the dream, Jung equated Siegfried with the will of the German people to impose their dominion on the world. In serving the interests of his No. 1 personality he, too, had been heroically asserting his will to get his own way. The brown-skinned man he recognized as a primitive shadow figure, a symbol of the unconscious, guiding him away from the Freudian Id to the archetypes of the collective unconscious. Although Jung makes no mention of this, it is clearly possible that Siegfried is the heroic image that Jung himself projected on to Freud, and that the murder (and his subsequent guilt) is to be interpreted as a wilful act of parricide.

By this time, however, he was suffering guilt from another source: he was involved in an extramarital affair.

Jung's anima problem

Though Jung was clearly in love with his wife, it became evident within a few years of their marriage that there was an aspect of his anima which Emma seemed unable to carry. The more preoccupied she became with her maternal responsibilities, the more the unattached portion of his anima caused Jung to be attracted by other women. We cannot know how often this occurred, but several instances have come to light. In the spring of 1907, for example, while he and Emma were on holiday in Hungary and Italy, Jung was for a while infatuated with a woman, and he wrote to Freud about it, confessing that he had 'polygamous components' in his nature. Not long afterwards, he allowed himself to be dangerously attracted by a disturbed and gifted patient, Sabina Spielrein, and he made such a mess of the relationship that he had to ask Freud to help sort it out for him.

These difficulties did not deter Jung, however, from taking Emma into analysis. Her analysis began in 1909, but, not surprisingly, it soon ran into difficulties on account of Jung's anima problem and the jealousy, anxiety and indignation that this provoked in his analysand. Jung wrote to Freud mentioning that Emma had staged a number of jealous scenes: 'Analysis of one's spouse is one of the more difficult things unless mutual freedom is assured. The pre-requisite for a good marriage, it seems to me, is the licence to be unfaithful' (30 January 1910).

Why should this be? We cannot be sure, of course, but Jung does give us some important clues – in his memoir, in his essay on marriage already mentioned and in his view that there exist for a man essentially two types of women: the wife and mother, and the '*femme inspiratrice*'.

In his memoir, Jung recalls the provision which was made for his care during the months of his fourth year when his mother was away in hospital. Responsibility for him was shared between an aunt and a young maid. The latter made an indelible impression on him:

> I still remember her picking me up and laying my head against her shoulder. She had black hair and an olive complexion, and was quite different from my mother. I can see, even now, her hairline, her throat, with its darkly pigmented skin, and her ear. All this seemed to me very strange and yet strangely familiar. It

> was as though she belonged not to my family but only to me, as though she were connected in some way with other mysterious things I could not understand. This type of girl later became a component of my anima. The feeling of strangeness which she conveyed, and yet of having known her always, was a characteristic of that figure which later came to symbolize for me the whole essence of womanhood. (*MDR*, p. 23.)

The traumatic loss of his mother at such an early age, associated with her thrilling replacement by a physically enticing young girl from outside the family, could well have produced the split in his anima which persisted well into middle age. The maid was the first embodiment of a maternal adjunct, the *femme inspiratrice*, the close companion and confidante, the consolation of his lonely inner journey, which began when his mother was taken away. Although well content with his excellent wife, his anima demanded the additional presence of a *femme inspiratrice*. What we yearn for in life, whether it be sexually charged or not, is what we need in order to achieve self-completion. This inner longing was an imperative as powerful as that which drove him to find gratification of his father hunger in Freud.

By taking Emma into analysis, Jung presumably intended that their marriage should be a 'conscious relationship', believing that a combination of analytic insight and good will would reduce the tensions existing between them. But, unfortunately, Jung, 'the container', with his 'many-sided nature', his unfulfilled anima longings, his extramarital interests and professional commitments, could not avoid afflicting the 'contained' Emma with 'too many rooms', thus causing her great insecurity and much unhappiness.

Commenting in general on the anguish suffered by simpler, 'contained' partners in relating to their complicated, multi-faceted spouses, Jung wrote that it is all too easy for them to 'lose themselves in such a labyrinthine nature, finding in it such an abundance of possible experiences that their personal interests are completely absorbed, sometimes in a not very agreeable way since their sole occupation then consists in tracking the other through all the twists and turns of his character' (*CW* 17, para. 331c). Poor Emma!

In some desperation she wrote to Freud in November 1911:

I am tormented by the conflict about how I can hold my own against Carl. I find I have no friends, all the people who associate with us really only want to see Carl, except for a few boring and to me quite uninteresting persons.

Naturally the women are all in love with him ... Yet I have a strong need for people and Carl too says I should stop concentrating on him and the children, but what am I to do? ... it is difficult because I can never compete with Carl. In order to emphasize this I usually have to talk extra stupidly when in company.

Emma's situation had been rendered unenviable by the arrival on the scene of a young, intense and compellingly mysterious girl called Antonia Wolff. She became a patient of Jung's towards the end of 1910, for treatment of a breakdown following the death of her father, a rich Zürich businessman and a member of an old, highly respected Swiss family.

Herr Wolff was twenty years older than his wife, and Antonia's excessive grief after his death points to 'unfinished business' – a sign that she too needed to encounter aspects of the father archetype which her own father had been unable to provide. She was twenty-two, and Jung, a powerful personality fifteen years her senior, seems to have been exactly what she needed. She responded readily to treatment and developed a devotion to him which was to last a lifetime. For his part, Jung was captivated by her. Hers was a subtle, brilliant, complicated nature, only marginally less 'labyrinthine' than his own, and by August 1911 he was writing enthusiastically about her to Freud, praising her 'remarkable intellect' and her 'excellent feeling for religion and philosophy'. He had found his *femme inspiratrice*, capable, as she would have to be during the years of his inner crisis, of containing *him*.

Writing years later of the anima and animus, Jung commented:

In a marriage it is always the contained who projects this image upon the container, while the latter is only partially able to project his unconscious image on his partner. The more unified and simple this partner is, the less complete the projection. In which case, this highly fascinating image hangs as it were in mid-air, as though waiting to be filled out by a living person. There are certain types of women who seem to be made by

> nature to attract anima projections; indeed one could almost speak of a definite 'anima type'. The so-called 'sphinx-like' character is an indispensable part of their equipment, also an equivocalness, an intriguing elusiveness ... an indefiniteness that seems full of promises, like the speaking silence of a Mona Lisa. A woman of this kind is both old and young, mother and daughter, of more than doubtful chastity, childlike, and yet endowed with a naive cunning that is extremely disarming to men. (*CW* 17, para. 339.)

It is not clear how long Toni Wolff's analysis lasted or when their love affair began. Nor do we know how or when Emma Jung found out about it. But Emma's letters to Freud in 1911 and 1912 show her to have been a troubled woman. In September 1911 Toni Wolff accompanied Emma and Carl Jung to the Weimar Conference of the International Psychoanalytic Association, and the affair became a subject of gossip at the Conference as well as in psychoanalytic circles in Zürich and Vienna. There seem to have been long and bitter rows between Carl and Emma, during which he insisted that Toni was far too crucial to his well-being to be dispensed with, and since there could be no question of divorcing or breaking up the family, Emma must adjust to the situation and accept Toni as part of Carl's life. The strain on both of them was terrible and may have been a major factor in Jung's breakdown towards the end of 1913.

By this time, then, his life was in crisis. He had broken not only with Freud and the International Psychoanalytic Association but also with Bleuler, the Burghölzli and the University of Zürich. Although *Symbols of Transformation* had been published, it brought him no acclaim. Once more he was totally isolated. 'After the break with Freud, all my friends and acquaintances dropped away. My book was declared to be rubbish; I was a mystic, and that settled the matter.... But I had foreseen my isolation and harboured no illusion about the reactions of my so-called friends. ... I had known that everything was at stake and that I had to take a stand for my convictions' (*MDR*, pp. 162–3).

In the weeks and months that followed he became withdrawn, depressed and perilously close to psychosis. It seems probable that had it not been for the care he received from both Emma and Toni the psychosis would have taken over and the ordeal that awaited him would not have been the 'creative illness' it was destined to be.

CONSEQUENCES FOR JUNG'S PSYCHOLOGY

Although this period of Jung's life seemed to end disastrously, it completed, in fact, a time of unparalleled growth and development. The odd, aloof schoolboy, son of a poor village pastor, had become a leading figure in the most original and influential cultural movement of the turn of the twentieth century.

On the personal level, he had not only discharged his social and economic duties, but he had also gone some way towards completing his 'unfinished business' with his parents – with his mother as well as his father. In this, Freud and psychoanalysis played a major role. As the more powerful parent, his mother had continued to 'contain' Carl – especially in the guise of her uncanny 'second personality' – far into adult life. Carl's situation in relation to her was symbolized in his first dream, where the masculine principle (the phallic god) was entombed in the feminine (the womb of the earth). He needed a strong father figure not only to compensate for his father's spiritual weakness but also to liberate him from thraldom to the maternal feminine. This was part of his problem with Emma, who inevitably caught his maternal projection and was experienced by Jung as an irritating constraint on his freedom. The drive to individuate decreed that he must free his masculinity from the mother. This inner need brought him to Freud (as well as to Toni Wolff) and committed him to the years of work necessary to produce *Symbols of Transformation*, with its central drama of the night sea journey, the hero's struggle with the monster of the deep, his transformation and rebirth. By the end of 1913 he was ready to give up the life of 'promising son' and undergo the ordeal of initiation into the mature life of the Self. The initiation was to take five years.

On the professional level much had been achieved. He had introduced and demonstrated the practical implications of three seminal notions – the unconscious complex, the primordial image and the mythopoeic function of the collective unconscious. He now had to *experience* these concepts as a *personal revelation* in order to develop them into a coherent, dynamic psychology out of which it would be possible to live, to work and to teach.

The crisis which afflicted him as he approached middle age was to be the most important experience of his life.

SUGGESTIONS FOR FURTHER READING

Adolf Guggenbühl-Craig, *Marriage Dead or Alive*
C. G. Jung, *Anima and Animus* (in *CW* 7)
—— *Marriage as a Psychological Relationship* (in *CW* 17)
—— *Symbols of Transformation* (*CW* 5)
Emma Jung, *Animus and Anima*
William McGuire, *The Freud/Jung Letters*

Chapter Eight

MID-LIFE TRANSITION

THE ARCHETYPAL PROGRAMME

As Jung well knew, he was not unusual in suffering a personal crisis in mid-life. Many people go through similar experiences. The period from thirty-five to forty-five is one of raised rates of suicide, depression and divorce, and for everyone it is a time of existential doubt and inner questioning. What have I achieved? What am I here for? What am I to do with the rest of my life? What is there left to look forward to except old age, infirmity and death?

When a man reaches mid-life, according to Jung, he comes to realize that 'what originally meant advancement and satisfaction has now become a boring mistake, part of the illusion of youth, upon which he looks back with mingled regret and envy, because nothing now awaits him but old age and the end of all illusions'. Joseph Campbell put it another way, defining the mid-life crisis as what happens when you climb to the top of the ladder – and discover it's against the wrong wall!

The devilish paradox of this time of life is that disillusionment sets in at the very moment that one reaches one's peak.

> Middle life [wrote Jung] is the moment of greatest unfolding, when a man still gives himself to his work with his whole strength and his whole will but in this very moment evening is born, and the second half of life begins ... the turnings of the pathway that once brought surprise and discovery become dulled by custom. The wine has fermented and begins to settle

> and clear. Conservative tendencies develop if all goes well; instead of looking forward one looks backward, most of the time involuntarily, and one begins to take stock, to see how one's life has developed up to this point. (*CW* 17, para. 331a.)

As often as not, one is unhappy with what one sees, and, not uncommonly, one's spouse bears the brunt of one's discontent: 'since one is not conscious of the real state of things one generally projects the reason for it on to one's partner' (*CW* 17, para. 331b). A highly critical atmosphere develops, which can threaten to blow the marriage apart; but it may also be a necessary prelude to full conscious recognition of each other as people. As Carl and Emma Jung both discovered, these insights do not come easily: they are gained only through the severest shocks; and this can be a time of deep anguish. But not for everyone.

Some people manage to slip through middle life without acknowledging that anything particularly significant is happening to them. They plod on through the routines of daily existence with no awareness of the fateful trudge of time. Each dawn is a preparation for business as usual, each year an example of *plus ça change, plus c'est la même chose*. They 'lose and neglect the creeping hours of time' (William Shakespeare, *As You Like It*, Act II, Scene vii), and there is no awakening. 'Time merely drives these lives that do not live/As tides push rotten stuff along the shore' (Stephen Spender, 'In Railway Halls'). Transformation eludes these somnambulists.

On the whole, men are more likely to get away with this existential anaesthesia than women, for men are spared the harsh initiation into the second half of life that menopause brings. Men are also more prone to seek solace for uncomfortable thoughts in drink and in sexual promiscuity. By such means they avoid waking up to the reality of their position and stay deaf to the call to individuate.

Yet for most men and women the mid-life transition is marked by various kinds of upheaval, and, disagreeable though these disturbances are, they do have the psychological advantage of providing stimuli sharp enough to wake one up (for one has to wake up if one is to individuate). This is particularly true when crisis hits dramatically – as, for example, when one loses one's spouse or one's job. It is less true when the crisis comes on gradually, with the vague feeling, so characteristic of mid-life, that life has become flat and the zest has gone out of it. Whichever mode of onset the crisis adopts, we are not helped by the fact that it is largely unexpected, since our culture does not prepare us for this time of profound transition or provide us with *rites of passage* to carry us through it. As a result, people commonly misunderstand the problem – not least doctors and psychiatrists, who tend to regard it less as an existential crisis rich in meaning for every person's development than as an illness to be attacked with electric shocks and drugs.

The etymology of the word 'crisis' is instructive. It comes from the Greek word *krinein*, meaning 'discrimination' or 'decision'. In Chinese the pictogram that signifies 'crisis' also implies 'opportunity'. The mid-life crisis can be approached, therefore, as a time for taking stock and making decisions and for turning something upsetting into a new opportunity. Generally, people find it easier to apply this insight, if they have it, to their outer circumstances than to their inner lives. They divorce, remarry, change jobs, sell up their homes and move elsewhere, not realizing that these outer changes are but the expression of inner restlessness and uncertainty and that what is needed is not so much a new spouse, a new job or a new home as a new orientation.

The trouble is, as Jung saw, that success in the first half of life so often demands the development of a one-sided approach to reality and a channelling of energy in one, highly specific direction, and this, over the years, can result in a serious 'diminution of personality' with much Self-potential falling into the unconscious. To change your outer circumstances will not usually affect this narrowness of vision, for you will continue to carry it with you. What is needed is an *inner* inventory – a taking stock of what has been achieved, certainly, but also of what has been missed and what remains in yourself to be fulfilled. If you can achieve this, then you will have taken a step towards your individuation.

JUNG'S MID-LIFE TRANSITION

Having climbed to the top of the psychoanalytic ladder, Jung's realization that it was against the wrong wall resulted in the loss of all that he had achieved – his friendship with Freud, the presidency of the International Psychoanalytic Association, the editorship of the *Jahrbuch* and his Lectureship in Psychoanalysis at the University of Zürich. Fortunately, he still had his private practice and, thanks to Emma, enough money to live in comfort; but his public reputation was tarnished and he found himself, yet again, isolated and alone. This, combined with the severe tensions in his marriage, has to be added to the usual problems of the mid-life crisis, and it is sufficient to account for the low state he had reached by the end of 1913.

It was at this time that he had the dream of killing Siegfried, which confirmed for him the need to abandon the attitudes, ambitions and ideals that he had embraced up to that time. He had no idea what could take their place, for he was living in a void and 'totally suspended in mid-air'. He felt that all the knowledge he had acquired up to that point was useless, and thought to himself, 'Since I know nothing at all, I shall simply do whatever occurs to me' (*MDR*, p. 168).

His decision to embark on his 'experiment with the unconscious' was taken shortly before the Siegfried dream and came after a period of playing like a child in his garden, building villages, waterworks and dams. This functioned as a kind of *rite d'entrée* to the work to come and it released in him a powerful stream of fantasies: 'I was living in a constant state of tension; often I felt as if gigantic blocks of stone were tumbling down upon me. One thunderstorm followed another' (*MDR*, p. 171).

Since there was no longer any outer authority for him to look to, he felt he had no alternative than to turn inwards and undertake an examination of himself. Although shaken to the core, it is a mark of his unusual quality that he conceived his confrontation with the unconscious as a scientific experiment: 'This idea – that I was committing myself to a dangerous enterprise not for myself alone, but also for the sake of my patients – helped me over several critical phases' (*MDR*, p. 172).

How was he to start? It seems likely that he found the inspiration for the mode in which he conducted his Self-confrontation in the work he had done for his doctoral thesis in 1899 and 1900, when he had investigated the séances of his cousin, the young medium Hélène Preiswerk. The emergence of the superior personality 'Ivenes', when Hélène was in the trance state, impressed Jung more deeply and more lastingly than is customarily realized. In his dissertation he wrote these significant words: 'It is, therefore, conceivable that the phenomena of double consciousness are simply new character formations, or attempts of the future personality to break through . . .' This insight was to become one of the basic concepts of Jungian analysis, namely, that the growth of new, more developed aspects of the Self is ever proceeding at the unconscious level and, if properly attended to, may be brought to birth in consciousness and integrated within the personality as a whole. It also provided Jung with a clue as to how he should proceed in dealing with his own 'state of disorientation', as he called it, following the break with Freud.

He tells us how the experiment eventually began: 'It was during Advent of the year 1913 – December 12th, to be exact – that I resolved on the decisive step. I was sitting at my desk once more, thinking over my fears. Then I let myself drop. Suddenly it was as though the ground literally gave way beneath my feet, and I plunged down into the dark depths' (*MDR*, p. 172).

Letting himself drop was like allowing himself, in the manner of Hélène Preiswerk, to fall into a trance, although he came to prefer the term *active imagination*. 'In order to seize hold of the fantasies, I frequently imagined a steep descent. I even made several attempts to get to the very bottom. The first time I reached, as it were, a depth of about a thousand feet; the next time I found myself at the edge of a cosmic abyss. It was like a voyage to the moon, or a descent into an empty space. First came the image of a crater, and I had the feeling that I was in the land of the dead. The atmosphere was that of the other world' (*MDR*, p. 174). In later life he would refer to these alarming and extraordinary experiences as his *Nekyia* – after the episode in Homer's *Odyssey* where Odysseus makes his journey to the Sojourn of the Dead.

On one occasion he encountered an old man with a white beard together with a beautiful young girl. He was able to converse with them, and they told him that their names were Elijah and Salome and that they had belonged together for all eternity. He recognized Salome as an anima figure and Elijah as a personification of the archetype of the wise old man. They were embodiments of the Eros and Logos principles. Not long after this, another personage arose out of the Elijah figure, and Jung called him Philemon.

Philemon first appeared in a dream, and what struck Jung most forcefully about him was that he had the wings of a giant kingfisher with its characteristic colouring. Jung painted this dream image in order to impress it upon his memory. While he was occupied with the painting, he found in his garden, by the lake shore, a dead kingfisher. This was an extraordinary happening because kingfishers are rare in the Zürich region, and as long as he lived there he never found one again. The coincidence of these two events was an example of what he was later to call *synchronicity* – the kind of meaningful coincidence that tends to occur when powerful psychic components are activated.

Philemon appeared to him on numerous occasions, and Jung learned many things from him, the most important being that there were events in his psyche that *produced themselves* on those occasions, as if they had a life of their own. 'In my fantasies I held conversations with him, and he said things which I had not consciously thought. For I observed clearly that it was he who spoke, not I. He said I treated thoughts as if I generated them myself, but in his view thoughts were like animals in the forest, or people in a room, or birds in the air, and added, "If you should see people in a room you would not think that you had made those people, or that you were responsible for them"' (*MDR*, p. 176).

Jung says that, among other things, it was Philemon who taught him the meaning of *psychic objectivity* and *the reality of the psyche*. For, as a result of these extraordinary encounters, he came to see clearly that the psyche is an objective expression of nature and is irreducible to any factor other than itself. The psyche is an *a priori* fact. Like 'Ivenes' for Hélène, Philemon represented 'superior insight' for Jung. 'At times he seemed to me quite real, as if he were a living personality. I went walking up and down the garden with him, and to me he was what the Indians call a guru' (*MDR*, p. 176). Jung would have liked nothing better than a real, live guru to help him at this stage. But in the absence of an outer guide, this task was undertaken by the figure of Philemon, whom he recognized as his 'psychagogue'. Like 'Ivenes', he was an 'attempt of the future personality to break through'.

It was also in the course of these fantasies that Jung first discovered the reality of the anima as an autonomous complex within himself. One day he asked himself, 'What am I really doing? Certainly this has nothing to do with science. But then what is it?' Whereupon he clearly heard a female voice within him

Figure 9 Philemon

say, 'It is art.' He was irritated by this interjection and replied emphatically, 'No, it is not art! On the contrary, it is nature' (*MDR*, p. 178).

He resented the imputation that what he was doing was 'art' because if his unconscious emanations were contrived, then they were not the spontaneous productions of the 'natural mind' that he took them to be. For him the distinction was crucial, and he could not allow this subversive suggestion to pass unchallenged. He was, nevertheless, greatly intrigued that a woman should interfere with him from within, and, after much reflection, he came to the conclusion that she must be the personification of his soul. In many traditions the soul is conceived of as feminine, and for this reason he gave her the Latin name 'anima'. 'I came to see that this inner feminine figure plays a typical, or archetypal, role in the unconscious of a man,' and 'anima' seemed the most appropriate name for her (*MDR*, p. 174).

The Salome figure was herself a personification of that aspect of the anima which Jung could not find in Emma but had found in Toni Wolff. In fact, Elijah and Salome were inner representations of the outer relationship between Jung and Toni. Jung had always seemed older than his years – his nickname at school was 'Father Abraham' – and Barbara Hannah, who became a close colleague of Jung, tells us that to see Jung and Toni together was to exaggerate the difference in age between them: 'He seemed the prototype of the wise old man, she had a quality of eternal youth' (Hannah, 1977, p. 117). Although Jung makes no mention of it in his memoir, Toni supported him throughout the protracted ordeal of his experiment with the unconscious. She was his companion of the way or, in alchemical terms, his *soror mystica*. The nearest he comes to acknowledging this is a passage in which he declares that anyone involved in work with the unconscious should have the benefit of another's point of view, for even the Pope has a confessor. 'Women are particularly gifted for playing such a part,' he says. 'They often have excellent intuition and a trenchant critical insight ... They see aspects that the man does not see' (*MDR*, p. 133).

Toni was particularly important to him at times when he felt that he was losing his sanity, and perhaps on this account Emma appears to have muted her hostility and agreed to a *modus vivendi* whereby Toni was admitted to the family circle, and the nature of her relationship with Carl was tacitly accepted. Barbara Hannah thinks that this was made possible because Jung had enough love for them both. She quotes Emma Jung as saying years later: 'You see, he never took anything from me to give to Toni, but the more he gave her, the more he seemed to be able to give me' (Hannah, 1977, pp. 119–20). More significant still, Emma told a friend of Laurens van der Post, 'I shall always be grateful to Toni for doing for my husband what I or anyone else could not have done for him at a most critical time' (van der Post, 1975, p. 177).

For her part, Toni must be given credit for not using her power over Jung to destroy his marriage and take him to herself – though she once admitted to Barbara Hannah that this required great self-control. Throughout this time she was stalwart. She carried the full burden of his anima projection, as well as his terrors and despair, until the personification of the anima in his fantasy life became sufficiently differentiated for him to be less in need of an outer woman to mediate his work with the unconscious. For the anima is not only a built-in anticipation of the woman to be encountered in the outer world but also the personification of all that is feminine in the male. Whatever one may think about the morality of their relationship, Toni evidently advanced Jung's individuation by enabling him to integrate the unlived feminine in himself and bring it to maturity. There is little doubt that the relationship was of equal importance to her.

Nevertheless, the whole experience brought him to the edge of madness. Not only did he hear voices, play like a child and walk about his garden holding lengthy conversations with an imaginary companion, but he believed his house to be invaded by spirits. He reports that on one occasion the front doorbell began ringing frantically when no one was there.

> I was sitting near the doorbell, and not only heard it but saw it moving. We all simply stared at one another. The atmosphere was thick, believe me! Then I knew that something had to happen. The whole house was filled as if there were a crowd present, crammed full of spirits. They were packed deep right up to the door, and the air was so thick that it was scarcely possible to breathe. As for myself, I was all a-quiver with the question: 'For God's sake, what in the world is this?' Then they cried out in chorus, 'We have come back from Jerusalem where we found not what we sought.' (*MDR*, p. 183.)

He dealt with this intrusion by writing his *Seven Sermons of the Dead*. It poured out of him, and within three evenings it was written. 'As soon as I took up the pen, the whole ghostly assemblage evaporated. The room quieted and the atmosphere cleared. The haunting was over.'

But experiences like this warned him how perilous a state he was in and how desperately he needed to keep a hold on reality. He would repeat to himself, 'I have a medical diploma from a Swiss university; I must help my patients; I have a wife and five children; I live at 228 Seestrasse in Küsnacht,' in order to remind himself that he really existed and that he was not 'a blank page whirling about in the winds of the spirit, like Nietzsche', who went mad when he had similar experiences (*MDR*, pp. 181–2). Jung recognized, of course, the irony that he, a psychiatrist, should run into the same psychic material as is found in the insane. He was exploring the same fund of unconscious images which fatally confuse the psychotic patient. But this only confirmed for him the truth of Bleuler's teaching, namely, that there is no fundamental distinction between the healthy and the abnormal mind. Through active imagination he was merely entering realms of the psyche which are normally inaccessible to people when they are sane.

What prevented these experiences from being destructive was the creative attitude he adopted to them: 'I took great care to try to understand every single image, every item of my psychic inventory, and to classify them scientifically – so far as this was possible – and, above all, to realize them in actual life. That is what we usually neglect to do. We allow the images to rise up, and maybe we wonder about them, but that is all. We do not take the trouble to understand them, let alone draw ethical conclusions from them.' Understanding, knowledge and insight are not enough. 'Insight into them must be converted into an ethical obligation ... The images of the unconscious place a great responsibility on a man' (*MDR*, pp. 184–5).

We begin to see that, starting at the age of 38, this was the turning point of Jung's life. It began with a regression to childhood, which was followed by a period of profound introversion and a movement of libido into the unconscious. Now there came a period of progression, of confident extraversion, and a new synthesis between his conscious and unconscious personalities. This immensely enriching phase reached its culmination in the months immediately after the Armistice in 1918, during which he was the commandant of a camp for British internees. Each morning he would work on a mandala in his notebook, an activity which increasingly absorbed him. He found, to his great satisfaction, that his drawings enabled him to objectify and observe the transformations which his psyche underwent from day to day. 'I had the distinct feeling that they were something central, and in time I acquired through them a living conception of the Self' (*MDR*, p. 187).

He began to understand that the goal of all psychic development is the Self. 'There is no linear evolution; there is only a circumambulation of the Self ... I knew that in finding the mandala as an expression of the Self I had attained what was for me the ultimate' (*MDR*, p. 188).

A series of insights flooded his consciousness at this time. The Self is the centre beyond which it is not possible to go. It is the goal to which everything is directed. It is the archetype of orientation and meaning. As one approaches it one comes under the power of its influence: then all oppositions are transcended and intrapsychic healing occurs. These ideas struck him with the force of a gnostic revelation: he *knew* them to be true. As a result, the stability that had eluded him for years came within his grasp: 'Gradually my inner peace returned' (*MDR*, p. 188).

Finally, the whole extraordinary 'experiment' ended with a dream. He found himself in Liverpool – which literally means 'pool of life'. The various quarters of the city were arranged radially about a square. 'In the centre was a round pool, and in the middle of it a small island. While everything round about was obscured by rain, fog, smoke and dimly lit darkness, the little island blazed with sunlight. On it stood a single tree, a magnolia, in a shower of reddish blossoms. It was as though the tree stood in the sunlight and was at the same time the source of light.' Some companions who were with him commented on the abominable weather. 'They spoke of another Swiss who was living in Liverpool, and expressed surprise that he should have settled here. I was carried away by the beauty of the flowering tree and the sunlit island, and thought, "I know very well why he has settled here"' (*MDR*, p. 189).

This dream brought him a sense of finality. The unpleasant black opaqueness of the fog represented what he had undergone up to that point. But now he had been vouchsafed an image of unearthly beauty and with that he could go on living in the 'pool of life'.

After that he gave up drawing and painting mandalas, for the dream had depicted the climax of the whole process of the development of consciousness. It satisfied him completely. 'When I parted from Freud, I knew that I was plunging into the unknown. Beyond Freud, after all, I knew nothing; but I had taken the step into darkness. When that happens, and then such a dream comes, one feels it as an act of grace' (*MDR*, p. 190).

CONSEQUENCES FOR JUNG'S PSYCHOLOGY

It seems that Jung's work as a student with his strange, mediumistic cousin was seminal to the later development of his ideas. It not only provided him with inspiration to discover his own psychic reality, but it also showed him how unconscious parts of the total psyche could 'personate' through free use of the imagination. It also gave rise to the fundamental concept of *individuation* and was the basis of the whole therapeutic orientation which came to be practised in his name.

Of all the figures he encountered in the course of his *Nekyia* none affected him more deeply than Philemon and his anima. If one considers Philemon in the light of Jung's life as a whole, it becomes evident that this intensely numinous figure performed two equally indispensable functions. First, having destroyed the surrogate father's authority in the persons of Siegfried and Freud and having suffered the bereavement of their loss, Jung now discovered his own inner authority in Philemon. Second, Philemon constituted a prefiguration of the charismatic personality that Jung was to become in later life – the guru, the spiritual father, the wise old man.

Discovery of the anima was no less a boon for him. The more differentiated she became as an inner figure, the more Jung found he could rely on her in dealing with the unconscious. He learned from his encounters with her that she could on occasion be cunning and destructive but that she also had a very positive aspect, which he came increasingly to value. For decades afterwards he would turn to the anima when he felt emotionally disturbed or when some unknown event was being prepared for

Figure 10 Jung's mandala, 'Window on Eternity'

in the unconscious. 'I would then ask the anima: "Now what are you up to? What do you see? I should like to know." After some resistance she regularly produced an image. As soon as the image was there, the unrest or the sense of oppression vanished' (*MDR*, p. 180).

That inner figures could assume such crucial importance for a man strikes many people as bizarre – particularly if they are extraverts and firmly grounded in their sensation function. Even to some introverts, it seems strange. Yet these psychic personages are present in all of us, if we but attend to them, and the knack of conducting inner dialogues with them is not hard to acquire. However, Jung was exceptional in the degree to which such figures were real for him and in the extent to which he acknowledged the power they had to influence his life. Dr Anthony Storr (1973) has commented that this was symptomatic of Jung's extreme isolation. Happily married people, he suggests, are not normally aware of any discrepancy between their partner and an inner representation of the opposite sex. To become vividly aware of unconscious fantasy figures requires a withdrawal into the wilderness reminiscent of the temptation of Christ or St Anthony. 'The completely isolated man has only fantasy figures,' says Storr, and he argues that 'the whole concept of the anima and animus arose from the fact that Jung was an emotionally isolated person' (p. 57).

As we have seen, Jung's isolation was also an important factor in the formulation of his hypothesis of the collective unconscious and his theory of psychological types. But this does not invalidate these hypotheses. Important discoveries are generally made by unusual people capable of pushing themselves to extremes and of tolerating conditions which ordinary men and women could not endure. If Jung was afflicted with feelings of isolation, he was also blessed with a supreme gift for introspection, and this more than adequately compensated for his loneliness. His isolation was the thorn in his flesh which drove him on to discover a world that escapes the attention of the socially adjusted (and less conscious) majority.

There are, in fact, numerous parallels to what Jung had experienced. Indeed, Odysseus' visit to the Sojourn of the Dead must in part have guided Jung, since it was read to him by his friend Albert Oeri during a cruise on Lake Zürich shortly before

Jung began his own descent into the underworld. The theme recurs in the epic of Gilgamesh, Virgil's *Aeneid*, Dante's *Divine Comedy* and even in early science fiction (e.g., Jules Verne's *Journey to the Centre of the Earth*). Present in all of them is the notion of regression and involution (descent and turning inwards), the turning point (*enantiodromia*, going over to the opposite) and progression and evolution (ascent and turning outwards). Thus, when Virgil accompanies Dante in his descent into the underworld, they do not retrace their steps until they have reached the deep point of Hell: only then do they commence the reverse journey – the ascent towards Purgatory and Heaven. This spontaneous reversal – Heraclitus' *enantiodromia* – is a natural expression of the homeostatic principle and is experienced by all those who have gone through a depressive illness. It is also characteristic of what Henri Ellenberger (1970) calls the 'creative illness'.

In his remarkable book *The Discovery of the Unconscious* Ellenberger describes the creative illness as a rare condition whose onset usually occurs after a long period of intense intellectual work. The main symptoms are exhaustion, depression and irritability, and it can present the picture of a severe neurosis and, sometimes, a psychosis.

During the illness the sufferer remains preoccupied with the problems that absorbed his attention before the onset. He feels isolated and develops the conviction that no one can help him. He is driven, therefore, to find ways of healing himself. Not infrequently, these attempts seem to increase his suffering, and the illness can last as long as three or four years. Recovery occurs spontaneously, is associated with feelings of euphoria and is followed by a transformation of the personality. The subject emerges convinced that he has gained access to a new spiritual truth which it is his duty to share with the world.

Examples of the illness can be found among Siberian and Alaskan shamans, among mystics of all religions and among certain creative writers, philosophers and artists. Ellenberger provides persuasive evidence to suggest that Gustav Theodor Fechner, the founder of psychophysics, suffered such an illness between his late thirties and early forties, as did Friedrich Nietzsche and Rudolf Steiner. As we noted in Chapter Two, this fate also befell Freud as well as Jung. Freud, suffering his crisis twenty years earlier when he had a neurotic breakdown, was extremely dependent upon his friend Wilhelm Fliess and conducted his own self-analysis through the use of free association.

The interesting point to emerge from this is that Freud's self-analysis was as crucial to the development of psychoanalysis as was Jung's experiment with the unconscious in the development of analytical psychology. For both it was the perilous journey of the hero, bearing the archetypal hallmarks of isolation, initiation and the return. Having undergone his superhuman ordeal, the hero re-emerges as a man transformed, possessed of great wisdom and the power to bestow benefits on his fellow men and women. Such experiences result in what Joseph Campbell calls a *hierophantic realization* – a profound intuition that carries the visionary into the realm of the sacred, which is inaccessible to those engaged in the profane matters of hunting and gathering, getting and spending. Properly understood, the mental suffering involved can transcend the usual life-maiming experience of a psychiatric breakdown because it brings insight, vision and understanding. Tragically, most doctors and most contemporary psychiatrists do not understand this. As I have already pointed out, they approach mid-life disturbances not as an opportunity for spiritual transformation but as a sickness to be suppressed. Their treatment is designed not to promote individuation but to bring about what Jung caricatured as 'the negative restoration of the persona' – that is to say, a reversion to the *status quo ante*.

There can be little doubt that Jung experienced his illness as a hierophantic realization or that he suffered any uncertainty about the importance of what he had to share with the world. 'There were things in the images which concerned not only myself but many others also. It was then that I ceased to belong to myself alone, ceased to have the right to do so. From then on, my life belonged to the generality ... It was then that I dedicated myself to service of the psyche. I loved it and hated it, but it was my greatest wealth' (*MDR*, p. 184). In old age he declared that he had never lost touch with those initial fantasies and dreams and that all his creative work had come out of them.

It took him the rest of his life to distil within his understanding all that he had experienced and recorded at that time. 'The years when I was pursuing my inner images were the most important in my life – in them everything essential was decided. It all began then: the later details are only supplements and clarifications of the material that burst forth from the unconscious, and at first swamped me. It was the *prima materia* for a lifetime's work' (*MDR*, p. 191).

What he suffered was not for himself alone but for mankind. A breakdown, such as afflicts many at the mid-point of their lives, was seized by him as an opportunity to learn how the psyche behaves at such times and how it finds the power to heal itself. Through this brave endeavour he found his own myth and his life's meaning. It brought him the realization that the psyche is a reality *sui generis*, irreducible to any other cause; that encounter with archetypal symbols at a critical phase of life brings radical transformation of the personality through which the ego acquires modesty and gives ground to the Self as the centre of all experience; and that the whole process is quintessentially religious, a true *vocation*, because heeding the 'inner voice' brings revelation. He now had the knowledge on which to base a new Psychology and a new therapeutic approach to the 'cure of souls'.

SUGGESTIONS FOR FURTHER READING

Mircea Eliade, *Shamanism: Archaic Techniques of Ecstasy*
Barbara Hannah, *Jung: His Life and Work*
Daryl Sharp, *The Survival Papers: Anatomy of a Midlife Crisis*
Murray Stein, *In Midlife: A Jungian Perspective*

Part III

FROM MID-LIFE TO DEATH

Chapter Nine

MIDDLE AGE

THE ARCHETYPAL PROGRAMME

In Chinese philosophy Confucianism and Taoism represent opposing yet complementary poles of human nature. Confucianism is concerned with extraverted life in society and Taoism with the introverted life of the Way. Confucianism is thus appropriate to what Jung saw as the goals of the first half of life and Taoism to those of the second. At the middle of life an *enantiodromia* occurs. 'At the stroke of noon the descent begins. And the descent means the reversal of all the ideals and values that were cherished in the morning' (*CW* 8, para. 778). Although the two halves of life are not simple mirror opposites, Jung's stark statement contains more than a grain of truth. What goes up must come down. Or as Estienne's aphorism has it: *Si jeunesse savoit; si vieillesse pouvoit* ('If youth knew; if age could').

The stroke of noon is a painful moment for all of us, as it carries with it inescapable intimations of mortality. 'And therefore never send to know for whom the bell tolls,' warned Donne: 'It tolls for thee' (*Devotions*).

> 'And so, from hour to hour we ripe and ripe,
> And then from hour to hour we rot and rot,
> And thereby hangs a tale.'
> (William Shakespeare, *As You Like It*, Act II, Scene vii)

The knowledge that one day we must surely die is one of the most disagreeable discoveries of childhood, but there are a number of ego-defence mechanisms at our disposal to take the sting out of this dreadful truth, and for the first forty years or so we live comforted by the thought that old age is far off and death too remote to bear worrying about. Then, suddenly, the realization dawns that it is not such a long way off after all – in fact, it is rushing up towards one like the ground towards a complacent parachutist. How apposite is the medieval symbol of human life as so much sand running through the aperture of an hourglass! At first, the level of the sand falls so slowly as to be imperceptible, but then, when more than half of the contents has passed out of the upper chamber, the level falls faster and faster until, in the last few minutes of the hour, the rush through the hole is positively unseemly. So it is with life.

> But at my back I always hear
> Time's winged chariot hurrying near.
> And yonder all before us lie
> Deserts of vast eternity.
>
> (Andrew Marvell, 'To His Coy Mistress')

Birth, reproduction and death – de-integration and re-integration in endless cycles – these are the very basis of existence on this planet, which none but the lowliest organisms escape. An amoeba or a bacterium does not die: it reproduces itself by simply splitting into two and thus lives on in its progeny more completely than we do. What made our evolution possible and our survival secure was nature's discovery of sexual reproduction, but with sex came its inevitable corollary – death. Nature demanded the mortality of the individual in return for the immortality of the species. Before each generation fades away its new conjunction of chromosomes enables, through sexual reproduction, the next generation to adapt to novel challenges in the environment, thus allowing the species to survive and, through mutation, new species to evolve. Individual death is the price of collective survival and involution the precondition of evolution.

Natural selection has therefore ensured that the archetypal programme for human life be ruthlessly finite, since to grant an unlimited lifespan to individuals after they had fulfilled their reproductive usefulness would be impossibly wasteful of the resources required by subsequent generations. And so we have to die; and, as sentient beings, we have to know it.

But one interesting question arises. If, once we have produced and reared our children, Nature regards us as expendable, why does she allow us to stay around for a further thirty or forty years before finally gathering us to her bosom? Is it because she is lazy, or is there method in her mildness?

Jung was sure there was a purpose: 'A human being would certainly not grow to be seventy or eighty years old if this longevity had no meaning for the species. The afternoon of life must have a significance of its own and cannot be merely a pitiful appendage of life's morning' (*CW* 8, para. 787). He argues that the function of people in the second half of life is to sustain the culture that supported their youth. He saw older people as essentially the repositories of wisdom.

In case this idea should seem unduly exalted, it is well to remember, when dealing with archetypal realities, that by far the most extensive period of our existence as a species was spent in a state of preliteracy. Not only did our forebears lack schools and universities, but they could not write things down, since no one had discovered how to do it. If the laws, myths and traditions of a people were to be passed on, there was no other means than by word of mouth. It was essential, therefore, that enough members of each society should achieve years advanced enough for them to be experienced and knowledgeable in interpreting the customs of the past. The integrity, indeed the very survival, of the culture depended on it.

Our species has, after all, been literate for a mere five thousand years. Before that, if one needed advice on an important matter in one's life, or if one needed to know the right way to do something, one turned to an older and wiser member of the community. Viewed in this global perspective, Jung's assertion does not appear far-fetched. The second half of life is a period of continued development. By following the archetypal imperative to individuate, we become as complete human beings as we can *within the context of our culture* and, in so doing, perform our highest spiritual function for the well-being of society as well as for the personal fulfilment of our lives.

Now that we have books and universities, mass-circulation periodicals and television, it might be thought that older people are no longer necessary to play this role, but this would be a facile conclusion to reach. Mere information is no substitute for accumulated experience and insight; the acquisition of 'book learning' cannot rival the inspiration to be derived from someone who *knows*; the young cannot see what fullness the human personality can achieve unless they encounter someone who has attained it.

The increased life expectancy of modern times has brought new emphasis to the second half of life. When times were harder and life much shorter for the great majority of people, the priorities of life concerned survival and reproduction. But now that more and more people are living into their eighties, the spiritual quality of our culture could be greatly enriched. The problem is that, in the years since the great symbols of Judaeo-Christianity began to lose their vitality, we have collectively become so preoccupied with material development and personal gratification that few of us seem aware of a deeper meaning or purpose to life than is represented by an increase in the Gross National Product. In other words, our values *as a culture* are predominantly adolescent ones. We are in need of a cultural shift in the direction of post-mid-life wisdom, and it is possible that, as the population becomes more weighted in favour of the older age groups, *enantiodromia* may occur – but only if more of us respond creatively to the challenges of mid-life and heed the call to individuate.

This does not mean to say that at the age of forty we all have to enter Jungian analysis or that we have necessarily to undergo the same profound inner transformation that Jung did during his confrontation with the unconscious. Individuation is essentially about waking up, becoming conscious and being constantly alive to the possibility in one's life for growth and development. Jung maintained that some people never wake up, but some wake up early, some in mid-life, others very late – perhaps during a terminal illness or on their deathbed. Possibly in our society those who never wake up are in the majority.

Jung saw two possibilities for people as they enter middle age: they either change or they become rigid. Either 'Certain traits may come to light which had disappeared since childhood; or again one's previous inclinations and interests begin to weaken and others take their place' or 'one's cherished convictions and principles, especially moral ones, begin to harden and grow increasingly rigid until, somewhat around the age of fifty, a period of intolerance and fanaticism is reached. It is as if the existence of these principles were endangered and it were necessary to emphasise them all the more' (*CW* 8, para. 773). Pope John XXIII put it more pithily: 'Men are like wine,' he said. 'Some turn to vinegar, but the best improve with age.'

Clearly, how we confront the mid-life crisis carries the utmost significance for how we live the rest of our lives, for it determines whether or not we choose the path of individuation.

The individuation principle

The idea of individuation is by no means new. Interest in the *principium individuationis* has recurred throughout the history of Western philosophy since the time of Aristotle. It is to be found in the work of Aquinas, Leibniz, Spinoza, Locke and Schopenhauer, but these great thinkers focused on the conscious aspects of the process, so their work is of limited usefulness in the development of a dynamic psychology. A small number of developmental theorists in the present century, such as Charlotte Bühler, Erik Erikson, Kurt Goldstein and Abraham Maslow, have observed the operation of the individuation process in their subjects and have used such terms as 'self-realization' and 'self-actualization' to describe it. But these concepts fall short of Jung's 'individuation' because they view the self-actualizing process as peculiar to humans. Jung, on the other hand, considered self-actualization to be a property of all living things. 'Individuation,' he wrote, 'is an expression of that biological process – simple or complicated as the case may be – by which every living thing becomes what it was destined to become from the beginning' (*CW* 11, para. 144). He eventually concluded that a similar principle was at work in inorganic matter as well – as when a crystal forms out of a hidden configuration within its pre-existent liquor. But it is in humans that individuation finds its highest expression.

As part of the order of nature, and because it is a natural homeostatic system, the psyche possesses the power to heal itself, and this is why dreams are so important – particularly series of dreams. In them one can perceive natural processes of healing and individuation taking place. For this reason, individuation is undoubtedly assisted if one attends to one's dreams, but it is not essential to have them analysed. The mere act of writing them down or illustrating them greatly enhances their effect on ego-consciousness. After all, the vast majority of dreams that have ever been dreamed have not been analysed. Yet they clearly perform a vital function because we all have them – as, indeed, do all mammals – and when human subjects are deprived of dream sleep for any length of time they become disorientated, hallucinated and deluded. The probability is that their function, in all species that dream, is to integrate the programme for life laid down in the genome (i.e., the entire genetic constitution of the species) with the daily experience of the individual.

Individuation, then, involves the progressive integration of the unconscious timeless self in the personality of the time-bound individual. And since the human psyche is itself a product of nature, it follows that individuation is a biological phenomenon proceeding in a cosmic context.

However, in the course of growing up, the degree to which the Self can be integrated is inevitably limited by circumstance – especially by the personality, culture and relationship of the parents. Just as no parent can ever hope to embody the totality of the parental archetype, so no individual ego can ever hope to incorporate the wholeness of the Self. In every case, certain aspects of the Self will prove unacceptable to the family milieu and will consequently be relegated to the personal unconscious to fill out the shadow personality, while others will remain unactualized and will persist as latent archetypal potential, which may or may not be activated at a later date. In the history of every one of us there will have been *some* distortion of primary archetypal intent, and none of us by middle age can hope to be any more than a 'good enough' version of the Self. The extent of the earlier distortion, however, will make all the difference between neurosis and mental health and will affect the degree to which one may be said to have started on the path of individuation.

At the organic level individuation proceeds with or without the participation of consciousness, and it has to be understood as a relative, not an absolute, phenomenon. There are differing degrees and various forms that individuation can assume. Natural, relatively unconscious individuation, for example, just happens and is virtually indistinguishable from normal maturation: the individual merely acts as a carrier of the process. This 'natural' individuation proceeds inexorably from the cradle to the grave. It is the imperative to develop that is imminent in every aspect of life from the very beginning.

However, the kind of individuation that was the focus of Jung's attention was the process *consciously lived* and *actively participated in* by the committed ego. This is the individuation that Jung saw to be the responsibility of the second half of life; and ego-consciousness is crucial to its fulfilment – not as director, stage-manager or *metteur-en-scène* but as collaborator, co-author and grateful recipient of all that the unconscious may offer. This is the initiation which is ushered in by the mid-life crisis – the time at which many people 'wake up'.

Involvement in life during the first thirty-five or forty years is usually so wholehearted that it is possible to live out the life cycle quite unreflectingly and still experience the joys of achievement, but if one goes on living biologically and economically into the second half without becoming conscious of oneself *existentially*, then one is missing the point; life, in all essentials, is finished. To choose individuation is to wake up to the prospect of ageing, to grow accustomed to the sound of time's wingèd chariot hurring near, to accept one's achievements and failures, weaknesses and strengths and to make ready to abandon the youthful ego-centred state for the mature state of ego-transcendence. Then the original promise of one's conception may be achieved – to become as complete a human being as it is in one to be.

Like individuation itself, the idea that each of us is but a pale replica of our potential Self is extremely ancient. When Pindar advised, 'Become what thou art,' he meant, 'Abandon your superficial persona, your social clichés, your worldly habits, and discover the ideal human being latent in your soul and befriend the personal daimon which lives there.' At Delphi the temple of Apollo bore the words 'Know thyself' – which is what Socrates meant when he said that the unexamined life is not worth living. Both Plato and Aristotle taught that to become your true self is to make explicit what implicitly you already are. Jung was indebted to these sources, as indeed he was to the great European discoverers of the unconscious, Carl Gustav Carus, Eduard von Hartmann, Arthur Schopenhauer, G. H. von Schubert and Ignaz Paul Vital Troxler. Particularly influential was von Schubert's belief that in each individual there coexisted a personal soul (the ego) and an aspect of the World Soul (the Self). For his part,

Troxler saw the centre of the personality not as the ego but as what he called the *Ich selbst*: the *Ich selbst*, he said, was the goal of this life and the starting point for life after death: it was indispensable for communion with God. Troxler also attributed major importance to dreams, insisting that in them we find the revelation of our own human essence and that dreams are the means through which we progress to a higher form of existence.

The Self, then, is both the origin and the goal of ego-consciousness. Everything unexperienced by the ego is unconscious and unknown. Individuation is about experiencing the unexperienced and knowing the unknown. Coming to Selfhood, therefore, in the second half of life, is more than a cultural commitment to being a good citizen; it is an ethical choice to fulfil one's individual humanity, to transcend one's fear of death and to recognize oneself as a unique expression of all creation. That realization made, one enters the religious dimension; one attains 'wisdom'. For the more conscious one becomes, the more conscious the universe becomes of itself.

JUNG'S MIDDLE AGE

A change came over Jung as he entered his fifties. It was apparent not only to those who knew him but also in the photographs which were taken at the time. Earlier pictures show a rather austere figure with close-cropped hair and small eyes behind rimless spectacles, but from fifty onwards the image is more open and sympathetic: the eyes twinkle with humour and intelligence and the whole countenance exudes integrity, kindness and human warmth. Many have mentioned the new authority which possessed him after he emerged from his confrontation with the unconscious and the absolute conviction with which he spoke of such matters as the anima, the Self and the union of opposites. As he grew older, the tendency to aloofness betrayed in his youth gave way to the altogether more genial persona revealed by the later photographs. Although still relishing seclusion, he displayed a talent for getting on with people in all walks of life and became increasingly sociable as the years went by. He wore his vast erudition lightly, and people who met him were impressed as much by his simplicity, humour and courtesy as they were by his wisdom and the force of his intellect.

If enrichment of the personality does indeed result from working with the unconscious in the manner advocated by Jung, then he was a good advertisement for his own theories. The degree of individuation which became apparent in him drew people to consult him from all over the world, and it accounts for the interest that has grown in him after his death.

The fascinating truth is that if he had perished at the age of forty, during the First World War, it is unlikely that his contribution to our culture would have received any greater recognition than a footnote in textbooks on the history of psychiatry. His true stature became apparent only as he *grew* into old age.

He emerged from his mid-life crisis not only as a wiser and more considerable man but also as a man with a life of extraordinary achievement ahead of him. Just as he had no doubts about his vocation on the threshold of early maturity, so now he knew exactly what he had to do with the second half of his life. He *must* understand what had happened to him during his confrontation with the unconscious. 'I had to find evidence for the historical prefiguration of my inner experiences. That is to say, I had to ask myself, "Where have my particular premises already occurred in history?" If I had not succeeded in finding any evidence, I would never have been able to substantiate my ideas' (*MDR*, p. 192).

First he turned to the Gnostic writers, convinced that they too had confronted the primordial world of the unconscious. Unfortunately, the major accounts that have survived of gnostic beliefs and experiences come from their opponents and persecutors, and Jung was unable to establish any real link with them over the issues burning in his mind.

However, with the immense energy of one who has emerged from a creative illness, he ransacked the histories of philosophy and religion and, on the basis of these researches, wrote *Psychological Types*, published in 1921. This, as we have already seen, was an attempt to put his differences with Freud on an objective basis and to develop a theory to explain how different individuals can develop different orientations to the same phenomena. It was also his first systematic attempt to organize his ideas about the structure and function of the psyche that had emerged during his experiment with the unconscious.

Then, in 1922, he bought some land at Bollingen, beside the beautiful upper lake of Zürich. There he began to build the simple dwelling that was to become his 'Tower', over whose entrance he eventually inscribed *Philemonis Sacrum – Fausti Poenitentia* (Shrine of Philemon – Repentance of Faust). At this stage, words and paper did not seem real enough to him; he felt that something more was needed. 'I had to achieve a kind of representation in stone of my innermost thoughts and of the knowledge I had acquired' (*MDR*, p. 212). Over the years he added to this building until it became a habitable mandala in stone. As he grew old this tranquil place beside the lake became more and more precious to him, and as a very old man he wrote: 'At Bollingen I am in the midst of my true life, I am most deeply myself.' Here he could be the No. 2 personality he had already experienced as a child. 'In my fantasies he took the form of Philemon, and he comes to life again at Bollingen' (*MDR*, p. 214).

Historical affirmation of all that he had been through up to the end of the First World War did not come, however, until he 'discovered' alchemy. This happened in 1927, when he was already fifty-two. The eminent sinologist Richard Wilhelm sent him the manuscript of a Taoist alchemical treatise called *The Secret of the Golden Flower*, with a request that Jung should write a commentary on it. This caused him great excitement, for he found in the text the most extraordinary confirmation of his ideas about the mandala and the circumambulation of the centre. He realized at once the crucial significance of this discovery. 'That was the first event which broke through my isolation. I became aware of an affinity; I could estabish ties with something and someone' (*MDR*, p. 189).

As was usual with Jung, when something as important as this was brewing, he had several dreams that prepared him for what lay in store.

In one of these he entered a previously unknown wing or annexe of his house. There he discovered a wonderful library, dating from the sixteenth or seventeenth century. Among the numerous fat folio volumes were several embellished with strange copper engravings containing curious symbols such as he had never seen before. Only much later did he recognize these as alchemical symbols. At the time he realized that the unknown wing of the house was an aspect of his own personality of which he was not yet conscious. But after fifteen years had passed he had assembled a library very like the one in his dream.

In another crucial dream he found himself in the south Tyrol. It was wartime, and he was driving back from the Italian front with a peasant in his horse-drawn wagon. Eventually they entered the courtyard of a fine old manor house. 'Just as we reached the middle of the courtyard, in front of the main entrance, something unexpected happened: with a dull clang, both gates flew shut. The peasant leaped down from his seat and exclaimed, "Now we are caught in the seventeenth century." Resignedly I thought, "Well, that's that! But what is there to do about it? Now we shall be caught for years." Then the consoling thought came to me: "Some day, years from now, I shall get out again"' (*MDR* p. 195).

Several years passed before Jung realized that these dreams referred to alchemy, which reached its peak in the seventeenth century. Meanwhile, his delight in *The Secret of the Golden Flower* stirred in him a desire to become better acquainted with alchemical texts. Accordingly, he commissioned a Munich bookseller to notify him of any books on alchemy that might fall into his hands. Gradually Jung assembled one of the finest alchemical collections in the world.

To begin with he could not understand a word that he read, but after a while an important realization dawned on him: the alchemists were writing in symbols. He decided he must learn to decipher them. 'By now I was completely fascinated, and buried myself in the texts as often as I had the time. One night, while I was studying them, I suddenly recalled the dream that I was caught in the seventeenth century. At last I grasped its meaning. "So that's it! Now I am condemned to study alchemy from the very beginning"' (*MDR*, p. 196).

He started to compile a lexicon of key phrases with cross references and filled volumes with these, working along philological lines, as if he were trying to decipher some unknown language. 'In this way the alchemical mode of expression gradually yielded up its meaning. It was a task that kept me absorbed for more than a decade' (*MDR*, p. 196).

Now he began to see that alchemy was a precursor of analytical psychology. 'The experiences of the alchemists were, in a sense, my experiences, and their world was my world. This was, of course, a momentous discovery: I had stumbled upon the historical counterpart of my psychology of the unconscious' (*MDR*, p. 196). His fate was sealed – not only for the next decade, but for the rest of his life. Indeed, his ideas about the psychological meaning of alchemy did not reach full maturity until he himself had entered old age. It is appropriate, therefore, that we should postpone examination of them until we come to consider Jung's late maturity.

Just as Jung's intellectual vitality fuelled his research and his literary output, so also it sustained his commitment to analysis and to his patients. He now conceived of analysis more as a method to promote individuation than a means to treat mental disorder, and he spent the rest of his life teaching others, whether as pupils or patients, to use the techniques he had perfected during his own confrontation with the unconscious.

CONSEQUENCES FOR JUNG'S PSYCHOLOGY

The major contributions to psychology made by Jung during this period of his life were his description of the psychological types and the development of analysis as a technique for the promotion of the individuation process. In this section we will briefly examine his theory of types and consider how Jungian analysis is used in the service of individuation.

Psychological types

Jung deduced that in the course of development individuals come to adopt differing habitual attitudes which determine how they experience life. With his own conflict with Freud in mind, he looked into famous quarrels of the past between such figures as St Augustine and Pelagius, Tertullian and Origen, and Luther and Zwingli. He also examined the major distinctions which Nietzsche made between Dionysian and Apollonian attitudes, Ostwald between Classical and Romantic attitudes, Spitteler between the characters of Prometheus and Epimetheus, and Goethe between the principles of diastole (expansion) and systole (contraction). He concluded that all were examples of the same fundamental dichotomy: on the one side there was an outward movement of interest towards the object, and on the other a movement of interest away from the object to the subject and his own psychology. The first typified the extraverted attitude and the second the introverted attitude. A major cause of his rupture with Freud, he believed, was Freud's extraversion and his own introversion.

The desire to detect common denominators and typical characteristics in human nature was not peculiar to Jung. It led to the description in classical times of four temperaments based, as we have seen, on the four elements of Empedocles, to Hippocrates' theory of four humours and to Aristotle's belief in the characterological influences of different types of blood. At about the same time as Jung published his book *Psychological Types* in 1921, Rorschach's *Theory of Types* appeared, as well as Kretschmer's *Physique and Character*.

While they are helpful in imposing some kind of order on the data, all such attempts at characterology are open to the same objection, namely, that they are Procrustian – they endeavour to confine the infinite variety of human psychological differences within a narrow, arbitrary structure. Jung was aware of this deficiency, and in proposing his own typology he did so with fitting modesty: 'One can never give a description of a type, no matter how complete, that would apply to more than one individual, despite the fact that in some ways it aptly characterizes thousands of others. Conformity is one side of a man, uniqueness is the other. Classification does not explain the individual psyche. Nevertheless, an understanding of psychological types opens the way to a better understanding of human psychology in general' (*CW* 6, para. 895).

Introducing the terms *introversion* and *extraversion*, Jung said it would be easy for him to give uncomplicated descriptions of both these fundamental attitude types, 'but everyone possesses both mechanisms, extraversion as well as introversion, and only the relative predominance of one or the other determines the type'.

He describes the extravert as 'an outgoing, candid and accommodating nature that adapts easily to a given situation, quickly forms attachments and, setting aside misgivings, will often venture forth with careless confidence into unknown situations'. The introvert, on the other hand, is 'a hesitant, reflective, retiring nature that keeps itself to itself, shrinks from objects, is always slightly on the defensive and prefers to hide behind mistrustful scrutiny'.

This distinction between introverts and extraverts has found widespread assent. Even that scourge of analysts, Professor Hans

Eysenck of London University, has confirmed the existence of an extraversion–introversion axis in the human personality, using carefully controlled quantitative techniques. Moreover, he equated extraversion with Galen's choleric and sanguine temperaments and introversion with the melancholic and phlegmatic.

There is, however, more to the development of one's psychological type than the adoption of an introverted or extraverted attitude. Jung found that once he had established to his satisfaction the universal applicability of these two categories, he still had to explain how it was that individuals within each category persisted in showing marked differences from one another. Clearly, additional factors were involved. He came to the conclusion that people, whether predominantly introverted or extraverted, further differed from one another in respect of the degree to which they developed the conscious use of one or more of four basic functions. As we noted in Chapter Two, he designated these *thinking*, *feeling*, *sensation* and *intuition*. He gives the most succinct definition of these four functions in his book *Modern Man in Search of a Soul* (1933), where he says: 'Sensation establishes what is essentially given, thinking enables us to recognize its meaning, feeling tells us its value, and finally intuition points to the possibilities of the whence and whither that lie within the immediate facts' (p. 107).

Jung considered feeling, like thinking, to be a *rational* function, since it has less to do with emotion or affect than with *evaluating* the significance of objects and events. Sensation and intuition, on the other hand, were to be conceived of as *non-rational* functions in that they proceeded beyond the confines of rationality. These non-rational functions are, nevertheless, of fundamental importance to the psyche because they give rise to *a priori* knowledge which is irreducible to any other mode of understanding.

Out of the two *attitude* types and the four *functional* types there emerge, theoretically, *eight* possible psychological types: introverted thinking types, extraverted thinking types, introverted feeling types, extraverted feeling types and so on. Jung observed that people tend to develop *one* rational and *one* non-rational function in addition to the introverted or extraverted attitude, while the other two functions remain relatively unconscious. Thus an extraverted thinking–intuitive would have an introverted feeling-sensation *shadow* and vice versa.

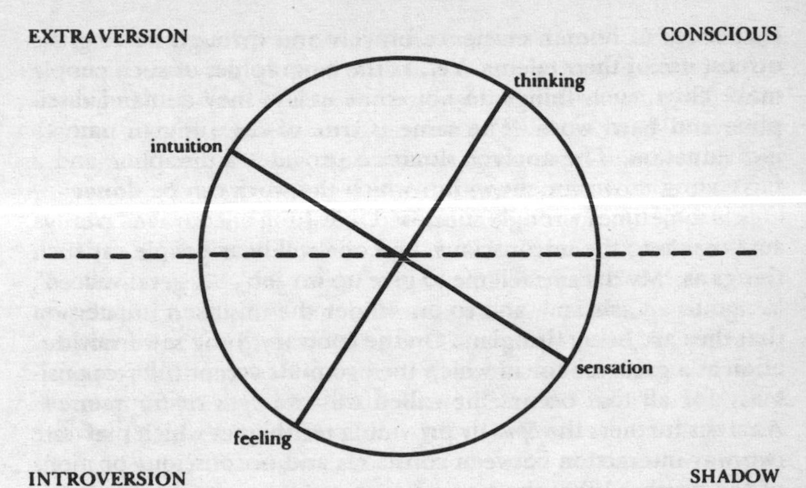

Figure 11 The attitudes and functions in an extraverted thinking–intuitive

Jung's typology provides a useful compass. To know somebody's type is to derive valuable insights into the characteristic assumptions on which he lives his life. It should not, however, be taken as a categorical description of that person. Jung believed that a typology could be useful only if it were an essentially dynamic set of concepts, and he insisted that we remember that *all* typological possibilities are inherently available in the Self. While it is true that in the course of growing up an individual tends to rely on one attitude, the other may always be developed and brought into consciousness as individuation proceeds. Viewed in this light, getting to know one's psychological type is not to put oneself in a straitjacket but to become aware of where there is room left for personal development. It is in this sense that the typology is used in Jungian analysis.

Individuation and analysis

To adopt individuation as one's goal does not demand that one goes into analysis. History abounds with figures who, long before the days of psychotherapy, won through to wholeness and wisdom through conscious commitment to life, through acceptance of themselves and their circumstances, through confronting the challenges of human existence bravely and through making the utmost use of their talents. Yet, as the biographies of such people make clear, such things do not come easily: they demand discipline and hard work. The same is true of the Jungian path to individuation. The analytic situation provides a discipline and a facilitating environment within which the work can be done.

It is sometimes wrongly supposed that Jung encouraged passive submission to the unconscious, and one will hear people say such things as, 'My dreams tell me to give up my job', '... get divorced', '... go to an ashram', and so on, under the mistaken impression that they are being 'Jungian'. On the contrary, Jung saw individuation as a great labour in which the ego must accept full responsibility for all that occurs: he called this the *opus contra naturam*. Analysis furthers the *opus* by providing techniques which promote two-way interaction between conscious and unconscious portions of the psyche. What the unconscious produces the ego responds to, and out of the dialogue between them a new position is achieved. For Jung, analysis carried the implications of a religious rite, for the work was furthering the purpose of the universe – namely, to become conscious of itself. Conscious and unconscious, sentient individual and nature, all then become two poles of a homeostatic system, and it is the purpose of the work to bring about a more balanced, and more conscious, relationship between them.

Writing of individuation, Jung's colleague, Gerhard Adler, declared: 'The whole problem consists in resolving the thesis of pure nature and the antithesis of the opposing ego into the synthesis of *conscious* nature' (*Studies*, p. 109). Adler discusses the relation of man and nature in terms of the subject and the object. '*Objectum* means literally what is in opposition, or facing you; *subjectum*, that which is subjacent, subordinate, or at the mercy of the object. But the object can only attain life through the subject. The task of the first half of life therefore consists in establishing this subject so firmly that it is capable of acting as an equal and opposite pole and as receiving agent to the objectum' (ibid., p. 109).

The psychic state reached as a result of interaction between these equal and opposing poles is both richer and better informed than one based on one or other set of intentions. The ultimate position is neither one nor the other but a third, previously unimagined, possibility, which negates neither the conscious nor unconscious position but does justice to them both. This achievement Jung attributed to the *transcendent function* of the psyche. And it is here that ethics becomes paramount. Ethics is concerned with the taking of informed decisions in the light of values one holds to be good. To live ethically is to 'choose' to develop the best possible personality that one's individuation will allow.

But if individuation is indeed the ultimate goal of the psyche, then the transcendent function is the mechanism indispensable to its achievement. The transcendent function is the psyche's means of evolution, through which it moves towards a fuller realization of its destiny to become whole. Moreover, intimate collaboration between No. 1 and No. 2 personalities is not only crucial for individuation but indispensable to the achievement of genius. Men like Shakespeare, Mozart, Leonardo da Vinci and Goethe all possessed the supreme knack of transforming unconscious intuition into the conscious lineaments of great art. Individuation, like art, depends on fruitful propinquity between the ego and the Self, producing a series of psychic metamorphoses and resulting in greater enrichment of the personality. In Jung's case, his anima was right. He was like an artist in the degree to which his No. 2 personality was accessible to him. But he lacked the gift of Shakespeare or Goethe in formulating the products of its bounty in words. For this reason, many find his books difficult to read.

Individuation is also about choosing one's own uniqueness. It involves not only self-realization but *self-differentiation*: the ethical decision to pursue one's individuation is a choice to differentiate oneself as a whole human being from all other human beings. The great paradox of the entire process is that in realizing one's full humanity one is, at the same time, actualizing one's unique individuality. To individuate, in the full Jungian meaning of the term, is to defy the tyranny of received opinion, to disengage from the banal symbols of mass culture and to confront the primordial symbols in the collective unconscious – in one's own unique way. Only thus does one become in-dividual, a separate, indivisible unity or 'whole'.

In adopting this view Jung is not advocating *individualism* – which is merely the arrogant assertion of the ego. Far from it: 'Individuation means precisely the better and more complete fulfilment of collective qualities' which are invested in the Self

(*CW* 7, para. 267). Nor is he advising a narcissistic withdrawal from the world, the termination of relationships or the abrogation of one's social responsibilities. On the contrary: 'Individuation does not shut out from the world, but gathers the world to oneself' (*CW* 8, para. 432). Thus the desire to individuate is quite opposite to the neurotic desire to be 'normal', that is to say, just like everyone else. The individuating person wants to be like everyone else (a full member of the human family) but in his or her uniquely individual way.

As we have seen from Jung's account of his own individuation experiences, it is a course fraught with danger. There are instances of others who tried to go the same way but came seriously to grief in the process. Levinson (1978) cites Friedrich Nietzsche, Dylan Thomas, F. Scott-Fitzgerald and Vincent van Gogh as examples of men who followed their creative daimon but were led into self-destruction or insanity. Defeat in mid- to late maturity is also a theme to which artists return again and again. The works of Chekhov, Ibsen and Strindberg come to mind in this connection, as do the later plays of Shakespeare – *King Lear* and *The Tempest*. In Lear's abdication of the throne, and in Prospero's breaking of his staff and the drowning of his book as he leaves his enchanted isle, we see a forewarning of Shakespeare's own withdrawal from the drama and the stage. Perhaps he had some foreboding that he was to die at the age of fifty-two.

As examples of writers and thinkers who successfully weathered the storm, however, Levinson cites Dante, Hesse, Mann, Frank Lloyd Wright and Bertrand Russell, as well as Freud and Jung, arguing that their later work had a depth and maturity derived from the creative energies released in them as they passed through their perilous mid-life experiences.

But it is evidently a risky business, and, although formal analysis is not essential, there is no doubt that the support of the analytic relationship – 'the league of the two through thick and thin' – can be of great benefit at this time. Not infrequently, however, individuals feel they have no choice in the matter: the mid-life crisis hits them so hard that they turn in desperation to a therapist to seek help. If that happens, then it is the analyst's duty to enable them to find the *meaning* of their suffering and help them discover the 'opportunity' that the 'crisis' entails. Within the protected, confidential intimacy of the consulting room, the past can be examined and the present circumstances assessed.

Where optimum conditions for individuation
the most comprehensive development possible will h
But such fortuitous circumstances are rare in the backg
those who have come into analysis, as indeed they ar
many who do not. More usually, the maturational proce as been inhibited or skewed at some stage, either by accident or by failure of the environment to meet essential archetypal requirements of the Self.

A person's individuational status at any stage in life represents the best possible achievement of personality growth which has been reached up to that point, and this may be either healthy or pathological as the case may be. Psychiatric conditions such as neurosis, psychosis, psychopathy, alcoholism, drug dependency, sexual deviations and so on can all be understood as *individuation gone awry*.

Health, on the other hand, is that desirable state in which archetypal need has been met by outer fulfilment, enabling the individual to pass freely from one stage of the life cycle to the next with a progressive widening and deepening of the personality. The purpose of analysis is to discover where development has been distorted, what aspects of the Self have not been lived, and then to give close attention to the unconscious in order to help the analysand work with the symbols emerging from his dreams and fantasies, to nourish them through conscious appreciation and to integrate their energy and meaning within the personality as a whole. In this way it is possible to bring to birth the attitude, functions, values, feelings and psychic components which have so far not been lived because, as the result of upbringing, they have remained repressed in the shadow.

For this to occur, the unconscious has to be rendered accessible, and this is where the analytic techniques of dream interpretation and amplification, free association, active imagination and spontaneous painting become important.

Techniques for rendering the unconscious accessible

The reader will already have formed some idea of the Jungian approach to dreams but may still be somewhat mystified by the procedure developed by Jung which he called *active imagination*. Jung described active imagination as *the art of letting things happen*:

'The art of letting things happen, action through non-action, letting go of oneself, as taught by Meister Eckhart, became for me the key opening the door to the way. We must be able to let things happen in the psyche' (1962, p. 93). Jung was intrigued to know what occurs when the mind is left to its own devices, so to speak, without any of the usual guidance or bullying by the ego. This he referred to as the *natural mind*, and he invariably wanted to know what it was up to. 'In sleep fantasy takes the form of dreams. But in waking life, too, we continue to dream below the threshold of consciousness' (*CW* 16, para. 125).

Active imagination is a matter of allowing the natural mind time and freedom to express itself spontaneously. It is important to make some record of what is produced so as to register it and make it lastingly available to consciousness, otherwise it is soon lost. The medium used is a matter of individual taste. The images may be written down, painted, modelled in clay, danced or acted. The important thing is to allow them to happen.

This is a knack which, given patience, anyone can acquire. Active imagination requires a state of reverie, halfway between sleep and waking. It is like beginning to fall asleep but stopping short before consciousness is lost and remaining in that condition. It is often helpful to adopt some little ritual as a *rite d'entrée*: Jung imagined he was descending into a cave; I prefer to use Aeschylus' notion (in the *Eumenides*) that when we pass into a reverie or dream our eyes revolve inwards and light up our souls so that we may perceive the truth about all that has been hidden from us during the day. On first achieving this state, one can usually sustain it for only a few minutes but, with practice, its duration can be extended, so that a session of active imagination can last up to anything between twenty minutes and an hour, depending on one's stamina and on the intrinsic interest of the fantasy as it develops before one's in-turned eyes.

To begin with, one is a mere spectator but, with growing confidence, one can actually participate in the action and so become committed to the absolute reality of the psyche. Only if you do this can you hope to grasp the essence of Jung's intention. You can know the reality and the transformative power of the psyche only if you experience it yourself: 'You yourself must enter into the process with your personal reactions, just as if you are one of the fantasy figures, or rather, as if the drama being enacted before your eyes were real. It is a psychic fact that this fantasy is happening, and it is as real as you – as a psychic entity – are real. If this crucial operation is not carried out, all the changes are left to the flow of images, and you yourself remain unchanged' (*CW* 4, para. 753).

It is necessary to stress this thoroughly Jungian credo because our sceptical age is even agnostic about the existence of the psyche itself, seeing it as a mere epiphenomenon of neurological functioning and therefore of less importance than the brain itself. Jung's standpoint was totally opposed to this soul-deadening view; 'It is indeed paradoxical,' he declared, 'that *the* category of existence, the indispensable *sine qua non* of all existence, namely the psyche, should be treated as if it were only semi-existent. Psychic existence is the only category of existence of which we have *immediate* knowledge, since nothing can be known unless it first appears as a psychic image' (*CW* 11, para. 769). For him the essence of life was *esse in anima* – to *be* in the soul – and this is achieved through the 'continually creative act' of fantasy. 'The psyche creates reality everyday. The only expression I can use for this activity is fantasy' (*CW* 6, para. 78). 'Being that has soul is living being. Soul is the living thing in man, that which lives of itself and causes life ... With her cunning play of illusion the soul lures into life the inertness of matter that does not want to live.' In other words, things come alive and are touched with soul when they come under the influence of imagination. 'With the archetype of the anima we enter the realm of the gods ... Everything the anima touches becomes numinous – unconditional, dangerous, taboo and magical' (*CW* 9, i, para. 59).

Jung insists that active imagination must be done in a spirit of utter seriousness: that the figures which emerge must be treated as *actual experiences*. They are most definitely not '"figments of the imagination" as rationalism would have us believe' (*CW* 5, para. 388). If we work with them hard and long enough, we begin to realize that, instead of deriving them from our psychic state, we derive our psychic state from *them*. 'It is not we who personify them; they have a personal nature from the very beginning' (*CW* 13, para. 62). For this reason it is necessary that we treat them as real people. In advising a certain Mr O. on relating to his anima, Jung wrote: 'Treat her as a person, if you like as a patient or a goddess, but above all treat her as something that does exist ...

you must talk to this person in order to see what she is about and to learn what her thoughts and character are' (7 May 1947).

The soul exists as a perpetual companion to consciousness; its utterances in words and symbolic images proceed ceaselessly below the threshold of everyday awareness. Normally we are unconscious of these priceless communications, just as we cannot perceive the stars in daytime because we are dazzled by the sun. But if we can cease to be dazzled by ego-consciousness, the soul becomes as apparent as the stars at night.

Analysis and the shadow

In practice, the first unconscious personality to emerge in the course of an analysis is not the anima but the shadow. In the early weeks, it is quite common for an analysand to bring a dream in which he is in a house, outside which there is some potentially dangerous or sinister figure that wants to get in. Alarmed, the dreamer goes round the house bolting and barring all the doors and windows but, as he does so, an uneasy feeling grows that these actions are futile and that, whatever he does, the intruder will get in.

Presented with such a dream, the analyst will encourage the dreamer to find out more about this intruder, in the hope that through active imagination the dreamer will begin to come to terms with him and eventually befriend him. This can be difficult to achieve, for, as we saw in Chapter Three, the shadow possesses all those qualities that the superego loathes and despises; normally one denies these qualities in oneself, unconsciously preferring to project them outside on to others, such as members of racial or sexual minorities, or social undesirables like vandals and football hooligans. This is why the hostile figure in the dream lurks *outside* the house; but it is characteristic of the individuation process that this figure should evidently wish to abandon his outsider status and *intrude* – that is to say, gain entrance to the conscious personality in order to promote wholeness.

Although a painful and disagreeable task, assimilation of the shadow can radically improve a patient's total situation. Jung saw neurosis to be the result of self-division. The sick personality is a house divided against itself. The more of the shadow that can be assimilated, the more the inner division is healed, and much previously repressed psychic energy is made available to consciousness.

Many a mid-life breakdown occurs because too much Self-potential has been locked away in the shadow, where it has remained unlived. If this persists, the personality becomes stultified. Indeed, whenever individuation comes to a halt one has the impression of futility – of losing touch with meaning, of no longer living in one's personal myth. At such times one feels like Hamlet: 'How weary, stale, flat, and unprofitable / Seem to me all the uses of this world.'

The Faust legend provides a good example of this. Faust has devoted the first half of his life to virtuous, academic achievement, and he is bored to death with it. His single-minded pursuit of knowledge has resulted in a one-sided, over-intellectualized development and in the suppression of so much Self-potential as to make him miserable, disorientated and utterly disillusioned with life. As usually happens in such cases, however, the repressed psychic energy demands attention, and in Faust's case it personates in the figure of the shadow-intruder, Mephistopheles. Unfortunately, not being in Jungian analysis, Faust does not recognize Mephistopheles as an unlived aspect of himself and, as a consequence, falls under his spell, projecting onto him all the power and energy which he would do better to own and develop himself.

Like Faust, Dr Jekyll, another intellectual bachelor with a similar problem, is fascinated by the charisma of the shadow, and, abandoning his ethical standpoint, he too falls completely under its power. Instead of assimilating the shadow, both Jekyll and Faust are possessed by it. As a result no individuation can occur: Faust becomes a drunk, a trickster and a libertine, and Dr Jekyll becomes the monstrous Mr Hyde. Thus, in dealing with powerful figures emerging from the unconscious at a critical stage in life, it is essential to hold on to the ethical values of ego-consciousness – but not so rigidly as to prevent oneself from confronting and assimilating what it is that these figures represent.

The reason why Faust and Jekyll fascinate us is because they are in a sense heroes: they dare to have dealings with the shadow instead of behaving, as most of us do, like Dorian Gray – striving to put on an innocent *persona* for the world, while keeping our unacceptable qualities hidden away in the hope that no one will discover they are there.

The stories of Jekyll and Faust, like the biblical story of Adam's fall, are cautionary tales which illustrate our theme: in each case a virtuous man, bored with his circumstances, decides to rebel against the prohibitions of the superego in order to liberate the shadow, encounter the anima, possess her and *live* as never before. Of the three, Adam fares best, for, although banished from the Garden of Eden, he retains his integrity as well as his bride, and together they go forth into the world to assume responsibility for their lives and for their eventual mortality. The others are less fortunate, for they lose their conscious hold on reality and are sucked into the maw of the unconscious. In Goethe's version of the Faust legend, however, Faust is redeemed through the profound transformation wrought in him by his anima.

Analysis and the anima/animus

In analysis it is usually not long after the first encounter with the shadow that the anima or animus puts in an appearance. As we have already noted in Jung's account of his own anima experiences, the contrasexual complex has a negative as well as a positive aspect. Now, as with other complexes, those aspects of the animus/anima experienced as negative are those which have been actively denied or repressed in response to environmental pressures. If they go unconfronted, these negative components can vitiate relations with the opposite sex, disturb the inner balance of the psyche and block all genuine creativity. For this reason, Jung regarded the work involved in confronting the contrasexual complex as the masterpiece of individuation. ('If the encounter with the shadow is the "apprentice-piece" in the individual's development, then that with the anima is the "masterpiece"' (*CW* 9, i, para. 61).

The anima and animus exist precisely because of the original hermaphroditic nature of the Self, which, however, begins in the womb to develop a gender bias in favour of the sex of the child. As they grow up, the conscious personality of boys and girls generally assimilates the characteristics regarded as appropriate to their sex. The contrasexual characteristics remain correspondingly unconscious.

Emma Jung, who in later life wrote an excellent book called

Animus and Anima, describes this as follows: 'In the development of masculine consciousness the feminine side is left behind and so remains in a "natural state". The same thing happens in the differentiation of the psychological functions: the so-called inferior function remains behind and, as a result, it is undifferentiated and unconscious. Therefore, in the man it is usually connected with the likewise unconscious anima. Redemption is achieved by recognizing and integrating these unknown elements of the soul' (1957, pp. 57–8).

But, as we have seen, the process of conscious/unconscious gender differentiation is not wholly induced by social pressures. There exist innate cerebral and hormonal biases for boys to develop masculine qualities and a masculine identity and for girls to develop their feminine equivalents. Equally, both males and females possess an innate anticipation of the essential 'oppositeness' of the opposite sex, which makes heterosexual attraction and heterosexual union the compelling and central phenomenon of life that it is. These are all *a priori* archetypal factors on which cultural factors then operate.

The anima/animus complexes, therefore, are not merely intrapsychic match-makers guaranteeing the procreation of the species but the living embodiments of all that is feminine in a man and masculine in a woman. For this reason the anima or animus is never projected *in toto* onto a member of the opposite sex, however beloved he or she may be. When we begin attending to our dreams or doing active imagination, unprojected aspects of the anima/animus emerge as autonomous figures, as daimons.

Jung equated anima with soul – 'My lady Soul', Spitteler called her – because he was working from the masculine point of view. This is why he also had much more to say about the anima than the animus – a deficiency which he left to his wife to make good. However, there is no implication that women lack soul. On the contrary, Jung believed soul to be less unconscious or repressed in women: soul is accessible to them in a way that it is not to most men. The soul aspect that remains unconscious in women is its *yang* or *hun* element carried by the animus, so that for women too the contrasexual archetype is imbued with soul. Jung makes this distinction clear when he identifies anima with *p'o* or *kuei* in classical Chinese philosophy – 'the feminine and cthonic part of the soul' (*CW* 9, i, para. 119), the embodiment of *yin*.

The confrontation with the inner soul image is, therefore, an indispensable stage in the individuation process. When persisted in with absolute commitment, vital resources are mobilized in the service of the psyche as a whole, bringing a fuller measure of personal freedom than has ever been experienced before, a broadening of psychic horizons and an enrichment of personality which is unmistakable to those in whom it has occurred. It is productive not only of wholeness but also of acceptance of one's independence and, it must be acknowledged, one's essential *aloneness* – even in intimacy. This inevitably results in a change in one's relationships, particularly sexual relationships. To a certain extent the opposite sex loses its mystery, and one is less likely to be bewitched or fettered in the same manner as in youth. Since the centre of gravity shifts from the outer object to the inner soul, one is less inclined to 'fall' for someone with the same force as in former years.

But this does not mean that individuation demands a sense of monastic detachment or that advancing years must produce a diminution of the capacity for love. Far from this being the case, understanding the contrasexual personality in oneself is associated with a greater appreciation of those qualities in one's companion and renders both partners more capable of sharing a deeper, more empathic love. As the contrasexual attributes become available to the conscious personality, so a man's *Logos* is complemented by a refined capacity for intimacy and a woman's *Eros* is tempered with rational purposiveness and intellectual understanding. This, indeed, seems to have occurred in Jung's own marriage as a result of his confrontation with the anima and Emma's work with the animus. Writing of her experience of animus assimilation, Emma Jung declared: 'Above all it makes possible the development of a spiritual attitude which sets us free from the limitation and imprisonment of a narrowly personal standpoint ... to raise ourselves out of our personal troubles to suprapersonal thoughts and feelings, which, by comparison, make our misfortunes seem trivial and unimportant' (1957, p. 40).

Again, Jung is insistent that the conscious encounter with the soul image is a task for the second rather than the first half of life. 'What I am saying here is not for the young – it is precisely what they ought not to know – but for the more mature man whose consciousness has been widened by experience of life' (*CW* 10, para. 272). In youth it is sufficient that mutual attraction be powerful enough to unite young couples for the purpose of procreation, rearing children and supporting them till they are old enough to fend for themselves. To become aware of the psychic *coniunctio* both without (in relation to the partner) and within (in relation to the soul-image), if it be attempted at all, is the work of maturity, when child-rearing responsibilities are at an end.

The vital contribution of the contrasexual attribute to the development of personality is apparent in people in whom no such contribution has occurred. People who habitually flee from the opposite sex, for example, usually do so because traumatic or inappropriate care from the contrasexual parent has led to repression, even atrophy, of the anima/animus. Such people will often grow up identifying in a compulsive manner with the members and attributes of their own sex. 'Confirmed' bachelors or spinsters are often of this type. When they do marry, they tend to function somewhat in isolation from their spouse. Psychically, they display what Jung called – using the anthropological term – 'loss of soul'. 'Younger people, who have not yet reached the middle of life (around the age of thirty-five), can bear even the total loss of the anima without injury . . . After the middle of life, however, permanent loss of the anima means a diminution of vitality, of flexibility, and of human kindness. The result, as a rule, is premature rigidity, crustiness, stereotypy, fanatical one-sidedness, obstinacy, pedantry, or else resignation, weariness, sloppiness, irresponsibility, and finally a childish *ramollissement* with a tendency to alcohol' (*CW* 9, i, paras. 146 and 147).

A quite other picture is presented by those who in childhood have experienced an intense *identification* with the parent of the opposite sex. Then the ego can become inflated with the contra-sexual archetype and there is a corresponding failure to actualize the sexual principle appropriate to the individual's biological gender. The result is either a 'butch' animus-dominated woman or a weak anima-dominated man. Although such people can certainly carry many of the good qualities of the opposite sex, these tend to be uncompensated by the qualities of their own gender. People of this type, especially when they are unrelated to a member of the opposite sex, tend to be moody, fussy and

emotional if th... ...ogative' (*CW* 10, para. 243). if they ... ...n were far more 'psychological' is... more concerned with 'logic': 'It is ... most direct exponent of psychology ...tent. Very many things can be perceived ...ost distinctness which in a man are mere ...in the background, whose very existence he is u...nt' (*CW* 10, para. 258).

H... ...cally masculine and feminine orientations as invariably c...terizing the attitudes of men and women to sex and marriage. To the woman, he maintained, marriage is always an exclusive relationship.

> She can endure its exclusiveness all the more easily, without dying of ennui, inasmuch as she has children or near relatives with whom she has a no less intimate relationship than with her husband. The fact that she has no sexual relationship with these others means nothing, for the sexual relationship is of far less importance to her than the psychic relationship ... In reality she is distributed among the children and among as many members of the family as possible, thus maintaining any number of intimate relationships. If her husband had as many relationships with other people she would be mad with jealousy. (*CW* 10, para. 255.)

Men, on the other hand, he saw as 'erotically blinded'. They committed 'the unpardonable mistake of confusing Eros with sex. A man thinks he possesses a woman if he has her sexually. He never possesses her less, for to a woman the Eros relationship is the real and decisive one. For her, marriage is a relationship with sex thrown in as an accompaniment' (*CW* 10, para. 255).

These statements, which were quite acceptable when they were first published in 1927, will strike the modern reader as somewhat sweeping, and Jung has been accused of 'sexism' on account of them. It should be remembered, however, that he was attempting to describe archetypal realities at a specific time in history. What he observed was the product of interaction between masculine and feminine archetypal principles and early twentieth-century European culture.

It is undeniable that since 1927 cultural attitudes have changed over such issues as the qualities, roles and behaviour patterns thought to be appropriate for men and women. But, far from opposing these changes, analytical psychology has both served and benefited from them. In the first place, Jung's recurring emphasis on the masculine and feminine as two great archetypal principles, existing as equal and complementary parts of a cosmic homeostatic system as expressed in the interplay of *yin* and *yang*, was deeply subversive of patrist culture which still, as Jung was writing, asserted male superiority as a right. Second, Jung's suggestion that an intact female personality existed in the unconscious of every man, and a male equivalent in every woman, was, unlike his views of the *conscious* psychology of men and women, found to be shockingly revolutionary when he first proposed it.

Both these contributions helped to free individual members of our society from narrow gender stereotypes and to create a social climate in which it became a less fearsome ordeal for men and women to assimilate their contrasexual characteristics in the quest for individuation. Moreover, Jung was aware that his psychology possessed a masculine bias because he knew it had grown out of his own experience. For this reason he encouraged women with whom he was in close contact to develop a feminine counterpoise to his work. Hence his encouragement of Emma Jung to train and practise as an analyst and to write about the anima and animus from the female point of view. Her attainments as an analyst, teacher and author were very considerable and required much unchauvinistic support from her husband in a country where the *Hausfrau* stereotype prevailed, where the education of females was considered wasteful and where no woman had a vote. In addition, Jung encouraged Toni Wolff to research and write her excellent paper *Structural Forms of the Feminine Psyche* and Esther Harding to publish her widely influential *The Way of All Women.*

Since these pioneering works were completed with Jung's blessing, many others have contributed to a growing Jungian understanding of female psychology – for example, Jean Bolen's *Goddesses in Every Woman* (1984), Linda Leonard's *The Wounded Woman* (1982), Sylvia Perera's *Descent of the Goddess* (1981), Bani Shorter's *An Image Darkly Forming* (1987), Ann Ulanov's *Receiving Woman* (1981) and Edward Whitmont's *Return of the Goddess* (1983). These are most welcome additions to the Jungian corpus and have served to widen Jung's original concepts of masculine and feminine psychology. Moreover, they have advanced female emancipation by making it possible for women to discover themselves in a truly Jungian perspective, namely, as an inner revelation which reflects their archetypal nature and transcends all repressive notions of woman's 'place'. The work of these writers has also enhanced the status of the animus, celebrating the richly positive role it can play in a woman's life (Jung, it must be admitted, was rather prone to harp on the animus's negative qualities). As Whitmont (1983) rightly says: 'Femininity can no longer be limited to responsiveness, passivity, and mothering. It will discover and express its active, initiating, creative and transformative capacity' (p. 189).

Over all, the influence of these new developments in feminine psychology has acted as a corrective to the (negative) animus-domination that has characterized the kind of militant feminism which glorifies pseudo-masculine attitudes. That militancy represented a necessary *enantiodromia* to the centuries of patriarchal repression that women have suffered, but we may now begin to hope that the age of the rebellious virago will give place to a more integrated and more assured feminine consciousness which will honour the *archetypal* feminine and bring about a new, more balanced accord with the masculine. Whitmont again: 'Self-affirmation for women means, first and foremost, acceptance of their difference from men, rather than identification, imitation and competitiveness with them by androlatric standards. Only by first finding this basic feminine stance can they also claim their Yang element and give expression to their masculine drives and capacities, in their own ways, as women' (p. 189).

Wishing to carry Jungian psychology to the forefront of feminist thinking, some modern Jungians have gone as far as to suggest that we should make a complete distinction between gender and sex, and liberate all our notions of masculine and feminine psychology from any biological context. For example, in a chapter entitled 'Gender Identity and Gender Rôles: Their Place in Analytic Practice', Katherine Bradway (1982) asserts, 'Linking traits to gender can perpetuate the stereotyping that women initially recognized, and that men have increasingly seen, as potentially limiting the development of both sexes' (p. 279). If we drop all question of sex-linkage, then we are free to discuss masculine and feminine components in the psyches of both women and men in a completely even-handed and non-discriminatory manner. Then, as Jungians, we can 'avoid implying that we support traditional stereotyping' (ibid.).

Several writers agree with this stance (e.g., Hillman, 1985; Samuels, 1985) and suggest that the time has come to reject Jung's generalizations concerning the Logos qualities of male consciousness and the Eros qualities of female consciousness, and to endow everyone, regardless of sex, with an animus *as well as* an anima: masculine and feminine capacities, Logos and Eros principles, anima and animus, should be equally accessible to all, whether they be men or women. Understandably, these developments have promoted interest in the notion of *androgeny*, which, since primordial times, has been represented by the symbol of the hermaphrodite.

The intentions behind these suggestions are laudable, for their purpose is clearly to free us all from outdated constraints that might inhibit our individuation and prevent us from becoming whole as *people*, irrespective of gender or sex. However, it is unlikely that Jung would have welcomed them – not because he was a died-in-the wool patriarch, but because he would have considered the assumptions upon which these proposals are based to be of dubious validity.

Since these issues attract much interest at the present time, it is necessary for us to examine in some detail the assumptions on which the new 'androgenous' position rests, so as to understand why it is largely incompatible with mainstream Jungian, and indeed modern scientific, thought.

In the first place, in order to separate gender from sex, it would be necessary to assume that psychology and biology are entirely separate disciplines, dealing with unrelated phenomena, and that our sex has no inherent influence on our personality or cast of mind. To make such an assumption would be to negate the advances made by neurophysiology and medicine during the last two hundred years and would reopen the Cartesian rift between mind and body that Jung's theory of archetypes sought to heal. It would mean the re-adoption of the *tabula rasa* theory of human development that Jung rejected as taking no account of the fundamental importance of archetypes and the collective unconscious. It would also be incompatible with Jung's cosmological view that body and mind, spirit and biology, are aspects of the same archetypal reality.

Second, the new androgeny would contravene the view shared by all human cultures that gender identity and physical sex are intimately related – that our gender is the psychic recognition and social expression of the sex to which Nature has assigned us. This universal understanding is in accord with palaeontological findings about how our species evolved and how natural selection endowed each sex with different, though complementary, psychophysical attributes in the interests of survival. Thus, as we have seen, there is very good reason to suppose that Nature has indeed endowed females with more Eros than males to enable them to meet the extraordinary demands that childbirth and child-rearing make of them.

It must be said in Jung's defence that he was talking not about roles or stereotypes but about age-old archetypal principles: Eros values intimacy and subjectivity – it is receptive and creative like the womb and like the earth; Logos embodies the word, law, power, meaning and objectivity. Both are equally necessary: each is needed to complement the other. Logos differentiates, while Eros 'unites what Logos has sundered' (*CW* 10, para. 275). It would, of course, be untrue to assert that Eros is exclusively the province of women and Logos entirely the prerogative of men. However, Jung never maintained that this was the case. When he addressed the matter specifically he made it clear that he used the terms relatively and not in the absolute sense of gender determinacy: 'The animus corresponds to the paternal Logos just as the anima corresponds to the maternal Eros. But I do not wish to give these two intuitive concepts too specific a definition. I use Eros and Logos merely as conceptual aids to describe the fact that woman's consciousness is characterized more by the connective quality of Eros than by the discrimination and cognition associated with Logos. In men, Eros, the function of relationship, is usually less developed than Logos' (*CW* 9, ii, para. 29). As this passage demonstrates, Jung was making a generalization that possessed, as it still possesses, *statistical* validity. *Individual* exceptions, of course, exist and are probably more numerous now than when Jung was writing.

Third, to divorce gender from sex and espouse an androgenous view of the psyche would be to overthrow the fundamental tenet of Jungian developmental psychology, namely, that both gender consciousness and the contrasexual complex are developed on an archetypal substrate. 'The autonomy of the collective unconscious expresses itself in the figures of the anima and animus' (*CW* 9, ii, para. 40). Jung insisted that these were fundamental components of human nature that had evolved for the purpose of making lasting relations between the sexes the profound and compelling mystery that they are and always have been. The contrasexual archetype is, therefore, irreducible: 'Though the contents of anima and animus can be assimilated, they themselves cannot, since they are archetypes. As such they are the foundation stones of the psychic structure ...' (*CW* 9, ii, para. 40).

Furthermore, advocacy of an even-handed distribution of masculine and feminine attributes, irrespective of sex, is to overlook the not unimportant matter of *polarity* between the sexes. What attracts males and females to one another is something more than the sum total of their physical attributes. A woman is attracted to a man who possesses the masculine *qualities* of her animus; a man is drawn to a woman who seems to carry the feminine qualities of his anima. The primordial attraction which the sexes have always exercised over one another is not merely a matter of penises and vaginas. It has to do with the essential 'otherness' of the opposite sex. If sexual otherness is abolished in the interests of sexual equality, what happens to sex?

The new hermaphroditism also overlooks the generative polarity between the conscious and unconscious aspects of the psyche. The existence of a dynamic personality of the opposite sex within the unconscious sets up a powerful energetic field between that personality and the conscious ego (which is normally identified with the same sex as the individual). By making the animus and anima conscious, Jung found that 'we convert them into bridges to the unconscious' from which all creative possibilities flow (*CW* 7, para. 339): 'Encounter with the anima logically leads to a greater expansion of our sphere of influence. The anima is a representative of the unconscious and hence a mediatrix' (letter, 13 March 1958). The fact that this inner figure is experienced as sexually 'other' enhances its importance and numinosity and hence its creative potential. To experience this, the ego must possess a clear and well-established same-sex identity.

Moreover, the anima and animus are also in direct relationship in a marriage. This is why the heterosexual relationship is productive not only of *physical* children but, through the *coniunctio* of souls, also of *spiritual* children. The good marriage is creative on both planes through the dynamics of polar opposition and complementarity.

Those innovators who wish to give an animus to a man and an anima to a woman justify this piece of generosity by the true observation that no man has so *fully* integrated the masculine principle into ego-consciousness as not to leave masculine components in the unconscious. It is also true to say that no woman is so *completely* feminine that feminine qualities never personate in her dreams. But to insist on renaming these unconscious elements of the same sex by using the term given by Jung to those elements in the opposite sex is to make an already difficult area of study almost Byzantine in its complexity. It is all very well to argue that we might possess greater psychic freedom if we ceased to attribute masculine qualities to males or feminine qualities to females, but people will continue to do so because they express what they see, know and feel. These worthy theoreticians would betray the empirical foundations of Jungian psychology, which is based on direct individual knowledge and experience.

Finally, the new advocacy of the hermaphrodite as the most productive symbol for masculine and feminine relations, both interpersonally and intrapsychically, is endorsing a configuration that is undifferentiated, unconscious and static. When imbued with consciousness, it proves unstable, displaying a propensity to dissociate and divide. As Katherine Bradway, herself sympathetic to the new proposals, suggests, a more fruitful symbol than the hermaphrodite is the *coniunctio* – a union of dynamic masculine and feminine elements inhering more creative vitality than the uroboric neutrality of the hermaphrodite. It performs no useful social or psychic service to nullify these opposing yet complementary forces: each must be acknowledged for the powerful daimon that it is. The alchemists declared that only what has been properly separated can be adequately joined, a sentiment that Jung shared when he said, 'There can be no consciousness without the perception of difference' (*CW* 14, para. 603). To individuate is not to become hermaphroditic but to become a whole woman or a whole man. This means the conscious integration of the contrasexual complex *in complementary relation to* the fully developed gender principle (femininity or masculinity) appropriate to one's sex.

While I feel it is important to reaffirm the classical Jungian position on these matters, I would not wish to detract from the immensely valuable developments of recent years, which have emancipated women and deepened our understanding of the feminine psyche. The essential fact is that we all agree with Jung's original dictum that feminine and masculine principles are to be held in equal esteem and that there is no question of one being superior to the other: each complements the other as mutually interdependent opposites whose constant interaction is homeostatically balanced and controlled. We can agree that males must feel free to develop their feminine side and females their masculine, but it still remains a principle of universal validity that males will establish a masculine identity and display predominantly masculine characteristics and females a feminine identity and feminine characteristics, particularly during the first half of life, and that they should not be made to suffer any confusion about it. No one should be under any compulsion to develop the qualities characteristic of their own sex, but, equally, they should not be made to feel guilty about it if they do. It is important when we have succeeded in detaching ourselves from old, restrictive stereotypes not to replace them with new stereotypes that are no less restrictive. It would surely be a mistake to abandon 'sexism' only to embrace 'neuterism'. As Jung said, all 'isms' are the devil.

What matters is that, regardless of sex, we all feel free to achieve our own individual realization of the Self. Arguments about what this involves are largely irrelevant in any case because, whatever we may think or say about them, the archetypes will prevail, and no archetypes possess greater power or salience than those of the Masculine and Feminine. Our egos may do what they like, but these great archetypal constellations will continue to have their way with us as long as our species survives.

SUGGESTIONS FOR FURTHER READING

Gerhard Adler, *The Living Symbol: A Case Study in the Process of Individuation*

H. J. Eysenck, *The Scientific Study of Personality*

Barbara Hannah, *Encounters with the Soul: Active Imagination as Developed by C. G. Jung*

Jolande Jacobi, *The Way of Individuation*
C. G. Jung, *Commentary on the Secret of the Golden Flower* (in *CW* 13)
—— *Psychological Types* (*CW* 6, especially Chapters 10 and 11)
—— *Woman in Europe* (in *CW* 10)
Demaris S. Wehr, *Jung and Feminism: Liberating Archetypes*

Chapter Ten

LATE-LIFE TRANSITION

THE ARCHETYPAL PROGRAMME

The late-life transition heralds the commencement of old age, and it is a less circumscribed and less predictable event than adolescence or the crisis of middle life. Now that many more people are living into their eighties there is a tendency for social statisticians to postpone the time of life at which old age is said to begin. Not so long ago it was commonly put at sixty-five; nowadays seventy-five is nearer the mark. I prefer the term *late maturity* for the period from sixty-five onwards because it avoids the pejorative connotations of the word 'old' and eschews any precise definition as to when 'old age' starts its course.

The transition which occurs during this stage is as much psychic as physical, and it is on the psychic aspect that we shall dwell – while acknowledging that both aspects are mutually dependent. Indeed, the psychic transition is often inaugurated by an accident or a physical illness that demonstrates just how precarious one's existence has become. What were previously mere intimations of mortality now become blunt warnings of fact. Moreover, at this stage illness and death come to increasing numbers of one's contemporaries, and when they begin to carry off one's nearest and dearest there is not only the grief to be dealt with but also the recognition that henceforth life must be lived in the imminent proximity of death.

Retirement, bereavement and physical infirmity can turn this period into a martyrdom of sickness, hopelessness and despair – unless the truth of one's situation is faced up to and dealt with honestly, creatively and, above all, *psychologically*. Jung found that the inner figures now become more important than ever: as one loses people in the outer world, increasingly one needs the Self. In late life isolation is something that many people suffer, at the very time when they are least able to adapt to it. Then a good relationship with the Self becomes invaluable. Moreover, the inner resourcefulness that this relationship brings can inhibit social withdrawal and enable one to increase one's cultural contribution. Creatively lived, retirement can be richly productive: so many things can now be done that could not be done in the past for lack of opportunity. As a result, late life can be the period when individuation proceeds apace. The fact that there are few outer goals left means that life is now essentially a process to be *experienced*: for many people, for the first time, *esse in anima* now becomes a practical possibility.

At this time of life, therefore, three strategies become apparent: first, people may feel so defeated by the implications of old age that they become depressed and helpless; second, they may retreat from the implications of age, *deny* mortality, lose touch with meaning and take refuge in day-to-day routines; or, third, they may manage to remain conscious of their situation, *grow* through the late-life transition and reach a point where they are ready, as Jung put it, 'to die with life'. To choose the latter strategy is to embrace life and death as a pair of profoundly related opposites and to declare one's participation in a process that transcends them both. Then one develops an awareness of 'ultimate concerns' and comes to an acknowledgement of the rhizome that exists beyond the blooming and dying of the tangible world.

As a stage in personal evolution from egohood to Selfhood, therefore, the late-life transition is both a preparation for the *ultimate* transition of death and the opportunity to accept one's personal existence as part of the immutable will of the cosmos.

JUNG'S LATE-LIFE TRANSITION

Jung's late-life transition probably began with a serious illness early in 1944, when he was sixty-eight. He fell while walking in the snow, broke his fibula and ten days later had emboli in his heart and lungs, which nearly killed him. As he hovered between life and death he had a series of visions that affected him deeply. In one of these he saw the earth from a thousand miles out in space. He felt he was detaching himself from the world and bitterly resented it when his physician brought him back to life. He had other visions of equal power, mostly filled with *coniunctio* symbolism, emphasizing an inner preoccupation with the archetypal theme of the reconciliation of opposites.

This period seems to have been in the nature of a second 'creative illness', for when he eventually recovered he entered what was perhaps the most productive period of his life. 'I no longer attempted to put across my own opinion, but surrendered myself to the current of my thoughts. Thus one problem after the other revealed itself to me and took shape' (*MDR*, pp. 276–7). For the last seventeen years of his life writing took precedence above all else.

His illness enhanced his sense of transition from his No. 1 to his No. 2 personality, and there were dreams that affirmed the significance of this transition. In one dream he entered a small wayside chapel: 'To my surprise there was no image of the Virgin on the altar, and no crucifix either, but only a wonderful flower arrangement. But then I saw that on the floor in front of the altar, facing me, sat a yogi – in lotus posture, in deep meditation. When I looked at him more closely, I realized that he had my face. I started in profound fright, and awoke with the thought: "Aha, so he is the one who is meditating me. He has a dream, and I am it." I knew that when he awakened, I would no longer be' (*MDR*, p. 299). He felt that the yogi was meditating his earthly form.

In another dream, which came fourteen years later, he experienced himself as the *projection* of a UFO, shaped like a magic lantern.

He understood both dreams as parables: they revealed that the Self assumes human shape in order to enter three-dimensional existence. They confirmed that the unconscious is the generator of the empirical personality: 'Our unconscious existence is a real one and our conscious world a kind of illusion ... this state of affairs resembles very closely the Oriental conception of Maya. Unconscious wholeness therefore seems to me the true *spiritus rector* of all biological and psychic events' (*MDR*, p. 300).

CONSEQUENCES FOR JUNG'S PSYCHOLOGY

These experiences confirmed for Jung his belief in the primacy of the Self and his conviction that the best possible life is the life lived *sub specie aeternitatis*. 'The decisive question for a man is: Is he related to something infinite or not? That is the telling question of his life. Only if we know that the thing which truly matters is the infinite can we avoid fixing our interest upon futilities, and upon all sorts of goals which are not of real importance' (*MDR*, p. 300). We count for something only inasmuch as we embody something *essential*, otherwise life is wasted. Only then can we proceed with vitality and meaning and be ready 'to die with life'.

SUGGESTIONS FOR FURTHER READING

Edgar Herzog, *Psyche and Death*
C. G. Jung, *The Soul and Death* (in *CW* 8)
Marie-Louise von Franz, *On Dreams and Death*

Chapter Eleven

LATE MATURITY

THE ARCHETYPAL PROGRAMME

The idea that even in old age we are growing towards realization of our full potential distinguishes the Jungian approach to developmental psychology from virtually all others. Most authorities see this stage primarily as one of decline and disengagement, stressing the degenerative changes that occur in the body and in the brain. Much writing on the psychology of ageing has the pessimistic ring of Jacques' description in *As You like It* (Act II, Scene vii):

> Last scene of all,
> That ends this strange eventful history,
> Is second childishness, and mere oblivion,
> Sans teeth, sans eyes, sans taste, sans everything.

While Jung naturally did not deny the element of decline in old age, he nevertheless insisted that the goal of this time of life was not senility but wisdom. Nor was he entirely alone in this view. His opinion was shared by one other eminent developmental psychologist of this century, Erik Erikson. According to Erikson, old age is a time when the individual is torn between the opposites of ego-integrity and despair: wisdom depends on the successful resolution of this conflict. When one attains wisdom one is able to accept that the life one has lived is 'something that had to be and that, by necessity, permitted of no substitutions' (1950, p. 268). Wisdom consists in acknowledging the legitimacy of other life-styles but at the same time defending the dignity of one's own.

would start one between my death and funeral in any case,' he told Barbara Hannah (Hannah, 1977, p. 296).

While his 'genius for propinquity' was more evident in him as the years passed, he never lost his love of solitude, and the peace of Bollingen, where he lived in great simplicity, was the main support of his spiritual life. The 'Tower' at Bollingen had no electricity, telephone or central heating. Water had to be fetched from the well, and food was cooked on a stove for which Jung chopped up all the wood himself. There was in the centre of the house a room, which no one was permitted to enter, where he could write and meditate undisturbed. At Bollingen he loved to sail his boat on the lake, carve inscriptions in stone, paint murals in the house and, from time to time, entertain close friends and members of his family to meals, often prepared by himself. There he enjoyed an existence that was in complete contrast to the more extraverted and worldly life he led at Küsnacht. As he got older he spent longer spells at Bollingen. It was as if the transition there from Küsnacht symbolized for him the transition from the ego to the Self – the path to individuation.

Two major kinds of disaster – illness and the death of loved ones – that break the spirit of many old people seem, in Jung's case, to have spurred him on to greater creativity. The creative daimon released by his illness of 1944 carried him through a second heart attack in 1946, through the recurrent bouts of paroxysmal tachycardia that afflicted him for the rest of his life, through the death of Toni Wolff in 1952 and of Emma Jung in 1955. He adjusted fairly quickly to the loss of Toni, but when Emma died he was distraught. For a while he gave himself up to stone carving, which brought some respite from his grief, and, characteristically, he pondered the meaning of why *he* should be the one to have survived. He began to feel under an even greater obligation to 'become himself' and decided to exteriorize this aim by adding to the house at Bollingen. He built an upper storey onto the low central section: this, he felt, represented his ego-personality. 'Earlier I would not have been able to do this, I would have rejected it as presumptuous self-emphasis. Now it signified an extension of consciousness achieved in old age. With that the building was complete' (*MDR*, p. 213). He moved his desk and writing materials into this new extension and was soon again hard at work.

CONSEQUENCES FOR JUNG'S PSYCHOLOGY

Although he applied his mind to many subjects during the second half of his life, there were three preoccupations to which Jung repeatedly returned – alchemy, psychotherapy and religion. He used his understanding of the first of these disciplines to make brilliantly original contributions to the other two. Since these were the crowning achievements of his life, we must examine them in some detail.

Alchemy

Jung began his serious study of alchemy when he was fifty-three, but it was not until he was sixty that he felt ready to make his discoveries public. He did so at the Eranos meeting at Ascona in 1935, but his key work on the subject, *Psychology and Alchemy*, was not published until he was sixty-nine.

Until Jung's work became known, alchemy was regarded less as the historical counterpart of depth psychology than as the precursor of modern chemistry. Jung realized, however, that the alchemist, in his efforts to treat base matter in such a way as to turn it into gold, was really working symbolically on the transformation of his own psyche. In other words, Jung discovered in alchemy a metaphor of individuation.

For what it is worth, it is my view that alchemy is also a metaphor of embryogenesis – that is to say, the alchemist was indulging in a form of compensation for his inability to emulate the female's capacity to create life. The objective of the alchemical opus is to separate two or more reagents out of a primary mass – the *prima materia* or *massa confusa* – within a womb-like retort; the recombination of these reagents to produce a miraculous new substance – variously called the philosopher's stone (*lapis philosophorum*), the elixir of life and so on – is symbolized by an act of sexual intercourse between a king and a queen in a water bath, resulting in the production of a child, a hermaphrodite or an androgyne.

To perceive a male embryogenetic fantasy at work in alchemy does not in any way undermine Jung's view of it: it is merely an amplification. The alchemical metaphor works on three levels: the material (gold-making), the embryological (life-making) and the psychic (soul-making). I add the embryogenetic element not as a *reductio* but for the sake of completeness – to throw *in* the baby, so to speak, with the alchemical bath water.

Moreover, the embryogenetic fantasy overlaps with a further metaphor, that of analysis. Alch[illegible] [illegible]nts the *opus* as occur-
[illegible] his female companion
[illegible] She is both his *femme*
[illegible] ing him to find the
[illegible] the labour of trans-
[illegible] himself and Toni
[illegible] nscious, has already
[illegible] he analytic process.
[illegible] ual transformation
[illegible] and patient: 'For
[illegible] different chemical
substances: if there is any combinatio[illegible] ll, both are transformed' (*CW* 16, para. 163). It is as if analyst and patient adopt the roles of alchemist and *soror mystica* in the course of the opus, namely, the analytic work towards individuation, the work of soul-making.

Equally important for Jung was the connection that the alchemists made between the macrocosmic and microcosmic dimensions, and the religious attitude they adopted to their work: 'This arcanum should be regarded, not only as truly great, but as a most holy Art,' says one text; all that occurs in heaven is duplicated on earth:

> Heaven above
> Heaven below
> Stars above
> Stars below
> All that is above
> Also is below
> Grasp this
> And rejoice
> (*CW* 16, para. 384.)

The holy Art consists in somehow connecting the microcosm with the macrocosm, the personal with the transpersonal, the ego with the Self.

European alchemy seems to have derived its origins from ancient Egypt, where it was associated with the worship of Thoth, who became Hermes in ancient Greece and Mercury in Rome. The notion of *primary matter* surfaced before the advent of Socratic philosophy in the belief that the world originated from a single substance, which separated out into the four elements, earth, air, fire and water and then recombined in various proportions to make up all the physical objects present in the world. Aristotle had refined this idea, teaching that primary matter existed first as pure potentiality, which then acquired form when it was actualized in reality – just like archetypes, in fact.

The alchemists adapted these ideas, reasoning that if they were to transform a base substance into the philosopher's stone, then it must first be returned to its original, undifferentiated state. To this thought they added an animistic view of nature, believing that all objects possessed spirits that, like the human spirit, were perfectable, in that they were capable of being transformed from lower into higher forms.

If one accepts these premises, alchemical endeavour begins to make some sense. Since all substances are composed of the same four elements, it should be possible to change one substance into another (for example, lead into gold) by performing a *solutio*, a *separatio* or a *sublimatio* to reduce the substance to the original elements, rearranging their relative proportions and then performing a *coagulatio* or a *coniunctio* to bring the new substance into being. Moreover, since the spirit of all entities is perfectable, there should be no insurmountable obstacle to transforming base matter into gold. The secret must lie in establishing the necessary stages through which the chemical operations must pass and also in discovering a miraculous agent – what today we might call a catalyst – capable of enabling the necessary transformation to occur. Many alchemists agreed on the appropriate stages necessary, but the miraculous agent proved more elusive.

Poring over the old texts in his library, Jung concluded that alchemy was an ancient tradition that attempted to make use of an eternally valid psychological truth, namely, that one becomes aware of new meanings arising from the unconscious by seeing them mirrored in outer reality. In other words, alchemy was a prime example of an elaborate discipline built entirely on the psychological phenomenon of *projection*.

Why should Jung reach this conclusion? What right had he to suppose that the alchemists were projecting their unconscious psyches into their retorts and into their texts? And was he suggesting that alchemy was in no sense the result of conscious ratiocination?

The answer is that the assumption was entirely intuitive. It was supported, however, by his clinical experience of the power of projection and by the many impressive parallels he found between alchemical symbols and the symbols produced by himself, and his patients, in dreams and in the practice of active imagination. In *Psychology and Alchemy* (1944), he published a series of dreams of a natural scientist (who had no knowledge of alchemy) and demonstrated how strikingly their content echoed the motifs contained in alchemical texts. Jung subsequently acknowledged (*CW* 18, para. 673, n. 9) that the scientist in question was none other than Wolfgang Pauli (1900–1958), the eminent Swiss physicist and Nobel Laureate. In *The Psychology of the Transference*, published two years later, he confessed that he was sure that the alchemists indulged in conscious speculation about the practical implications of their work but insisted that this would in no way impede the process of unconscious projection: 'For wherever the mind of the investigator departs from exact observation of the facts before it and goes its own way, the unconscious *spiritus rector* will take over the reins and lead the mind back to the unchangeable, underlying archetypes, which are then forced into projection by this regression' (*CW* 16, para. 405).

Moreover, the alchemists remained true to the Aristotelean doctrine of the unity of matter and therefore made no distinction between the psyche and the substance that was the subject of the *opus*. Indeed, they acknowledged that the work required the total commitment of the whole man: *ars requirit totum hominem*. So, inevitably, processes that they believed to be occurring in matter were indistinguishable from the parallel processes occurring in their own minds. The quest for perfectibility in the one was indistinguishable from the quest for perfectibility in the other. They were both aspects of the same event.

It was precisely because the alchemist had little knowledge of the real nature of matter that he projected his own unconscious processes into physical events in order to illuminate them. As he worked on his experiments, he had psychic experiences that he identified with the chemical processes themselves. Because projection is of its very nature entirely unconscious, the alchemist was unaware that his experience had little to do with matter itself. 'He experienced his projection as a property of matter; but what he was in reality experiencing was his own unconscious' (*CW* 12, paras. 345ff.).

What fascinated the psychologist in Jung was the way in which the alchemists attempted to give a systematic account of the stages through which the transformative process progressed, their odd, primordial, scientific words standing as symbols for the psychic transmutations involved. Thus, liberating gold from the *massa confusa* was bringing the Self to consciousness from the dark chaos of the unconscious. Making gold is creating the Self. Like analytical psychology, alchemy represented a discipline designed to promote Self-realization, though in the former case this is conscious and deliberate and, in the latter, largely unconscious and accidental. Just as Jung conceived the role of the Self in the individuation process, so the alchemists believed the philosopher's stone to be the starting point, the goal *and* the agent of transformation.

What is more, Jung also believed that alchemy stood in compensatory relationship to medieval Christianity. To the Christian it was man who needed to be redeemed by God, but to the alchemist it was God – 'the divine world soul slumbering and awaiting redemption in matter' – who needed to be redeemed by man (*CW* 12, paras. 456–7). This insight enabled Jung to restate the redemptive process (as traditionally conceived) in psychological terms, using the alchemical *opus* as his authority. He was thus able to make a cultural contribution of great moment, but at the subjective level he was evidently still attempting to solve the religious problem bequeathed to him by his father. Thus he says approvingly: 'The alchemists ran counter to the Church in preferring to seek through knowledge rather than to find through Faith' (*CW* 12, para. 41).

Jung was particularly excited by the alchemists' use of the terms *meditatio* and *imaginatio* in connection with their work: 'The word *meditatio* is used when a man has an inner dialogue with someone unseen,' says Ruland in the *Lexicon Alchemiae*. 'It may be with God, when He is invoked, or with himself, or with his good angel.' This, Jung points out, proves that the alchemists were advising not cogitation but 'explicitly an inner dialogue and hence a living relationship to the answering voice of the "other" in ourselves, i.e., of the unconscious' (*CW* 12, para. 390). Alchemical meditation is 'a creative dialogue, by means of which things pass from an unconscious potential state to a manifest one' (ibid.). For Jung the *imaginatio*, as the alchemists understood it, was the key that opened the door to the secret of the *opus*.

To turn to the study of alchemy was not, therefore, such an eccentric thing for a psychologist to do. Psychology differs, after all, from all other sciences in one fundamental way: other scientists use their minds to investigate data derived from observations of events proceeding in the world outside themselves; the psychologist, however, is using his psyche to investigate data derived from observations of itself. In many ways this is an impossible undertaking, like trying to smell your own breath or lick your own tongue. One way round this dilemma, taken by academic psychologists, has been the use of *projection tests* in which subjects are invited to say what they see in ink blots or ambiguous figures. Jung studied alchemy on the basis of precisely the same assumption, namely, that anything uncertain or unknown is filled by the observer with psychological projection.

The stages of the *opus*

From a synoptic scrutiny of many texts Jung was able to elucidate the stages of the alchemical *opus* and relate them to his own insights into the individuation process. Originally four stages were distinguished according to the colour changes characteristic of each stage. These were described by Heraclitus as *melanosis* (blackening), *leukosis* (whitening), *xanthosis* (yellowing) and *iosis* (reddening). Much later in the fifteenth or sixteenth century the colours were reduced to three (the yellowing stage being omitted), and their Latin names were mostly used: *nigredo* (blackening), *albedo* (whitening) and *rubedo* (reddening). Alchemy continued to treat with four elements, however, and four qualities (hot, cold, dry and moist). The change from three to four stages cannot have been for experimental reasons because the process never led to the desired practical goal, so it must be attributed to 'the symbolical significance of the quaternity and the trinity; in other words, it is due to inner psychological reasons' (*CW* 12, para. 333).

The nigredo, then, is the initial stage. In some traditions blackness is present from the very beginning as a quality of the *prima materia*; in others the blackness results from separation (*separatio, divisio, solutio*) of the elements. In yet another tradition elements are assumed to be separated at the outset. They are then grouped into male and female opposites, which are brought together in a union (*coniunctio, coitus*); the product of this union then dies (*mortificatio, putrificatio, calcinatio*) to produce the blackening of the *nigredo*.

Psychologically the *prima materia* is identical with the primal Self, containing all the potential, all the dynamic oppositions, necessary to achieve the goal of the *opus*. The *separatio* and *divisio*, like the division and multiplication of cells in the developing embryo, are necessary to get the process started. The *separatio* is also paralleled in the initial stages of Jungian analysis, differentiating the adult situation from the childhood complexes, the ego from the shadow, from the anima/animus and from the Self. 'Separate the earth from the fire, the subtle from the gross, acting prudently and with judgement,' says *The Emerald Tablet*, the most sacred of alchemical texts.

The *black* aspect of this stage has to do with the depression, the *melancholia*, that is so often the initial stage causing one to examine one's life, that brings one into analysis and that deepens when one encounters the shadow. The encounter with the shadow is invariably experienced as a *mortificatio*: humiliating, despicable parts of oneself have to be confronted and integrated; the feelings of guilt and worthlessness have to be suffered, taken on and worked through. All alchemists agreed that the *nigredo* was dangerous: poisonous vapours of lead or mercury were generated and the *vas* might explode. The texts advise perseverance, fasting and prayer: *orare et laborare* (pray and work).

The *albedo*, the second stage, results from the *washing* (*ablutio, baptisma*) of the products of the *nigredo*. Psychologically, this represents the later stages of shadow integration within the intimacy of the analytic 'retort' – the process of washing one's dirty linen in private.

According to some traditions, the *nigredo* constitutes the 'death' of the *prima materia* (in analysis, a dying to the old neurotic way of life, to childhood dependencies and so on); at the moment of 'death' the soul (*anima*) is released, refined and then reunited with the revitalized *materia* to produce the glorious stage of many colours – the 'peacock's tail' (*cauda pavonis*), which then transforms into white (*albedo*), which contains all colours, like 'white' light. This moment is highly prized. Jung compares it with daybreak, the preparation for the next and final stage, which is the sunrise.

In this stage, the *rubedo*, the white becomes 'united' with red through the raising of the heat of the fire. The white is associated with the queen and the red with the king, who now arise and perform their *coniunctio oppositorum*, the union of all opposites as symbolized by the conjunction of the archetypal Masculine and Feminine in the 'chymical marriage', the *hieros gamos*. This results in the grand climax, the achievement of the goal – the *lapis philosophorum*, the hermaphrodite embodying the united king and queen, the *filius microcosmi*, 'a figure we can only compare with the Gnostic Anthropos, the divine original man' (*CW* 12, para. 335).

In preparing *Psychology and Alchemy* Jung worked on 400 dreams and visual impressions, collected mostly from Wolfgang Pauli by a woman colleague of Jung, away from all contact with himself. Fifty-nine of these were reported in the book and analysed in the light of their alchemical and individuational symbolism. It is not, of course, possible to do justice to this exegesis here, but a few examples will give some insight into Jung's method.

Dream 13: 'In the sea there lies a treasure. To reach it, the dreamer has to dive through an opening. This is dangerous, but down below he will find a companion. The dreamer takes a plunge into the dark and discovers a beautiful garden in the depths, symmetrically laid out, with a fountain in the centre.'

In discussing this dream Jung interprets the treasure in the sea, the companion and the garden with the fountain as all referring to one and the same thing: the Self. The garden is evidently a mandala, with the fountain at its centre, and alchemy affords many examples of the centre of the circle as an analogue of the *lapis*.

'By descending into the unconscious, the conscious mind puts itself in a perilous position, for it is apparently extinguishing itself. It is in the situation of the primitive hero who is devoured by the dragon' (*CW* 12, para. 437). Jung observes that the dread that everyone feels at digging too deeply into himself is, at bottom, the fear of the journey into Hades and the danger of succumbing to the fate of Theseus and Peirithous, who descended into the Underworld and *grew fast to the rocks* there.

However, 'the purpose of the descent as universally exemplified in the myth of the hero is to show that only in the region of danger (water, abyss, cavern, forest, island, castle, etc.) can one find the "treasure hard to attain" (jewel, virgin, life-potion, victory over death)' (*CW* 12, para. 438).

Dream 14: 'The dreamer goes into a chemist's shop with his father. Valuable things can be got there quite cheap, above all a special water ...'

Jung sees the chemist's shop as a vestigial reminder of the alchemist's laboratory, and the 'special water' is literally the *aqua permanens* that is vital to the production of the philosopher's stone. The *commonness* of the water was often emphasized by the alchemists. Thus, according to one source, 'What we are seeking is sold publicly for a very small price, and if it were recognized, the merchants would not sell it for so little' (*CW* 12, para. 159n). The father leads the dreamer to the source of life because he is the source of the dreamer's life. He is also the archetype of the father, the wise old man.

The idea of the special water being cheap and easily obtained is richly symbolic of life itself. The unlived life is one that takes everything for granted. It sees nothing remarkable in anything, not even personal existence. One is 'just like everyone else'. Nothing is special. The miracle of life becomes apparent only when one makes it the focus of one's concentration. Then one's whole perception of reality is transformed. 'Life that just happens in and for itself is not real life; it is only real when it is known' (*CW* 12, para. 105). Jung comments that although the water of life is ready at hand, the stupid despise it 'because they assume that every good thing is always outside and somewhere else'. Other texts express the same notion – that the makings of the philosopher's stone are available everywhere: 'This Matter lies before the eyes of all; everybody sees it, touches it ... loves it, but knows it not' (*Hermetic Museum*, 1:13). 'It is said that the stone is refuse of little value, and lies accidentally on the road, so that rich and poor have it ready to hand' (*Atlanta Fugiens*).

Jung underlines the profound truth contained in these statements: 'People will do anything, no matter how absurd, in order to avoid facing their own souls. They will practise Indian yoga and all its exercises, observe a strict regimen of diet, learn theosophy by heart, or mechanically repeat mystic texts from the literature of the whole world – all because they cannot get on with themselves and have not the slightest faith that anything useful could come out of *their* souls' (*CW* 12, para. 126).

The series of dreams in *Psychology and Alchemy* culminates in an extraordinary vision: the vision of the World Clock.

The subject saw a vertical and horizontal circle, having a common centre. This was the World Clock. The vertical circle was a blue disc with a white border divided into 4 × 8 = 32 partitions. A pointer rotated upon it. The horizontal circle consisted of four colours. On it stood four little men with pendulums and round it was a ring that was once dark and was now golden. The clock had three pulses. For every complete revolution of the pointer on the vertical circle, the horizontal circle advanced by one thirty-secondth. Thirty-two pulses of the horizontal circle equalled one revolution of the golden ring. (*CW* 12, para. 307).

This vision made a deep and lasting impression on the dreamer and induced in him a sense of the 'most sublime harmony'. It was a three-dimensional mandala, a profound symbolic representation of the Self, parallel to the achievement of the goal in alchemy.

Mysterium coniunctionis

When he published *The Psychology of the Transference* Jung was seventy-one. It was the fruit of nearly two decades spent in the study of alchemy and four decades in the practice of analysis. It contains the crux of his analytic theory.

The central insight that he brought to the analytic relationship, as well as to the individuation process, grew out of the great theme that preoccupied him throughout the latter part of his life: the *mysterium coniunctionis*. The inherent affinity between opposites, drawing them together into a union to yield a new form that was more than its parts, became the central inspiration of his life and work: the *thesis* of the unconscious statement, the *antithesis* of the ego response, *synthesis* through the transcendent symbolic function, with the birth of new consciousness – repeated and repeated, round and round, up and down, circumambulating the goal of the *opus*.

Several of Jung's followers have confirmed and extended the application of his alchemical insights to analysis – for example, Edward Edinger in his *Anatomy of the Psyche: Alchemical Symbolism in Psychotherapy*, and Molly Tuby in an essay entitled 'The Search and Alchemy':

> Every time we make a new discovery linking inner and outer, we feel that we are getting closer to that intangible and elusive something that we are circling in a spiralling movement. It is spiralling because of inevitable setbacks. In alchemical parlance, the operation fails many times; the retort can even explode, and the work must be started all over again. Just like analysis, 'the same old thing all over again'! 'Seven hundred and seventy times', one alchemist suggests! However, at each new integration we experience more oneness, and as our centre of consciousness shifts closer to the Self (as the making of the stone proceeds) the underlying unity of all things becomes more obvious. (p. 12.)

The king and queen perform their *coniunctio* and melt into a single being with two heads. But their son, the *filius philosophorum*, is 'not born of the queen, but queen and king are themselves transformed into the new birth' (*CW* 16, para. 473). Jung translates this mystery into the language of psychology: 'The union of the conscious mind or ego-personality with the unconscious personified as anima produces a new personality compounded of both ... Not that the new personality is a third thing midway between conscious and unconscious, it is both together. Since it transcends consciousness it can no longer be called "ego" but must be given the name of "self" ... the self too is both ego and non-ego, subjective and objective, individual and collective. It is the "uniting symbol" which epitomizes the total union of opposites.' In other words, 'The one born of the two represents the metamorphosis of both.'

This can only be expressed by means of symbols, which occur in dreams and fantasies and find objective form in mandalas. Jung stresses that the Self is not a doctrine or a theory but a living reality that is expressed in the form of a psychic image, like the Golden Flower – 'an image born of nature's own workings, a natural symbol far removed from all conscious intention' (*CW* 16, paras. 474 and 475).

Psychotherapy

Like alchemy, Jungian analysis is an *ars spagyrica* – a spagyric art. 'Spagyric' is derived from two Greek words, *span* meaning to rend, to separate, to stretch out (i.e., to analyse) and *ageirein*, to collect together or assemble (i.e., to synthesize). The alchemical slogan *solve et coagula* (dissolve and coagulate) expresses precisely these two steps: 'The alchemist saw the essence of his art in separation and analysis on the one hand and synthesis and consolidation on the other' (Foreword to *CW* 14). The first stage corresponds to the reductive method of Freud and the initial stage of Jungian analysis, but it is the second stage that is the primary concern of analytical psychology.

Where Jung was able to make a contribution to psychotherapy that went far deeper than Freud's was in his application of insights gained from alchemy into the phenomenon of transference.

The psychology of the transference

Freud introduced the term 'transference' to describe the unconscious process by which a patient attributes to the analyst feelings, ideas and attitudes that were, in fact, possessed by significant people in his past and relates to the analyst *as if he were* a significant figure from his past (the so-called *transference relationship*). The transference relationship has to be distinguished from the *analytical relationship* or the *therapeutic alliance*, which refers to the total relationship between the analyst and patient as actual people.

At their first meeting in 1907, when they talked non-stop for thirteen hours, Freud asked Jung, 'And what do you think of the transference?' Jung replied, with the deepest conviction, that he considered it to be 'the alpha and omega of the analytical method'. Freud said, 'Then you have grasped the main thing' (*CW* 16, para. 358).

But later on, after the break, Jung had second thoughts. He began to feel that the transference, as Freud conceived it, was only of relative importance. With some patients it happened; with others it did not; and the outcome of the analysis was not necessarily affected one way or the other. Freud's technique of sitting behind the patient, remaining out of sight and keeping relatively silent, was more likely to evoke projections because the analyst remained an enigma. Jung, on the other hand, sat face to face with his patient and participated fully in the analytic relationship as a real person, which meant that transference phenomena were less evident in the analytic situation as he conducted it. On the whole, Jung confessed, he preferred it when there was only a mild transference or when it was practically unnoticeable. Then the analysis could proceed on the basis of a collaborative investigation of the patient's unconscious material. When a powerful transference did occur, however, it became an important part of the analysis, and it was usually a complicated matter. But he believed that Freud and Adler had both over-simplified what was involved, Freud seeing the transference as both erotic and neurotic, Adler seeing it as an expression of power longings that were a compensation for feelings of inferiority. Jung did not deny that these factors could play a part, but he was sure that there was much more to it than that. 'The transference is far from being a simple phenomenon with one meaning' (*CW* 16, para. 362).

First, as he discovered again and again in his practice, archetypes were stirred up by the analytical relationship that, when projected onto the person of the analyst, could confer upon him great therapeutic (or destructive) power. In his own experience, such archetypal figures as the magician, shaman, witch-doctor and wise old man were most commonly projected.

Second, the analyst could receive the projection of previously unfulfilled archetypal anticipations (e.g., the strong father that the patient lacked in childhood; as we have seen, this was unquestionably an important component of Jung's own transference to the person of Freud).

Third, the transference was further complicated by the fact that unconscious activity in the patient caused reciprocal activity in the unconscious of the analyst, with the result that the bond between them was transformed into something that went beyond the conventional doctor–patient relationship. Although this is of great importance for the successful outcome of the analysis, it is not without its dangers, and Jung believed that these could be minimized only if the doctor had been thoroughly analysed and made aware of his 'personal equation'.

As a result of this insight it was Jung, and not Freud, who first proposed the idea that the analyst himself must be analysed and that the essence of analytic training must be the training analysis.

Otherwise the patient, 'by bringing an activated unconscious content to bear upon the doctor, constellates the corresponding unconscious material in him, owing to the inductive effect which always emanates from projections in greater or lesser degree. Doctor and patient thus find themselves in a relationship founded on mutual unconsciousness' (*CW* 16, para. 365). The doctor is always in danger of becoming infected with the patient's psychic illness, and this opens up the dangerous possibility that the illness may be transferred, quite literally, to him. While the training analysis is no guarantee that this will not occur, it does at least enable the doctor to use his insight as a 'flickering lamp' to illuminate the darkness that would otherwise prevail.

Jung found that the light from his own flickering lamp was much strengthened by the illumination afforded by the alchemists. At the unconscious level both doctor and patient were participating in a *coniunctio*. Like two chemical substances, they were drawn together by *affinity*, and their interaction produced change: 'When two chemical substances combine, both are altered. This is precisely what happens in the transference' (*CW* 16, para. 358). For this reason it is important not only that the analyst be analysed but that he put himself completely *in* the analytic situation – not sitting behind the supine patient, out of sight, but sitting *with* the patient, both in similar chairs, as in a normal social encounter. 'The doctor must emerge from his anonymity and give an account of himself, just as he expects his patients to do' (*CW* 16, para. 23).

From the alchemical standpoint, the relationship between analyst and patient also resembles that between the alchemist and his *soror mystica*, when the analyst is male and the patient female (as

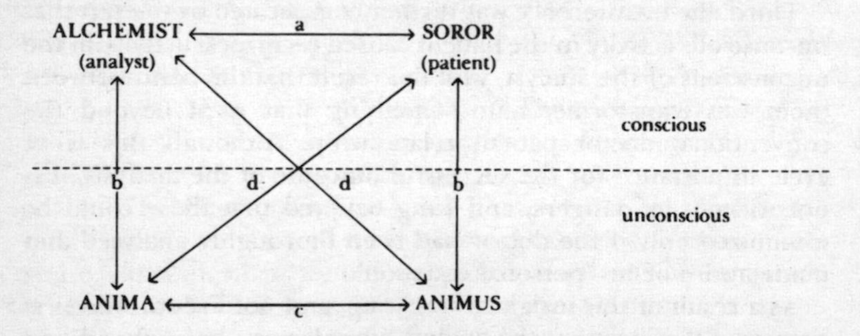

Figure 12. The 'marriage quaternity'

was usually the case in Jung's practice). The arrows in Figure 12 represent the pull from masculine to feminine and from feminine to masculine:

a = the uncomplicated, direct conscious personal relationship;
b = the relationship between the man and his anima and the woman and her animus;
c = the unconscious relationship between his anima and her animus;
d = the relationship between the woman's animus and the man and between the man's anima and the woman.

In real life these relationships are all mixed up together.

Jung saw this diagram as the key to the work. To succeed, the *opus* requires *relationship* and *feeling*. In this the analytic relationship resembles the marriage relationship as much as the alchemical relationship. Indeed, Jung refers to the diagram as the 'marriage quaternity' (*CW* 16, para. 425).

In the alchemical texts the *coniunctio* is symbolized not only by the union of the king and queen but also by the union of the sun and moon (*coniunctio Solis et Lunae*), the sun – the day-time principle – representing lucid consciousness, the moon – a nocturnal light – representing the unconscious. Because the unconscious partner in the *coniunctio* cannot be known directly, it is projected onto the 'other' with whom one has an emotional bond. This is associated with a subjective sense of wholeness or completion. 'The unrelated human being lacks wholeness, for he can achieve wholeness only through the soul, and the soul cannot exist without its other side, which is always found in a "You". Wholeness is a combination of I and You, and those show themselves to be parts of a transcendent unity whose nature can only be grasped symbolically, as in the symbols of the *rotundum*, the rose, the wheel, or the *coniunctio Solis et Lunae*.' (*CW* 16, para. 454.)

The relationship between the two partners exists as an objective fact, of course, but this is not as important as the *subjective experience* that each has of the relationship, and in this the unconscious activities of the animus and anima are crucial. They contribute to the formation of the bond in the first place and ensure that it possesses a powerful charge of feeling and libido in the second. The danger for both partners is that they will be tempted by the other's anima or animus to become identified with it through the 'inductive effect that always emanates from projections'. Therefore real progress in analysis begins only when this identification is refused. 'The supreme aim of the *opus psychologicum* is conscious realization, and the first step is to make oneself conscious of contents that have hitherto been projected. This endeavour gradually leads to knowledge of one's partner and to self-knowledge, and so to the distinction between what one really is and what is projected into one, or what one imagines oneself to be' (*CW* 16, para. 471).

Analysis thus makes therapeutic use of the natural mechanism of projection and, in so doing, it channels and strengthens the drive to individuate. In the same way the alchemist believed himself to be the servant of the work, believed that not he but Nature brought his efforts to fruition. Individuation drives us to constellate the royal pair in our intimate relationships and to seek in the other what we lack in ourselves. Analysis succeeds inasmuch as it makes this process conscious.

Transference itself is a perfectly natural phenomenon, not the result of a special 'technique' employed in the consulting room. Where the analytic relationship differs from most other relationships is in the use to which it puts the transference. 'Medical treatment of the transference gives the patient a priceless opportunity to withdraw his projections, to make good his losses, and to integrate his personality (*CW* 16, para. 420).

Analysis and feeling

In contrast to analysts of other schools, Jung laid stress on the vital importance of *feeling* – not only the patient's for the analyst but also the analyst's for the patient. Without feeling an indispensable catalyst is lacking: it is the *aqua permanens* that is necessary for the *opus* to succeed. Feeling has to be present not only in the analytic relationship but also in the ego's relationship with the unconscious, and this is particularly so when patient and analyst are both men, success depending on each being in a feeling relationship with the other's anima. In psychotherapy some over-rational patients 'try to understand with their brains only ... And when they have understood, they think they have done their full share of realization. That they should also have a *feeling relationship* to the contents of the unconscious seems strange to them or even ridiculous' (*CW* 16, para. 489). Yet unless feeling is present no real growth or transformation will occur.

The alchemists understood this perfectly. If books and intellect were given undue emphasis, the work got stuck, and the soul did not return to the inert conjoined couple of the *mortificatio*. 'The alchemists thought that the *opus* demanded not only laboratory work, the reading of books, meditation, and patience, but also love' (*CW* 16, para. 490).

Similarly, Faust was shaken out of his intellectual rut by the realization that 'feeling is all'. It required the intervention of the devil 'to transform the ageing alchemist into a young gallant and make him forget himself for the sake of the all-too-youthful feelings he had just discovered! That is precisely the risk modern man runs: he may wake up one day to find he has missed half his life' (*CW* 16, para. 491).

The analytical relationship, therefore, is a form of 'individuation marriage'. Its success depends on a *coniunctio* between Masculine and Feminine, *Logos* and *Eros*, in which each is transformed through conscious integration of the opposite in the other: 'The soul which accrues to ego-consciousness during the *opus* has a feminine character in the man and a masculine character in the woman. His anima wants to reconcile and unite; her animus tries to discern and dominate. This strict antithesis is depicted in the alchemists' *Rebis*, the symbol of transcendental unity, as a coincidence of opposites ...' (*CW* 16, para. 522).

From his study of alchemy, therefore, Jung was able greatly to enhance our understanding not only of the transference but also of the counter-transference as well. When first introduced, the term 'counter-transference' was used to describe *distortions of the analyst's view* of the patient arising out of his own past. Later it became more generally, and more loosely, used to designate the analyst's emotional reactions to the patient, which might, or might not, contribute to the treatment by assisting him to pick up the patient's true but unconscious intentions. What Jung's application of alchemical experience enabled him to do was to demonstrate that the counter-transference does not come wholly from the analyst or his past but is also itself a response to the unconscious influence on him of the patient. As a result Jung insisted that the psychotherapist must understand himself as much as his patient and that the analysis of the analyst must be the absolute precondition of analytic training. 'In the training analysis the doctor must learn to know his own psyche and to take it seriously. If he cannot do that, the patient will not learn either' (*MDR*, p. 132). It is not enough for an analyst to acquire a system of concepts or a range of methods and techniques: he must commit himself entirely to the analytic process in his own unique way. 'Every psychotherapist not only has his own method – he himself is that method' (*CW* 16, para. 198). In any thorough analysis the personalities of both doctor and patient are fully engaged. The doctor must keep constant watch over his own reactions: he must repeatedly ask himself how his unconscious is reacting to the situation, observe his dreams and study himself as carefully as he studies the patient. 'The doctor is effective only when he himself is affected. "Only the wounded physician heals." But when the doctor wears his personality like a coat of armour, he has no effect' (*MDR*, p. 133).

Jung's understanding of analysis as an alchemical operation inevitably leads to comparisons between the analytic situation and the *vas* – the retort in which the elements of the *prima materia* are separated and recombined to bring about the transformation of base matter into gold and the revelation of the *lapis*. For the alchemists the retort was no ordinary piece of laboratory apparatus: it was the *vas Hermetis*, something truly marvellous, a *vas mirabile*. 'It is a kind of matrix or uterus from which the *filius philosophorum*, the miraculous stone, is born . . . the vessel is more a mystical idea, a true symbol like all the main ideas of alchemy' (*CW* 12, para. 338). In the same spirit, the analysis is the matrix that gives birth to the Self; it contains both analyst and patient and, through their mutual interaction, brings about lasting transformations in the personality, thus advancing the progress of individuation.

Two decades spent 'trapped in the seventeenth century' therefore yielded impressive results. These years of alchemical study provided Jung with historical validation of his own experiences, with a paradigm of the individuation process and with a series of metaphors for analysis and for the phenomena of transference and counter-transference. It is true to say that all schools of psychotherapy have benefited from these insights, often applying them with enthusiasm, while preferring to neglect the source from which they derived.

In *Psychology and Alchemy* Jung asks himself what motivated the alchemists to go on with the *opus*. It never worked; they never succeeded in their declared intentions. Why did they not give up in despair? One might well ask the same question of Jung. What kept him in the seventeenth century so long? As if answering for himself, he says of the alchemists that we must never underestimate the 'sense of satisfaction born of enterprise, the adventure, the *quaerere* (seeking) and the *invenire* (finding)' (*CW* 12, para. 341). What fascinated Jung all his life was the *unknown*. Almost anything unknown was *numinous* for him. It was like matter for the alchemists: he would project his psyche into it. The unknown drew him on and on, as an inexhaustible field for projection. Having made his projections and recorded them, he could then stand back from them, assimilate them and test them against the projections of others. Kinship, as much as the drive to individuate, made him keep company with the alchemists for so many years. It was time well spent.

Religion

'Among all my patients in the second half of life,' wrote Jung, '– that is to say over thirty-five – there has not been one whose problem in the last resort was not that of finding a religious outlook on life' (1944, p. 264). He did not regard this as a problem confined to his patients, however: it was the collective problem of a culture no longer capable of meeting the religious needs of its members. He considered the need for a religion to be a basic, archetypal requirement of human nature. 'The idea of the moral order and of God belong to the ineradicable substrate of the human soul' (*CW* 8, para. 528).

This is not as extreme a claim as at first sight it might appear. There is a growing body of scientific opinion that is in accord with Jung's belief that we possess a 'natural religious function'. Comparative anthropology, for example, has revealed religious belief and practice to be a universal characteristic of human communities – as fundamental, it seems, as hunting, gathering, fishing, marrying and rearing children. Sociobiologists regard religions to be biological phenomena that, like other biological phenomena (such as large brains in proportion to physical build), enhance the welfare of those who have them. Some religions promote the survival of their adherents better than others. It is not unreasonable to assume, therefore, that in religious phenomena there are archetypes at work.

After all, religion performs crucial functions in the life of any human community: it provides a mythic explanation of how things began and how a special relationship came to be formed between the community and its gods; it ensures group cohesion by attributing absolute validity to the moral code on which society is based; it prescribes rituals that rejuvenate the beliefs and values of the collective and rites of passage that mark crucial stages in the life of each individual; and, most important of all, it gives a transcendent context for human experience, making possible a spiritual awareness of participation in a higher purpose that soars above the mundane preoccupations of the purely personal ego. In other words, a living religion grants access to the *numinosum*. This, for Jung, was religion's most essential function: 'The term "religion" designates the attitude peculiar to a consciousness which has been changed by the experience of the *numinosum*' (*CW* 11, para. 9).

The *numinosum* is *primary religious experience*. The creeds, dogmas and rituals of organized religion are secondary elaborations of this primary experience that are worked out over the centuries. As an example of such an experience Jung cites the 'vision of threefoldness' of the Swiss mystic Brother Klaus. The vision, when it appeared to him, was so terrible that his whole face was changed by it, and people were horrified when they saw him. After years of contemplation Brother Klaus came to the conclusion that what he had gazed upon was the Holy Trinity itself, and he recorded the vision in a painting on the wall of his cell. The painting, which is preserved in the parish church at Sachseln, is a mandala divided into six parts, in the centre of which is the crowned countenance of God. Thus Brother Klaus came to terms with his awe-inspiring experience on the basis of dogma, and this may have saved him from going mad or being burned as a heretic.

Such direct experience of the God-image, which for Jung was synonymous with the archetype of the Self, is so powerfully numinous that it can overwhelm and destroy the ego unless there is some religious framework in which the vision can be contained. Religion both provided this context and rendered the *numinosum* accessible to multitudes of people for many generations. The systematization of primary religious experience in dogma and ritual, therefore, contributes to the welfare of both individual and society. Unfortunately, it may ultimately lead to spiritual stultification, so that the *numinosum* departs from the dogma, and life withdraws from the creed. This is a state with which Jung was wholly familiar, having observed it so intimately in his father.

Jung's hypothesis of a religious archetype raises a most important question. Since our archetypal endowment is derived from the evolutionary adaptation of our species to the real world, it follows, as Konrad Lorenz (1977) has suggested, that archetypal reality must mirror cosmic reality. Now, if part of our archetypal reality is concerned with religious experience, does that mean that such experience, when it occurs, must be objectively real – as real, say, as our experience of a sweetly scented rose on a summer evening? Does the fact that you experience God mean that there must be a God for you to experience? Jung appears to imply that there is: 'When I say as a psychologist that God is an archetype, I mean that the "type" is in the psyche. The word "type" is, as we know, derived from the Greek word τυπος "blow" or "imprint"; thus an "archetype", presupposes an imprinter' (*CW* 12, para. 15). However, he denies that the existence of God can be proved; it can only be experienced: 'Religious experience is absolute, it cannot be disputed. You can only say that you have never had such an experience, whereupon your opponent will reply: "Sorry, I have." And there your discussion will come to an end' (*CW* 11, para. 167).

Where did Jung stand on this? In his famous television interview with John Freeman he was asked if he believed in God, and he replied: '*I know*.' In another interview with Frederic Sands, he was less enigmatic. He said of God: 'I do not take His existence on belief – I *know* that He exists.'

This conviction must have grown out of his own primary religious experiences as a boy, and the nature of God – especially His moral nature – remained a central preoccupation to the end of Jung's life. The God who had sent him the vision of the turd shattering Basel Cathedral was the same God who had tempted Adam in the Garden of Eden (who put the serpent there?), instructed Abraham to slay Isaac, subjected Job to hideous torments and allowed six million Jews to perish in Nazi concentration camps. The shock of two heart attacks seems to have made the problem of God's ambiguity all the more urgent for him, since Jung's seventies were a time of intense intellectual activity and literary output. Among other books and articles, he published

Aion in 1951, *Answer to Job* in 1952 and *Mysterium Coniunctionis* in 1955–6. All these were concerned with the opposites and attempts at their reconciliation in God and man.

In *Psychology and Alchemy* (*CW* 12), completed before his near-fatal illness, he had already drawn parallels between Christ and the *lapis* as symbols of the Self and examined the manner in which alchemy compensated Christianity. He developed these ideas in *Aion* (*CW* 9, ii) and traced the clash, interaction and union of the opposites throughout the history of Christendom. The symbolism of the fish fascinated him, for it recurs as a symbol both of Christ *and* the devil. Moreover, the Christian era has coincided exactly with the Great Astrological Year under the sign of the Fishes, and he was intrigued by the possibility that the Self manifests itself collectively both in religious symbolism and in time. The last part of *Aion*, entitled 'The Structure and Dynamics of the Self', demonstrates the way in which quaternities representing the Self seem to possess an inherent spiralling tendency that is related to the achievement of higher levels of consciousness as individuation unfolds.

Answer to Job (*CW* 11) is an altogether more subjective and passionate book, in which he gives rein to his personal indignation with God for His 'divine savagery and ruthlessness'. Jung expresses outrage that humanity should be expected to bear complete responsibility for the evil in the world: God must share his part of the burden. Jung describes the paradoxical nature of Yahweh – a god of immoderate emotions, who can be consumed with jealous rage as well as loving-kindness. That he can conduct Himself in this way points to a lack of conscious reflection on the part of the Almighty. Jung goes on to argue that the underlying meaning of the Christian belief that God became man is that God actually needs man in order to become conscious of Himself and His creation.

The germ of this extraordinary insight, which was to cause much perturbation among theologians, came to him in 1925, when he visited the Athai Plains in East Africa. He and his travelling companions stood on a hill looking down on the magnificent savannah stretching before them.

> To the very brink of the horizon we saw gigantic herds of animals: gazelle, antelope, gnu, zebra, warthog, and so on.

> Grazing, heads nodding, the herds moved forward like slow rivers. There was scarcely any sound save the melancholy cry of a bird of prey. This was the stillness of the eternal beginning, the world as it had always been, in the state of non-being; for until then no one had been present to know that it was this world. I walked away from my companions until I had put them out of sight, and savoured the feeling of being entirely alone. There I was now, the first human being to recognize that this was the world, but who did not know that in this moment he had first really created it.
>
> There the cosmic meaning of consciousness became overwhelmingly clear to me. 'What nature leaves imperfect, the art perfects,' say the alchemists. Man, I, in an invisible act of creation put the stamp of perfection on the world by giving it objective existence ... Now I knew what it was, and knew even more: that man is indispensable for the completion of creation; that, in fact, he himself is the second creator of the world, who alone has given to the world its objective existence – without which, unheard, unseen, silently eating, giving birth, dying, heads nodding through hundreds of millions of years, it would have gone on in the profoundest night of non-being down to its unknown end. Human consciousness created objective existence and meaning, and man found his indispensable place in the great process of being. (*MDR*, pp. 240–1.)

Towards the end of *Answer to Job* Jung interprets the psychological meaning of why the New Testament should culminate in the Revelation of St John the Divine. Such great emphasis throughout the New Testament on God as a loving, compassionate father, worthy of total trust, is bound, by the law of *enantiodromia*, to constellate its opposite – hate, cruelty and destruction. Indeed, it is likely, Jung argues, that the John who wrote the Epistle is also the John of the Apocalypse, who prophesied the end of the world in terms disagreeably suggestive of nuclear holocaust. If we are to escape that catastrophe, we must assist God to become man and thus more conscious. The Book of Revelation brings home to us once more that God is to be feared as well as loved. Man now has a new and terrible responsibility. 'He can no longer wriggle out of it on the plea of his littleness and nothingness, for the dark God has slipped the atom bomb and chemical weapons into his hands and given him the power to empty out the apocalyptic vials of wrath on his fellow creatures. Since he has been granted an almost god-like power, he can no longer remain blind and unconscious' (*CW* 11, para. 747).

Since God cannot reconcile the opposites in Himself, life in this nuclear age has become a race between consciousness and catastrophe – a race that can be won only, if won at all, by the transcendent function of the human psyche. Only the living symbol has the power to unite opposites so that they no longer clash but mutually supplement one another. In this transcendent power lies the meaning of the Christian myth of the *necessary* incarnation of God in man. For God Himself can become whole only through man's creative confrontation with the opposites and through their synthesis in the Self – the wholeness of the individual human personality. 'That is the meaning of divine service, or the service which man can render to God, that light may emerge from the darkness, that the Creator may become conscious of His creation, and man conscious of himself' (*MDR*, p. 312).

This is the one purpose that fits humanity meaningfully into the cosmic scheme of things, for it confers meaning on human life and, through humanity, on creation. The decline in religious faith that has occurred in the last hundred years makes no difference to this truth. God does not need us to prove His existence; He does not even need us to believe in Him: Summoned or not summoned, He will be there. Nature has placed a high premium on the development of consciousness precisely because it is only consciousness that can make creation *known*. Only consciousness can turn the inert world into the phenomenal world; only consciousness can confirm creation, and only consciousness can confirm the Creator. 'If the Creator were conscious of Himself, He would not need conscious creatures' (*MDR*, p. 312).

The division between light and darkness, begun by God in Genesis and perpetuated by the Church, with its separation of God from the devil and good from evil, is an expression of the same biological principle that makes us distinguish between what is familiar and known and what is unknown and strange. The Church's rejection of darkness extended even to matter, whose nature was, after all, largely unknown: it was left to alchemy to redeem this material principle, so profoundly opposed to light and the spirit, from oblivion and to reunite it with its opposite. The separation of spirit from matter, followed by their reunion in the *coniunctio oppositorum*, was, of course, the concern of all alchemists, but there was one alchemist who particularly impressed Jung and he was the sixteenth-century adept Gerard Dorn.

The eternal Ground

Mysterium Coniunctionis, the preparation of which occupied Jung throughout his seventies, was finally published in two parts in 1955 and 1956. In this work, which he regarded as his *magnum opus*, he went in detail into the stages of the alchemical *opus* as described by Dorn, comparing them, as before, with the stages of individuation and the practice of analysis. The importance of Dorn lay in his belief that the *coniunctio* and realization of the *lapis* did not mark the end of the work. Completion of the *opus* came only with the achievement of union of the whole man with the *unus mundus* – the unitary world, the potential world of the first day of Creation, when nothing had yet become differentiated, and everything was still one. The *unus mundus* was the 'eternal Ground of all empirical being, just as the Self is the ground and origin of the individual personality past, present and future. On the basis of a self known by meditation and produced by alchemical means, Dorn "hoped and expected" to be united with the *unus mundus*' (*CW* 14, para. 760). Here Dorn is articulating a profound idea at the heart of all religious intuition – the perception of the 'relation or identity of the personal with the suprapersonal atman, and of the individual tao with the universal tao' (*CW* 14, para. 762).

The symbol of union with the *unus mundus* was one that moved Jung as deeply as it had Dorn, for it represented the fulfilment of everything his No. 2 personality had ever made him feel – the intimation of closeness to 'God's world' that he had found by the lakes of his childhood, that his father gave him at the top of the Rigi and that he *knew* when he gazed on the Athai Plains. Union with the eternal Ground, the source of all purpose, all meaning and all creation, was an image that brought stillness to his seldom silent fears of inner fragmentation and made it possible for him to view death as a goal. Dorn's vision revealed to him that, at the moment of full realization of the Self, a window opens on eternity. Filled with anticipation of that prospect, he continued to work at his individuation till the very end of his life.

SUGGESTIONS FOR FURTHER READING

Jean Shinoda Bolen, *The Tao of Psychology: Synchronicity and the Self*
Edward F. Edinger, *Anatomy of the Psyche: Alchemical Symbolism in Psychotherapy*
—— *Ego and Archetype: Individuation and the Religious Function of the Psyche*
James Hillman, *Insearch: Psychology and Religion*
Wolfgang Hochheimer, *The Psychotherapy of C. G. Jung*
Aniela Jaffé, *The Myth of Meaning in the Work of C. G. Jung*
C. G. Jung, *Answer to Job* (in *CW* 11)
—— *Psychology and Alchemy* (*CW* 12)
—— *Psychology of the Transference* (in *CW* 16)
—— *Synchronicity: An Acausal Connecting Principle* (in *CW* 8)
Konrad Lorenz, *Behind the Mirror: A Search for a Natural History of Human Knowledge*

Chapter Twelve

CONCLUSION

DEATH

Jung's last years were enviably tranquil and productive. He remained committed to the process of *becoming*, and he continued to honour the teleological imperative at work in him. The unknown held as much fascination as ever. When, at eighty-two, he began his autobiography with the words 'My life is a story of the self-realization of the unconscious', it is significant that he wrote 'the' unconscious, not 'my' unconscious, for what concerned him was the universal human unknown that, generation after generation, seeks incarnation in the world. The work with his inner life went on: 'The inner images keep me from getting lost in personal retrospection. Many old people become too involved in their memories. But if it is reflective and is translated into images, retrospection can be a *reculer pour mieux sauter*. I try to see the line which leads through my life into the world, and out of the world again' (*MDR*, p. 296).

In contrast to most people of his age, his interest in the world itself did not contract – if anything, it expanded: for example, he was immensely intrigued by the world-wide 'sightings' of Unidentified Flying Objects, collected volumes of information about them and published a book on the subject in 1959; deep disquiet about the future of our species also haunted him into his eighties, and this concern is much in evidence in *The Undiscovered Self*, published in 1958, and in the chapter he wrote for *Man and His Symbols*, which was published three years after his death. Looking back on his life, he wrote, 'In my case it must have been a passionate urge towards understanding which brought about my birth. For that is the strongest element in my nature' (*MDR*, p. 297).

His fame brought him many visitors, and he was much fêted in later years, but celebrity never went to his head. He preferred the solitude of Bollingen, where he could smoke his pipe in peace, work on the 'inner images', carve stone and chop wood. Although at times he fell prey to an old man's doubts about the true value of what he had achieved in his life, his capacity to enjoy nature, good food and good company persisted to the end.

For him, ageing was not just the shortening of life; it was a process of refinement through which he sharpened his perception of the *essential*. In the shadow of death, the wonder, the miracle, the magnificence of life become vividly perceptible, and it is by recognizing how brief is our own personal time here that we become conscious of the infinite. In his mid-fifties he observed that it is 'hygienic' to discover in death a goal towards which one can strive: shrinking from death only robs the second half of life of its purpose (*CW* 8, para. 792). He thought, 'It is better to go forwards with the stream of time than backwards against it.' 'To the psychotherapist,' he wrote, 'an old man who cannot bid farewell to life appears as sickly as a young man who is unable to embrace it.' (*CW* 8, para. 792). He was of a mind with Shakespeare's Julius Caesar (Act II, Scene ii):

> Cowards die many times before their deaths;
> The valiant never taste of death but once.
> Of all the wonders that I yet have heard,
> It seems to me most strange that men should fear;
> Seeing that death, a necessary end,
> Will come when it will come.

Jung had many premonitions of approaching death, mostly in dreams, and he took these as both a preparation and a reassurance. For example, in one dream he saw the 'other Bollingen' bathed in a glow of light, and a voice told him that it was completed and ready for habitation. He knew that dying has its onset long before death and was impressed by how little fuss the unconscious makes about the matter: it seems to be concerned only with *how* one dies, that is to say, whether the attitude of ego-consciousness is adjusted to dying or not.

Although he believed in the possibility of survival after death, he was not adamant about it. All he knew with any certainty was that there exists in the unconscious an archetypal assumption that we do survive: it is not only apparent in dreams but is also expressed in the universal belief in some kind of afterlife that is found in human communities virtually everywhere. On the whole, he felt it best to give credence to these archetypal intimations: to do so, he argued, is just as right or as wrong as rejecting them. Anyone who gives up all belief in survival merely marches towards oblivion, but one who puts faith in the archetype follows a living path right up to the moment of death. 'Both, to be sure, remain in uncertainty, but the one lives against his instincts, the other with them' (*MDR*, p. 284).

As always, Jung put his own faith in the archetype, and this, together with the 'passionate urge towards understanding', kept him going until June 1961, when, at the age of 85, he had two strokes within a week of one another and died peacefully at Küsnacht, surrounded by his family. His last words to his housekeeper, Ruth Bailey, were: 'Let's have a really good red wine tonight' (Brome, 1978, p. 273).

JUNG'S CONTRIBUTION

There is a story that Jung tells about his childhood that gives us the key to his Psychology. From a slope in the parsonage garden at Klein-Hüningen there jutted out a large stone. This was *his* stone.

> Often, when I was alone, I sat down on this stone, and then began an imaginary game that went something like this: 'I am sitting on top of this stone and it is underneath.' But the stone could also say 'I' and think: 'I am lying here on this slope and he is sitting on top of me.' The question then arose: 'Am I the one who is sitting on the stone, or am I the stone on which *he* is sitting?' This question always perplexed me, and I would stand up, wondering who was what now. The answer remained totally unclear, and my uncertainty was accompanied by a feeling of curious and fascinating darkness. But there was no doubt whatsoever that this stone stood in some secret relationship to me. I could sit on it for hours, fascinated by the puzzle it set me. (*MDR*, p. 33).

Thirty years later he returned to that slope. He was now a married man, with children, a house, a place in the world and a head full of ideas and plans. All at once, he was a child again, sitting on the stone and not knowing whether it was he or he was it. Then, he says:

> I thought suddenly of my life in Zürich, and it seemed alien to me, like news from some remote world and time. This was frightening, for the world of my childhood in which I had just become absorbed was *eternal*, and I had been wrenched away from it and had fallen into a time that continued to roll onwards, moving farther and farther away. The pull of that other world was so strong that I had to tear myself violently from the spot in order not to lose hold of my future. (ibid.)

In this story of the child of seven or eight we see already at work the fundamental dualism of the mature man's thinking. 'Am I the one who is sitting on the stone, or am I the stone on which *he* is sitting?' We find echoes of this question repeating again and again throughout his life: Am I the No. 1 personality who is sitting on No. 2, or am I No. 2 on whom No. 1 is sitting? Which is the mover and which is the moved? Do I have complexes, or do they have me? Do I need God, or does He need me? Is religion something I do for God, or is religion something God does to me? Does mother mean '*That* is the man-eater' or 'That is the *man-eater*'? Am I the plant that lives on its rhizome, or am I the rhizome on which the plant lives? Do I dream, or am I dreamt? Do I have this certainty, or does it have me? Repeatedly the same need emerges – the need to see how things are from the other side. 'The difference between most people and myself,' he wrote, 'is that for me the "dividing walls" are transparent. That is my peculiarity. Others find these walls so opaque that they see nothing behind them and therefore think nothing is there. To some extent I perceive the processes going on in the background, and that gives me an inner certainty' (*MDR*, p. 327).

The game with the stone was both a product of his isolation and his means of compensating for it through use of his imagination. The imaginative relationship between subject and object took the place of the actual relationship between person and person, and this occurred through the mechanism he came to understand better than any other psychologist – the mechanism of *projection*.

'The stone could say "I" and think: "I am lying here on this slope and he is sitting on top of me."' It was this experience of projecting his psyche into the stone that gave him the clue to solving the mystery of alchemy and to appreciating what lay behind all human relationships.

In this game he discovered the life-saving power of the imagination and of the symbol, for the stone was his transitional object. In the absence of basic trust in the world of people, the stone became the source of his security, his link with Hermes ('he of the stones'), the underground phallic god. Turning from the outer world, he must find life and meaning in this 'other': knowledge of the world must come from there. *Private* experience, *inner* knowledge, *gnosis* are primary, but if the isolation is to be endured, these must be established on an objective, *universal* base – the archetype, the collective unconscious, the objective psyche, God – and to achieve this becomes a lifetime's work.

The need, born of desperation, to affirm the objective value of his subjective vision led him into psychiatry, psychoanalysis, Gnosticism and alchemy and explains his ecstatic response to Krafft–Ebing's 'subjective' view of medical psychology, to Freud's conviction that he had fathomed the unconscious and to alchemy's secret of the Golden Flower.

From intimacy with the stone came his love of stone carving, his fascination with the *lapis philosophorum* and his appreciation of the supreme value that lies in base and 'unimportant' things. 'The same stone which the builders refused: is become the head-stone in the corner,' says the Book of Common Prayer. (When the builder at Bollingen was furious with the quarrymen for delivering a corner stone of the wrong measurements and ordered them to take it back, Jung cried: 'No. That is *my* stone. I must have it!' And he set about carving on it inscriptions that epitomized all that the Tower had ever meant to him.) His care for what was generally despised made him love the alchemists, love the unconscious, love the inferior function and want always to look through the opposite end of any telescope that life presented to him. It made him question every orthodoxy. 'I would never have sided with you in the first place,' he wrote to Freud in March 1912, 'had not heresy run in my blood.'

Moreover, his childhood game provided the origins of his theory of psychic functioning – the tension between opposites and the homeostatic principle of *enantiodromia* (going over from himself to the stone and from the stone to himself). His relationship with the stone anticipated his relationship with the unconscious and with God – the thesis, antithesis and synthesis of the transcendent function to produce higher consciousness. The stone's fascination was the fascination of the unknown. Lacking all other friends, he had to *animate* the stone and *know* it. He was the means of bringing the stone to consciousness, of rendering the stone conscious of itself. The experience was repeated on the Athai Plains. The stone was his first encounter with the 'eternal Ground', his first revelation of the *unus mundus*. With the stone he was in the presence of eternity.

It is extraordinary that so much should come out of a game played by a child in his parents' garden, and it demonstrates, yet again, how deeply dependent is Jung's contribution to psychology on his personal experience of life. This is seen by some as sufficient reason for rejecting the whole corpus of analytical psychology.

Criticisms

Criticisms of Jung are not in short supply. It has been argued, for example, that Jung's view of human life is too constrained by his class, nationality, intellectual background, time of birth and formal education for his ideas to be taken as universal truths. It has been alleged that his theory of individuation cannot possess general validity, since it is too closely linked with his own experience and with his own psychological type; that his therapeutic approach is too inner-directed for life in the modern world, since it places too much emphasis on archetypes and mythology and too little on the problems of relationship and social adjustment; that he is élitist in his assumptions; and that, as a method of treatment, analytical psychology is suitable only for the leisured, cultivated and rich (Staude, 1981.) Moreover, Jung's whole cast of mind has been attacked as mystical and unscientific, encumbered with an outdated religiosity and characterized by a degree of naïvety that ill-equips his followers to treat the problems of modern men and women.

The grain of truth in these criticisms becomes apparent when one views Jung's achievement from the standpoint of Western scientific materialism. They are obscure, however, if one sees them in a transcultural perspective. It is precisely because he was so withdrawn from the world in which he grew up that he was able to stand outside and see beyond it. ('The difference between most people and myself is that for me the "dividing walls" are transparent.') Like William Blake, another introverted visionary, he lived in complementary relationship to his Age. Herein lay the essence of his contribution: as a psychologist he was the twentieth century's great compensator.

Jung the compensator

The capacity to see both sides of an issue, so apparent in his stone game, made him a natural enemy of all one-sidedness and dogmatism, all narrow-mindedness and bigotry. If he upheld the primary reality of the psyche, it was in part out of a need to heal his own isolation, it is true, but it was also because of a need to redress what he saw as the crudely materialistic bias of Western society. To one possessing the clarity of his two-way vision, the principle of homeostasis was indispensable: the ideas of compensation and psychic balance were as central to the maintenance of his sanity as they are to an understanding of his Psychology. It was no accident that *Psychological Types* should be the first major work he published after his confrontation with the unconscious, for in the course of his illness he came to terms with how profoundly his approach differed from that of Freud and most other psychologists, who emphasized the importance of *extraverted* adjustment – the attainment of social goals and mastery of the environment. He *had* to stand by his own intuition and follow his own 'flickering light'. If that provoked hostility or incomprehension, it could not be helped: 'I feel it is the duty of one who goes his own way to inform society of what he finds on his voyage of discovery. Not the criticism of individual contemporaries will decide the truth or falsity of these discoveries, but future generations. There are things that are not yet true today, perhaps we dare not find them true, but tomorrow they may be. So every man whose fate it is to go his individual way must proceed with hopefulness and watchfulness, ever conscious of his loneliness and its dangers' (*CW* 7, para. 201).

It is not possible, at this late juncture, to examine in detail all the ways in which Jung's lonely, introverted contribution has served to compensate for the one-sided biases of our culture, but I will attempt to summarize some of the more significant of them in relation to experimental psychology, psychoanalysis, science, society and religion.

Jung and experimental psychology

Having made a major contribution to experimental psychology through his use of the word-association test, Jung abandoned it soon after the publication of his findings. 'Whosoever wishes to know about the human mind,' he wrote, 'will learn nothing, or almost nothing, from experimental psychology' (*CW* 7, para. 409). Between the 1920s and 1950s psychology was dominated by the behaviourists, and Jung was driven increasingly into a compensatory position. Where, for example, the behaviourists concentrated on rigorous study of quantifiable responses to outer events, Jung stressed the importance of symbolic representations and inner events. Where they sought to ban the psyche from their laboratories and to prohibit the use of introspection, Jung insisted that the psyche was the primary datum of existence and that introspection was the only means by which it could be known directly. While they declared that all observations must be quantified and analysed statistically, Jung maintained that statistics alienate us from our personal perception of life and prevent us from experiencing its meaning. For him the measure of all things was the human individual and his or her unique experience of what it universally and eternally means to be alive.

Jung and psychoanalysis

In the course of this book we have already examined a number of respects in which Jung compensated for what he saw as the limitations of Freudian psychology, but it is as well, for the sake of clarity, to summarize them here.

As we have seen, the fundamental distinction between the two schools is the view that each adopts of the unconscious. Whereas Freud assumed that most of our mental equipment is acquired individually in the course of growing up, Jung asserted that all the essential characteristics that distinguish us as human beings are with us from birth and encoded in the collective unconscious.

While Freud insisted on an exclusively sexual interpretation of human motivation, Jung saw this as dogmatic reductionism – he referred to it as 'nothing but' psychology. To Jung, Freud's sexual theory was like equating the whole achievement of Greek civilization with the Dionysiad or Rome with the Colosseum. Instead Jung maintained that libido or psychic energy was pure life force (like Bergson's *élan vital*) of which sexuality was but one important mode of expression.

Whereas Freud espoused the principle of causality and proposed an almost mechanistic form of determinism, Jung insisted on the freedom of the will, which he defined as free psychic energy at the disposal of the ego. Where Freud's orientation was causal, Jung's was teleological.

Where Freud confined his attention to the problems of libidinal development in childhood and their malign consequences for later adult life, Jung conceived of the life cycle as a whole of which childhood was but a highly significant part. No less important than childhood was development in adult life – especially in the second half of it.

Where Freud's approach was clinical and focused on pathology, Jung stressed that the healthy functioning of the psyche was of primary concern. Only the healthy psyche could be used as a satisfactory basis from which to understand pathology. For Jung, to put pathology first was to put the cart before the horse.

Where Freud was interested primarily in signs and symptoms, Jung was interested in meanings and symbols. While Freud stressed adjustment to 'actual reality', Jung was concerned more with 'psychological reality', maintaining that clinical material does not have to be *historically* true so long as it is *subjectively* true and filled with meaning for the patient.

Finally, where Freud considered religion an expression of infantile longings for parental protection and an obsessional means of expiating guilt, Jung saw religious practice as representing a fundamental archetypal need. Deprived of religious symbolism, individuals were cut off from meaning, and societies were doomed to die. To Jung the problem of the second half of life was essentially religious.

Jung and science

Jung's unashamed adoption of a religious or cosmic perspective has caused many to dismiss his work as 'unscientific'. In so doing they have often made statements that demonstrate that they have not understood him and have betrayed their own want of vision. It is not that Jung's thought was unscientific. Rather, it went *further* than science – and for good reason: 'Science', he said, 'comes to a stop at the frontiers of logic, but nature does not – she thrives on ground as yet untrodden by theory' (*CW* 16, para. 524). He allowed his imagination to carry him beyond the disciplinary constraints of pure science.

At the same time he had much respect for the empirical method – the collection and collation of facts, the testing of hypotheses against hard evidence and so on – and he attempted to apply this method in the development of analytical psychology, while admitting the difficulties involved. 'Analytical psychology is fundamentally a natural science,' he wrote, 'but it is subject far more than any other science to the personal bias of the observer. The psychologist must depend therefore in the highest degree upon historical and literary parallels if he wishes to exclude at least the crudest errors in judgement' (*MDR*, p. 192).

His use of the word-association test (which later earned notoriety in 'lie detector' proceedings), his application of the physiological principle of homeostasis to the phenomena of developmental psychology and his collaboration with the physicist Wolfgang Pauli in the study of scientific epistemology all show that Jung was no stranger to scientific method. But he refused to commit the fallacy of *scientism* – which denies the validity of any phenomenon not susceptible to scientific investigation. It was more his style to adopt an open-minded attitude, which permitted him to give due weight to the irrational, acausal elements in life that science disregards as irrelevant but Jung saw as full of significance.

He knew that an insistence on pure reason that excludes the irrational from life stifles the spirit and shackles the soul. 'The more the critical reason dominates, the more impoverished life becomes; but the more of myth we are capable of making conscious, the more of life we integrate. Overvalued reason has this in common with political absolutism: under its domination the individual is pauperized' (*MDR*, p. 280).

Reason may connect us with the real world, but it has little to do with the use of the imagination, which is the essence of psychic vitality. In itself reality is of little worth. It is what we make of reality through the psyche that gives it meaning. Through the imagination we *animate* the world in the same way as young Carl animated his stone. Creation is not something God completed in six days. Every moment of life is a continuing act of creation. It goes on in us through the life-enhancing power of symbols. Reason, science and technology pin us down to the literal fact, but symbols nourish the soul by pointing to something beyond what is known. Symbols quicken reality with meaning. 'Cut off the intermediary world of mythic imagination,' said Jung, 'and the mind falls prey to doctrinaire rigidities' (*MDR*, p. 292).

It was in order not to fall 'prey to doctrinaire rigidities' that he kept an open mind on all things, particularly those that shocked the scientific psychologists. He knew there to be more things in heaven and earth than were dreamt of in their philosophy. If he abandoned the word-association test and turned to mythology, alchemy and religion, it was because these contained psychological truths that were ignored by the scientists. For Jung psychology was the endlessly fascinating frontier zone between biology and spirit, body and mind, conscious and unconscious, the individual and the collective. Psychology was about *all* of life – rational and irrational, explicable and inexplicable: hence his willingness to give serious attention to the phenomena of parapsychology, spiritualism, precognition, astrology, life after death, synchronicity, UFOs, the spontaneous fragmentation of tables and knives and so on. That he was ridiculed for these interests did not unduly upset him. Loneliness and the incomprehension of critics were a way of life for him. In any case, many criticized him without bothering to read what he wrote. What interested him about flying saucers, for example, was less the question of whether they actually existed than why it was that so many people all over the world *reported* 'seeing' round objects in the sky. He concluded that UFOs were a modern myth, a compensation by the collective unconscious for our rational scepticism and our need for symbols of wholeness in a deeply divided world.

Similarly, his interest in astrology did not derive from a desire to divine the future but arose from his insight that astrology, like alchemy, was an attempt to develop psychology through projection of the unconscious psyche into matter, namely, the planets. Where astrology differed from alchemy was in the significance that it attributed to time. Like the ancient Chinese, the astrologers perceived that meanings are constellated within the context of the moment. The heavens were mirrors in which they saw their inner psychic patterns reflected within discrete moments of time.

These thoughts led him onto the formulation of his theory of *synchronicity*, the 'acausal connecting principle' that creates meaningful relationships between events occurring at the same time. This principle is at the root of the ancient Chinese acausal approach to reality that is embodied in the *I Ching* or *Book of Changes*. Since all life is pattern, it follows that time functions as an aspect of that pattern. Anything that happens is related to everything else that happens through the time at which the happening occurs. The Chinese attempted to determine empirically how patterns of meaning unfold in the universe through time. The *I Ching* used this empiricism to provide a meaningful context for events occurring at any particular moment.

Jung was sympathetic to this approach because it corresponds to how we *experience* meaningful coincidences and also to how we experience time. We may be taught that time is an abstract measure, but it never feels as if it is. Rather, time is felt to have a character of its own, which colours all events as they occur. The whole 'nostalgia industry' is based on this simple truth. It is as true of physical events as of mental events that may, as a consequence, appear to be causally related – as when a door slams at the same moment as one reads of a door slamming in a novel. The Western mentality dismisses such coincidence as meaningless, but life reaches beyond the significance of mere causality. We are not prisoners on a mechanistic treadmill driven by abstract time. Through awareness of acausal relationships between the phenomena of life we enter a wider reality capable of liberating us from the intellectual chain-gang whose warders are Cause and Effect. Jung was saying, in other words, that not only life has its seasons but meaning has them too, and all meanings bear the imprint of the time at which they come into existence.

Those who accuse Jung of being unscientific are right, of course, if they mean by 'science' the use of the experimental procedures of physics and chemistry rather than the growth of *scientia* (knowledge). It is a fact that in developing his Psychology,

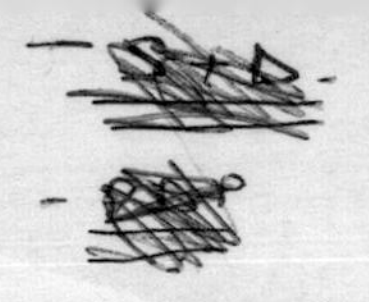

Jung did not propose hypotheses that he then subjected to experimental test. Instead he began with his own experiences and those of his patients. The hypotheses he proposed were attempts to comprehend these experiences. And it must be acknowledged that for him a living experience of the individual psyche was far more important than any theory about it. 'I cannot experience myself as a scientific problem,' he wrote. 'Myth is more individual and expresses life more precisely than does science. Science works with concepts of averages which are far too general to do justice to the subjective variety of an individual life' (*MDR*, p. 17). Ultimately it is a matter of ethics. Stalin, who of all people knew what he was talking about, summed it up when he remarked that a single death is a tragedy, whereas a million deaths is a statistic.

If analytical psychology is not, strictly speaking, a science, what then is it? There has been much debate about this. Henri Ellenberger (1970) probably offers the most accurate classification when he describes analytical psychology, like psychoanalysis, as a form of *hermeneutics* – the art or science of *interpretation*. Ellenberger compares both disciplines with the philosophical 'schools' of Graeco-Roman antiquity. Just as the Platonists had their Academy, the Aristoteleans the Lyceum and the Epicureans the House and Garden of Epicurus, so the Freudians and Jungians have their Institutes, and their bodies of knowledge and wisdom into which new members are initiated through the ritual of the training analysis. This is not to demean analysis, for the ancient philosophical schools made a contribution of the highest importance to our civilization, but it does divest analysis of any unwarranted pretension to being an experimental science.

Jung and society

Because he went his own introverted, lonely way and remained stubbornly resistant to hostile criticism, Jung's Psychology has been attacked as self-centred (i.e., ego-centred) and anti-social. Since everyone grows up and lives within a social context, it follows that personality development must be sensitive to social influences and that any effective school of psychotherapy must take account of these. Jung was aware of this, but it is an index of the profundity of his introversion that he tended to put the inner relationship with the Self before the outer relationship with people in the environment. This is not to say that he devalued outer relationships – on the contrary he regarded them as of the greatest importance – but he clearly believed that good relations with people grew out of good relations with the Self. Integration of the Self was the primary good out of which all other goods followed: 'Relationship to the Self is at once relationship to our fellow man, and no one can be related to the latter until he is related to himself' (*CW* 16, para. 445). However, he acknowledged that there is in all of us a longing for kinship – an expression of what he termed *kinship libido* – which drives us to seek the specifically *human* connection and that, without this, inner integration will not take us very far: 'Without the conscious acknowledgement and acceptance of our kinship with those around us there can be no synthesis of the personality.' The longing for human connectedness, he says, is the 'core of the whole transference phenomenon' and 'behind it there stands the restless urge towards individuation' (*CW* 16, paras. 444–7).

Individuation, therefore, has two principal aspects: 'In the first place it is an internal and subjective process of integration, and in the second it is an equally indispensable process of objective relationship. Neither can exist without the other, although sometimes the one and sometimes the other predominates' (*CW* 16, para. 448). In other words, individuation has both its introverted and its extraverted modes of progression, and if Jung gave greater emphasis to the former, it was indeed because of his psychological type.

It was also an aspect of his compensatory contribution to our culture. He was staunchly opposed to the collectivism and materialism of the modern world, which encourages exploitation of the physical resources of the planet but neglects the creative resources of the Self. In his view, we are collectively committing the same fallacy as the alchemists by projecting our spiritual aspirations into matter in the belief that we are pursuing the highest values. By denying the soul we treat each other as economic commodities. Instead, he believed, we must pay due attention to the inner life of the individual if we are to change the soullessness of European culture.

On the whole, those who accuse Jung of denying the importance of social adjustment do him an injustice, for he maintained that each of us has a primary duty to our culture, time and place and that we have to purchase our individuation at the cost of equivalent work for the benefit of society (*CW* 18, para. 1099). 'You cannot individuate on Everest,' he said (Hannah, 1977). The emphasis of his therapeutic approach was to induce in his patients an awareness of their *total* situation, which necessarily embraced their social as well as their intrapsychic circumstances. He always encouraged them to plough analytic insights into *life*, to assume personal responsibility for their own shadows and to stop projecting them onto others.

For all that, he was never in sympathy with the practice that grew in many psychiatric centres during his lifetime of treating patients in groups. This was because of his conviction that therapeutic groups eroded the individual's sense of personal integrity and caused him to 'render himself obsolete'. While Jung had no quarrel with the notion that patients often need help to achieve a more fruitful adaptation to society, he nevertheless considered it essential that everyone should make this adaptation in his or her unique way. The one attempt to apply analytical psychology on a group basis of which he approved was that of Irene and Gilbert Champernowne, who established a Jungian therapeutic community at the Withymead Centre in England in 1942. At Withymead, however, all residential patients were in individual analysis, and the only group meetings that took place were those confined to members of the staff. The therapeutic value of living in a community while undergoing personal analysis was held to be largely unconscious and based on the effective constellation of the archetype of the extended family (Stevens, 1986).

In his own life Jung was conscientious in discharging his social duties, taking very seriously his commitment to the Swiss Army and to his municipality, following political developments in his country and elsewhere, always voting in referenda and making a point of getting on with people of all kinds. Nevertheless, his fundamental belief was that our behaviour in the world is shaped and determined by our inner (largely unconscious) life and that our relation to people is contained in our experience of the Self. Thus the more an individual becomes 'what he is' the more truly sociable he will be. When Jung declared that individuation does not shut one out from the world but gathers the world to oneself (*CW* 8, para. 432) he was, as usual, stating a general truth based on his own experience.

Finally it must be admitted that the charge that Jungian analysis is élitist contains an element of truth. Any form of analysis is necessarily only for a few, since the number of analysts is limited, and only people with above-average intelligence, verbal ability and a capacity for working with symbols can hope to benefit from the procedure, even if they can afford it. However, it can be argued that classical Jungian analysis is less élitist than other forms of analytic treatment. Patients are seen two or three hours a week to begin with; then sessions are reduced to one hour a week as soon as possible. Moreover, Jung advocated that the treatment be broken off every ten weeks so as to throw the patient back into life and into a personal relationship with the Self. Patients are encouraged to work on their own dreams, paint their symbols, read related material and collaborate actively throughout the whole course of the analysis. The advantage of this procedure is that it tends to prevent infantile regressions and dependencies, to foster personal responsibility for individuation and to reduce the possibility that the patient will become alienated from his surroundings or divorced from everyday life (*CW* 16, paras. 26 and 43). It also has the advantage of making classical Jungian analysis considerably less expensive than its Freudian or Kleinian equivalents, which require up to four or five sessions a week for anything up to three or four years. Because Jungian analysands do so much of the work on their own, success depends more on the energy that they put into the analysis than on the money that it costs them.

It would be less than honest, however, to obscure the fact that there are some patients with whom it is not helpful to work in the manner advocated by Jung – namely, those who, as a result of defective parenting in early life, suffer from what Bowlby calls 'anxious attachment' (see p. 102 above). Such patients need time to establish with their analyst a working relationship on which they *know* they can depend, so that they can experience a sense of 'basic trust' and conceive of themselves as capable of sustaining a lasting bond of intimacy. Only when this has been achieved can they begin to benefit from the kind of imaginative work with the Self that Jungians regard as the crux of analysis. Deprived of the opportunity to form a lasting and uninterrupted bond of attachment with their analyst, there is a danger that such patients may be reinforced in their schizoid personality structure and may continue to show what one of Bowlby's colleagues has called 'compulsive self-reliance' (Parkes, 1973), adopting an attitude of prickly independence and detachment, denying all need for love or support and rigidly insisting on doing everything for themselves. Apart from this important exception, however, the classical Jungian approach can be applied with benefit to patients with widely differing types of personal maladjustment or existential need.

Patients whose 'anxious attachment' has been relieved through a close and enduring relationship with their therapist can themselves proceed with benefit to use the inner-directed techniques devised by Jung. This, indeed, appears to have happened to Jung when, through his intimacy with Emma Jung, Freud and Toni Wolff, he was able to proceed to his confrontation with the unconscious and the later development of his psychology. There is something to be said for the argument that contemporary schools of psychotherapy (with the exception of the Jungian school) place excessive emphasis on the importance of 'object relations' and 'analysis of the transference' while neglecting the value of retreat and the capacity to be productively alone. Endorsing Edward Gibbon's dictum 'solitude is the school of genius', Anthony Storr (1988) has developed the thesis propounded in his earlier *Dynamics of Creation* that many of the world's most original thinkers and artists have lacked close personal ties and that creative achievement, as well as personal happiness, can find their chief source in solitude: 'Development of the capacity to be alone is necessary if the brain is to function at its best, and if the individual is to fulfil his highest potential. Human beings easily become alienated from their own deepest needs and feelings. Learning, thinking, innovation and maintaining contact with one's own inner world are all facilitated by solitude' (Storr, 1988, p. 28). The capacity to achieve fruitful enjoyment of one's own company is every bit as much a mark of emotional maturity as the capacity to form intimate relationships and should be no less significant a goal for analytic treatment.

Jung and religion

During his lifetime Jung witnessed the decline of organized Christian belief. He compensated for this by developing a religious attitude based on personal experience of the numinous power of archetypes and by reaffirming the need for a *mythic* connection between the individual and the cosmos. To be spiritually alive, he believed, we must perceive ourselves to be part of a cosmic purpose, and this truth was reinforced for him when he talked to people whose lives had been shaped by cultures other than that of Western Europe.

He was deeply impressed, for example, by a Pueblo chief whom he met on his visit to New Mexico during the winter of 1924–5. The chief described the alarm that white Americans inspired in him: 'See how cruel the whites look,' he said. 'Their lips are thin, their noses sharp, their faces furrowed and distorted by folds. Their eyes have a staring expression; they are always seeking something. What are they seeking? The whites always want something; they are always uneasy and restless. We do not know what they want. We do not understand them. We think they are mad.' Jung asked him why he thought the whites were mad. 'They say that they think with their heads,' the chief replied. 'Why, of course. What do you think with?' Jung asked him in surprise. 'We think here,' the chief said, indicating his heart (*MDR*, p. 233).

Jung saw that the pre-eminence of 'head-thinking' had enabled Europeans to master the world through science, technology and armed might but that, in the process, they had lost the capacity to think with the heart and live through the soul.

As they sat together high about the Taos plateau, the Indian confided to Jung, 'We are a people who live on the roof of the world; we are the sons of Father Sun, and with our religion we daily help our Father go across the sky. We do this not only for ourselves, but for the whole world. If we were to cease practising our religion, in ten years the sun would no longer rise. Then it would be night for ever' (*MDR*, p. 237).

This belief sustained his dignity and composure, which, Jung observed, 'springs from his being a son of the sun; his life is cosmologically meaningful, for he helps the father and preserver of all life in his daily rise and descent. If we set against this our own self-justifications, the meaning of our own lives as it is formulated by our reason, we cannot help but see our poverty ... Knowledge does not enrich us: it removes us more and more from the mythic world in which we were once at home by right of birth' (*MDR*, p. 237).

Encounters like this taught Jung that unless we assume responsibility for our own part of the universe, everything of importance is lost. This is the primordial religious intuition of our kind. All early religions, in their various ways, portray man as the messenger between heaven and earth. More advanced religions express the same idea. To the Muslim man is the viceroy placed by God over creation; to the Hindu the human spirit is one with the eternal and infinite Brahman; to the Christian man is made in the image of God.

Those who would dismiss Jung's religious orientation as anachronistic fail to appreciate the incomparable value of the sacred view, which elevates human life above the mundane practices of subsistence and enhances all human acts by revealing the duty we owe to each other, to our fellow creatures and to our planet. It grants us a vision of our dual nature – we are both microcosm and macrocosm, both temporal and eternal, and, though we may be subject to the constraints of daily existence, we nevertheless transcend them by virtue of our humanity.

While all religions teach this, Jung was the one psychiatrist of stature to perceive its fundamental importance to the human spirit and to incorporate it in his therapeutic work. To belittle his perception as an anachronism is to disavow one of Jung's most extraordinary gifts – his ability to live *in* his time and, simultaneously, to step out of it, to share an affinity with men of all the times that have ever been. Everything he wrote bears the stamp of that affinity. It has been well said of him that his ideas were too fundamental, in a sense, to be modern (von Franz, 1975, p. 11).

Although he never stated his creed as an analyst, the text that would come nearest to expressing it, I believe, is contained in the alchemical treatise *Rosarium philosophorum* (Frankfurt, 1550), on which Jung based his *Psychology of the Transference*. It runs as follows: 'He who would be initiated into this art and secret wisdom must put away the vice of arrogance, must be devout, righteous, deep-witted, humane towards his fellows, of a cheerful countenance and a happy disposition, and respectful withal. Likewise he must be an observer of the eternal secrets that are revealed to him' (*CW* 16, para. 450). In this spirit Jung practised his art which, he said, must always be undertaken with the kind of attitude that is required in the execution of a religious work.

But he was much more than a brilliant exponent of the art of psychotherapy. Since his death Jung has been compared with such men as Columbus, Copernicus and Livingstone. Whether or not such comparisons are justified, it cannot be denied that his was a gigantic work of exploration into all the 'prodigies of Africa' that lie within us. Though he subsequently discovered that the alchemists had been there before him, he experienced his own perilous expedition as if he were the first man ever to have attempted it. Like any geographical explorer, he kept a detailed log of his voyage, making drawings of the significant features he encountered, and, on his return, published them for the edification of mankind.

So if he could not aspire to be a natural scientist, he was at least a cartographer of the soul. At the end of his life and at the height of his fame he was modest about his achievements: 'A man once dipped a hatful of water from a stream . . .' (*MDR*, p. 327). What, then, did his discoveries amount to? Perhaps to nothing more than the *true* gold of the alchemists. It is enough.

SUGGESTIONS FOR FURTHER READING

Peter Homans, *Jung in Context*
C. G. Jung, *The Undiscovered Self (Present and Future)* (in CW 10)
R. K. Papadopoulos and G. S. Saayman (eds), *Jung in Modern Perspective*
Ira Progoff, *Jung's Psychology and its Social Meaning*
Anthony Storr, *The School of Genius*

JUNG'S ADVERSARY: RICHARD NOLL

Since the original publication of *On Jung* in 1990, two influential books have appeared which are highly critical of Jung and his Psychology. These are *The Jung Cult: Origins of a Charismatic Movement* (Princeton University Press) and *The Aryan Christ: The Secret Life of Carl Jung* (Random House) by Richard Noll, a clinical psychologist and post-doctoral Fellow in the History of Science at Harvard University. Since Noll makes serious allegations against Jung and impugns the integrity of Jungian analysts, I propose to take advantage of the publication of a second edition of my book to examine the gravest of Richard Noll's charges. This is necessary, I believe, because he has been so effective in promoting his ideas that there is a danger that they will enter public consciousness as received wisdom. Should that be allowed to happen, it would represent a gross injustice to Jung's memory and to the whole tradition of psychotherapy practised in his name. It is important, therefore, that the record should be put straight.

Essentially, Noll's charges are that Jung and his followers were less interested in developing a school of psychotherapy than in establishing what he calls 'an institutionalized capitalist enterprise', with training institutes distributed throughout the world. This enterprise, he says, is at the same time a 'secret church' or religious cult, centred on the 'pseudo-charismatic' figure of Jung (who, Noll insists, actually believed himself to be the 'Aryan Christ'), and run by an élitist group of acolytes, who sell initiation into the 'fantasy of individuation' at an exorbitant price. Noll marshalls extensive evidence designed to prove that Jungian psychology shares precisely the same Germanic, Aryan, '*völkisch*', Nietzschean sun-worshipping roots as National Socialism – though he acknowledges that Jung put this tradition to the service of a 'religious' rather than a political objective.

Richard Noll directs his most sustained attack against Jung's theory of archetypes which, he maintains, is based on deliberately falsified evidence and is wholly lacking in scientific validity. As a result, he felt justified, in an article published in the *Times Higher Educational Supplement* (22 November 1996), in making a comparison between the attitude Jungians adopt to their patients and that of Ben Johnson's *Alchemist*, who 'deceives one customer after another . . . stringing each dupe along with scientific sounding jargon'. Jungian analysts, he says, 'most of whom have no formal medical, psychological or scientific training', having remained silent on the issues of what he calls 'Jung's deliberate fraud'. What is more, Noll accused Jungian analysts of ducking his criticisms and refusing to examine the scientific status of Jung's theoretical constructs because 'new patients would stop knocking at their door if the truth were more widely known'. Since I am fortunate enough to have received a formal medical, psychological and scientific training, it is appropriate that I should use this opportunity to pick up the gauntlet that Noll has thrown down.

Readers of *On Jung* will find it hard to reconcile Noll's charges with the facts of Jung's life and the development of his Psychology as I have presented them. However, Noll's books have received very favourable reviews and, when *The Jung Cult* was published in 1994, it was that year voted the 'Best Book on Psychology' by the Association of American Publishers. When *The Aryan Christ: The Secret Life of Carl Jung* was published in 1997 it was to similar acclaim. Yet most of the critics who so warmly endorsed Noll's books are not noted for their familiarity with Jung's work, and their enthusiasm betrays the ease with which they have been persuaded by Noll's imputations and the strength of what seems to be a growing prejudice against Jung. Why should this be? Reflecting on this question, it has struck me that a progression (or perhaps a regression) is discernible in the history of biographical writing over the last hundred years. Up to the end of the First World War biographies tended to focus on their subjects' public life. Then, between the wars, the focus shifted from the public to the private life. In our own more salacious and intrusive times, the primary concern has become centred on the secret life, prying into those aspects which, during their lifetime, and after their death, the subjects, and their families, would rather have kept discreetly to themselves. It is as if biographic interest has moved from the persona to the shadow. For this reason, some recent biographers of Jung have been loud in their condemnation of the Jung family for continuing to keep certain diaries, letters and documents out of the public domain. This is true of Richard Noll and of Frank McLynn, who published a hatchet biography of Jung in 1996. Evidently, these authors detect hidden dirt and they resent not being able to lay their hands on it and serve it up for public delectation. Anyone who achieves eminence is now vulnerable to this peculiarly modern form of investigative prurience. However, possibly because of the family embargo, anyone who bought Noll's *Secret Life of Carl Jung* in the hope of picking over the minutiae of the great psychiatrist's sex life was disappointed. Instead, Noll concentrated on the 'hidden agenda' which he perceived as providing the key to Jung's life and work.

Jung, says Noll, presented himself as a psychologist and a Christian, not because he was either, but as a deliberate deception designed to disguise his 'magical, polytheistic, pagan worldview' and to conceal his fantasy of bringing redemption to all members of the Aryan race. Through his use of active imagination and the rituals of analysis, Jung was in fact proselytizing a form of 'spiritual elitism, a Neitzschean new nobility of the individuated' based on the pattern of his own inflated experience of 'deification'. In all seriousness, Noll goes on to imply that, by developing the use of techniques to mobilize the transcendent function and promote individuation, Jung was dedicating himself to the production of an Aryan 'master race'. 'Jung was waging war against Christianity and its distant, absolute, unreachable god and was training his disciples to listen to the voices of the dead, to worship the sun, and to become gods themselves' (Noll, 1994, p. 224). To anyone conversant with Jung's writings and experienced in the practice of Jungian analysis this seems a travesty of the facts. What evidence does he provide to support his apparently grotesque interpretation? This seems to have been derived from three sources: (1) Jung's discussion of solar symbolism in *Symbols of Transformation*; (2) the account of inner experiences which Jung gave to a closed seminar in 1925; and (3) a recently discovered text which Noll alleges to be the inaugural address made by Jung to the Psychology Club in Zurich in 1916.

Because Jung writes at length about solar symbolism and solar renewal in *Symbols of Transformation*, Noll jumps to the conclusion that he must have been a 'sun-worshipper'. And since Jung exposed himself to the experience which he and many other introspective people have described as 'the god within', he believed he *was* a god. Noll makes much of the account of inner experiences which Jung gave in his 1925 seminars, which contain material additional to that published in *Memories, Dreams, Reflections.* Jung reported that during one episode of active imagination 'a most disagreeable thing happened. Salome became very interested in me, and she assumed I could cure her blindness. She began to worship me. I said "Why do you worship me?" She replied "You are Christ". Inspite of my objections she maintained this. I said, "This is madness", and became filled with sceptical resistance.'

Noll interprets this to mean that 'Jung believed he had undergone a direct initiation into the ancient Hellenistic mysteries and had even experienced deification in doing so.' In the course of Jung's active imagination, a snake approached him, encircled and gripped his body. He assumed the attitude of the crucifixion and felt that his face had taken on the aspect of a lion or a tiger. Jung proceeded to amplify this experience in terms of Mithraic symbolism, identifying the lion-headed god gripped in the coils of a snake as Aion, the eternal being, a statue of which is in the Vatican Museum.

In the course of his discussion of this and other episodes experienced by Jung during his 'confrontation with the unconscious', Noll demonstrates that he has only the crudest conception of symbolism and has no idea how it is possible to make therapeutic use of the symbols which people produce in the course of an analysis. His stolid literal-mindedness leads him into absurd misinterpretations. He does not appreciate that at critical points in their lives people commonly experience initiatory symbolism in their dreams, or that it can be of enormous therapeutic help to them to enter imaginatively into the spirit of this drama so as actually to experience the emotions and psychological changes of the initiation being symbolized. He also fails to appreciate the significance of Jung's discovery of the dynamic *power* of symbols to act as 'transformers of energy' and their central importance in the processes of psychic transformation and healing. As a result, Noll insists on taking Jung's experience of Aion not symbolically but concretely. Clearly it suits his purpose to assume that Jung was crazy enough to think that he had actually *become* a god. Noll writes as if the creative act of entering the symbolic life and exposing oneself to the seemingly limitless vitality of unconscious resources was a pathological aberration. Yet such experiences have been reported by innovative people engaged in all forms of creative endeavour, whether it be literature, music, mathematics, philosophy, science, sport, the plastic arts, or even analysis itself. Nor does he understand that to feel the power of a symbol is to enter a world of make-believe. For the devout Catholic, at the moment of consecration, the bread and the wine *become* the body and blood of Christ. When in a primitive ritual, a man puts on the mask of a god, then for the duration of the ritual, he *is* the god. The profane object is transformed into the sacred object through a culturally sanctioned act of imagination. We have all experienced similar transformations, not only those of us who have been analysed, but at a more simple, more personal level, as children at play.

A sceptic, like Noll, can, of course, refuse to participate, and then the magic does not work. He stands outside it and scoffs. For him there is no transformation because he declines to have anything to do with the whole charade. He eschews the imaginal realm that others wish to enter. It is as the scoffing outsider that Noll has produced his caricature of Jung's achievement.

On the basis of these distortions Noll builds his case that Jung believed himself to be 'the Aryan Christ' and the founder of a neo-pagan cult. Where did he get his absurd but catchy title 'The Aryan Christ' from? Jung never used it to describe himself, nor does Noll provide any evidence that he did so. But this does not prevent him from confidently asserting, 'Jung became conscious that he was the Aryan Christ for a new age', as if this were a fact rather than Noll's own interpretation. He derives the term 'Aryan Christ' from a belief which he says was current in certain Germanic '*völkisch*' circles that Christ's whole cast of mind was 'Aryan' rather than Jewish and that his biological father was either a Roman centurian or a 'Hellene'. As the 'Aryan Christ', Noll assures us, Jung believed he 'could redeem those biologically capable of rebirth – Aryans –

by returning them to their natural pagan roots, to the archaic man still within. He could save the world. Having been blessed with the direct knowledge of the divine, who better than he to be the prophet of the new age?'

This is the 'secret agenda' which Noll claims that Jung concealed behind his imposture as a psychotherapist and a man of science. 'To make his spiritual movement a success', says Noll, 'Jung had to adopt at least three false faces or masks'. In the first place, Jung passed himself off as a psychologist, devising various *Decknamen*, or cover names, such as 'personal unconscious', or 'collective unconscious', 'persona', to disguise his true intention. Thus, in his publications and lectures, 'Jung was careful to always speak and write *in code* [my italics]'. At this point an unmistakable whiff of paranoia enters Noll's argument. The term 'psychological reality', says Noll, is 'itself a *Deckname* – still very much used by Jungians today – for direct mystical experience of the spiritual world of the divine. This was his first mask'. Second, 'he stuck close to Christian metaphors to hide the pagan undertow of his stream of thought. This was his second mask.' Third, 'he assumed the role of a religious prophet or leader of a charismatic cult of individuals looking up to him for guidance. This was his third mask' (Noll, 1997a, pp. 159–60).

Insofar as Noll has had a scholarly contribution to make to Jungian studies it has been to lay bare the cultural sources of much of Jung's thought, and it is unfortunate that he has found it necessary to put a paranoid spin on these discoveries to make them fit into his 'conspiracy theory' that all his life Jung was following a secret mission as an Aryan redeemer. What is particularly disturbing about Noll is his attitude of Olympian condescention to all that Jung experienced and described, and his dismissal of the notion that it can have any relevance to the human condition merely because it is 'Germanic' and 'Aryan'. Moreover, he writes as if sun-worship were a peculiarly Aryan invention and therefore culturally determined and without archetypal implications. But sun divinities are apparent in Egypt, early Europe, Asia, Peru and Mexico. The notion that the sun is the eye of a sky god is evident not only in Egypt but among the Bushmen of the Kalahari Desert, the Semang Pygmies, and the inhabitants of Tierra del Fuego, encountered by Charles Darwin on his voyage in HMS *Beagle*. Mithras began life as a sky god, was transformed into a sun god, and later became a hero-saviour (*sol invictus*), while at the same time ensuring the continuance of life by slaying the bull from which all plants and grains originated. Such a career is common to many sky gods. As with Mithras, the solarization of the sky god coincides with his decline to the semi-human status of the solar hero, who, having been swallowed up in the Underworld in the West, emerges triumphantly next morning in the East. This motif is linked to initiation rites world-wide, such as those practised in Australasia, through which the initiate becomes identified with the solar hero, and, in the process, himself becomes the son of the sky god. The initiation is, like all other initiations, a death and rebirth experience, whereby the symbolism of the setting and rising of the sun is symbolically repeated and ritualized.

Although sun-worship has never been as widespread as once thought, the sun is nevertheless the origin of heat and light, and its resurrection every morning as well as its return after the winter solstice are matters of primary concern to every human being who has ever lived. It is not surprising, therefore, that sun symbolism, like sun-worship, is widespread. The swastika, one of the oldest and most complex of all solar symbols, is far from being peculiar to Germanic peoples. It has been found in virtually all parts of the world, including pre-Columbian America. Its form suggests rotation about a central axis, and there are in fact two kinds of swastika: the right-handed *swastika* and the left-handed *swavastika*. These have been variously interpreted as male and female, solar and lunar, the rising vernal sun and the descending autumnal sun, and so on. In China the two swastikas depict the forces of *Yin* and *Yang*. Sun symbolism is thus no mere Aryan curiosity. Indeed, it is so universal that it leads one to suspect that somewhere in his psyche there still lurks a sun-worshipping Richard Noll.

It would thus appear that we can safely dispose of Noll's attempt to brand Jung as a lunatic, self-proclaimed, Aryan Christ. But what of the recently discovered text on which Noll bases his argument that by founding the Psychology Club in Zurich in 1916 he was setting up his own redemptive cult? This document, declares Noll, 'appears to be a summary transcript of a talk Jung gave in 1916 at the meeting at which the Psychology Club was founded. It has been found among the papers of Fanny Bowditch Katz, an American patient of Jung's and Jung's Dutch associate, Maria Moltzer, who underwent analysis with the two of them in 1912 and

1913. Moltzer, however, remained her primary analyst, and as is apparent from their mutual correspondence, they remained in touch long after Katz's return to America. The document concerning the Psychology Club is probably an original English transcript typed by Moltzer in Zurich and, it is assumed, mailed to Katz in America. In the upper right-hand corner of the document "Frl. Moltzer" is written in an unknown hand.'

These assertions have been examined by the noted Jungian scholar, Sonu Shamdasani, and he has published his findings in *Cult Fictions: C.G. Jung and the Founding of Analytical Psychology* (1998). Shamdasani establishes that the text was not by Jung but in all probability by Maria Moltzer herself. Previously a nurse at the Burghölzli Hospital, Maria Moltzer became an analyst, and worked as Jung's assistant. Among Fanny Bowditch Katz's papers are diaries containing notes of her analytic sessions with Moltzer. Katz translated several of Moltzer's papers from German into English, and if Moltzer was the author of the document's contents this would explain why it exists in English and why it is among Bowditch Katz's papers. Furthermore, there are parallels between Moltzer's known views and those expressed in the document.

If Jung were indeed the author, and had the text formed the basis of his inaugural address to the club, as Noll claims, then a copy would almost certainly have existed in German among Jung's papers as well as in the club's archives. That Jung gave so important an address would be recorded in the minutes of the inaugural meeting and its contents summarized. However, no trace of such a text has been found in Jung's papers, nor has a copy been found at the club, though the manuscripts of two papers that Jung is known to have delivered to the club were found there, signed and dated by Jung, October 1916, and these manuscripts are in German. Moreover, the minutes of the Psychology Club exist, including those of the first meeting held on 26 February 1916. Jung was present, but all he did was read out a Deed of Donation!

Jung's own account of the founding of the club shows that he had not the slightest intention of establishing a cult, but wished merely to overcome the limitations of the one-to-one analytic relationship: 'I agreed with the idea of the Club,' he wrote in a letter to Alphonse Maeder, 'because it seemed to us to be of the greatest importance to experience how analysed people met together without compulsion, and where the flaws in our analysis of the collective function lay. I have up till now learnt an extraordinary amount in the Club.' That Jung had no wish to impose his religious beliefs on the club or to manipulate or dominate its members for his own cultic purposes is evident from his refusal to accept executive office and his insistence on remaining an ordinary member. As he wrote, in italics, in his letter to Maeder, *'I am absolutely prepared, in every respect, to withdraw and leave others a free path.'* This is hardly the language of a charismatic cult leader or of an Aryan Christ mobilizing devoted disciples around his divine person. Moreover, the statutes of the club, which Shamdasani also publishes, make it clear that they reflect none of the proposals contained in the text which Noll insists is Jung's inaugural address. If Jung were indeed the author, and had he really intended it to form the basis of a new cult, it would seem to have been a dismal failure.

According to the advance publicity circulated by Noll's publishers, his books purport to be 'ground-breaking works of historical reconstruction' bringing Jungian scholarship to 'a new level of sophistication', Sonu Shamdasani has demonstrated the hollow nature of this claim, and has, by contrast, produced a balanced and meticulously researched contribution to the study of Jung and his Psychology.

While it is true that many others have spoken of a cultlike atmosphere among Jung's early followers, precisely the same could be said about the groups that collected around Freud and Adler in Vienna, Lacan in Paris, Melanie Klein and Anna Freud in London, to say nothing of Aristotle, Plato and Socrates in Athens. It is inevitable that when charismatic leaders arise they will attract followers, and a cultlike atmosphere will develop around them. But analytical psychology was never a religious cult in the sense that Noll tries to impose on it and it is certainly not true of analytical psychology today. By so overstating his case, Noll destroys it. What could have been a scholarly examination of the cultural antecedents of Jung's thought, and a creative exposure of the shadow side of Jungian training and practice, becomes a burlesque – a gross distortion of the truth.

The Theory of Archetypes and the Solar Phallus Man

The second major thrust of Noll's attack on Jung is his attempt to disprove the theory of archetypes with its basis in biology. Noll's case against the theory of archetypes and the collective unconscious is that it is based upon falsified evidence (i.e. the case of the Solar Phallus Man) and upon outdated and erroneous biology. In an article published in *The Times* on 5 June 1995, Noll is quoted as acclaiming Jung 'the most influential liar of the twentieth century'. This was widely noted and commented upon. The article paraphrases pages 181–7 of *The Jung Cult* in which Noll accuses Jung of falsifying the details of a piece of evidence which Jung frequently cited in support of the theory of the collective unconscious. It concerned the schizophrenic patient who is said to have told Jung that if he stared at the sun with half-closed eyes, he would see that the sun had a phallus and that this organ was the origin of the wind. Years later, so Jung said, a Greek text was published describing an almost identical vision. The patient, a poorly educated man, could not have seen the text, even if he could have understood it, since it was published after his admission to hospital, where no such literature was available.

Noll's researches revealed certain discrepancies between Jung's frequently repeated account of the facts – discrepancies to which Noll attributed great importance. These are: (1) the patient was not Jung's, but one of Jung's assistants, J. J. Honegger, who committed suicide in 1911; (2) the case was reported in 1909 and not 1906 as Jung later claimed; (3) the first edition of the book in which the Greek text appeared (*Eine Mithrasliturgie*) was published by Dieterich in 1903; Jung's copy, which first brought the solar phallus image to his attention, was a *second* edition published in 1910; and (4) earlier authors, such as Creuzer and Bachofen, had made references to the solar phallus before that date, and since these were published in German it is possible that the patient could have read them and they could have influenced the content of his hallucination. Noll castigates Jung for not making these facts known and for persisting with this original story, implying that this invalidates Jung's theory.

Although the Solar Phallus Man seems to have been Jung's favourite example to illustrate his hypothesis of the collective unconscious, it has never seemed a particularly felicitious example. The hallucination is not readily explicable as the result of an archetype of the collective unconscious operating in different individuals living in different places at different times in history. Much more persuasive examples could have been given, such as the behaviour of generations of mothers and children as they work out their personal variations on the basis of the mother–child archetypal programme, or global parallels surrounding the ubiquitous symbolism of the snake. To explain Jung's example it is necessary to postulate three archetypal objects (sun, phallus and wind), an archetypal principal (that of masculine generativity) and an archetypal association between them (the sun's phallus generating the wind). Although such an association is statistically improbable, it is not impossible, but Jung could certainly have found a more persuasive example to support his theory.

In fact, the validity of Jung's hypothesis is in no way dependent upon the case of the Solar Phallus Man. It is striking how many workers in different fields have rediscovered the archetypal hypothesis and proposed it in their own terminology to explain their own observations. A number of evolutionary psychologists and psychiatrists both in Britain and the United States have detected and announced the presence of neuropsychic propensities virtually indistinguishable from archetypes. Paul Gilbert (1989) refers to them as 'psychobiological response patterns', Russell Gardner (1988) as 'master programmes' or 'propensity states', while Brant Wenegrat (1984) borrows the sociobiological term 'genetically transmitted response strategies'. David Buss (1995) refers to 'evolved psychological mechanisms' and Randolph Nesse (1987) to 'prepared tendencies'. These response patterns, master programmes, propensity states, response strategies, evolved psychological mechanisms, and prepared tendencies are held responsible for crucial, species-specific patterns of behaviour that evolved because they maximized the fitness of the organism to survive, and for its genes to survive, in the environment in which it evolved. These strategies are inherently shared by all members of the species, whether they be healthy or ill. Psychopathology intervenes when these strategies malfunction as a result of environmental insults or deficiencies at critical stages of development.

The importance of this work is not only its extension of

archetypal theory to psychiatric aetiology but the historic fact that it represents the first systematic attempt to acknowledge the phylogenetic dimension in psychiatry and to put psychopathology on a sound evolutionary basis. These are all exciting developments and Noll either ignores or is completely unaware of them.

The question remains as to whether Jung deliberately falsified his data. Though Noll wishes to convince us that he did, the evidence he produces is not sufficient to support his contention. As Noll himself admits, Jung did attribute the case to Honegger in his first published account of it in 1911 (in *Transformations and Symbols of the Libido*, Part I). Twenty years later, it is true, Jung claimed the case as his own in his essay '*Die Struktur der Seele*' in 1930. This is not such a base slip as Noll would imply since Jung was the consultant under whom Honegger came to work in 1909, whereas the man had been at the Burghölzli under Jung's overall care since Jung took up his appointment there in 1901. As Jung was deputy superintendent of the hospital the man was technically Jung's patient. Honneger was merely the assistant who recorded the patient's solar delusions. The truth, therefore, is less sinister than Noll would wish to imply.

Yet in *The Aryan Christ* he persists in building a mountain out of this particular molehill, giving the incident a bold headline: 'The disappearance of J. J. Honegger from history'. Under this heading he attributes the worst possible motives to Jung: 'by 1930 [Honegger] had been dead for almost twenty years, and with no living heirs to complain, Jung saw no reason why anyone would object if he removed J. J. Honneger from history and took credit for the case himself' (p. 269). This is pure hostile surmise.

That Jung claimed he had gathered the information in 1906 rather than 1909 could not, according to Noll, possibly have been an innocent slip of memory many years later, but was a deliberate lie to cover up the fact that Jung had wrested the case from Honneger, who had not joined the staff of the Burghölzli until 1909, 'surmising that no one would catch him or care very much in the years to come' (p. 269). This again is surmise on Noll's part rather than Jung's.

He acknowledges that Jung's editors inserted a footnote in *The Collected Works* which drew attention to the fact that there was indeed a 1903 first edition of Dieterich's *Eine Mithrasliturgie*, but, characteristically, Noll goes on to accuse them of 'covering up' for

Jung, when they added, 'the patient had, however, been committed [to the Burghölzli] some years before 1903' (p. 270). However, this is evidently not a cover up, but a plain statement of fact. If the editors had wished to indulge in a cover up they would surely have omitted the footnote altogether.

It is undeniable that all his life Jung retained a fondness for the Solar Phallus Man. The case had provided a Eureka experience which strengthened his intuition that beneath our personal intelligence a deeper intelligence is at work – the evolved intelligence of humanity. In his famous 'Face to Face' BBC television interview Jung was specifically asked if he felt that the case of the Solar Phallus Man 'proved that there was an unconscious which was something more than personal' and he replied: 'Oh well, that was not a proof to me, but it was a hint, and I took the hint.' Yet Noll would have us believe that the whole concept of the collective unconscious stands or falls on the basis of this one case. That Jung may have exaggerated the unlikelihood of the Burghölzli patient knowing about the Mithraic cult, which specifically celebrated the phallic sun, probably represents nothing more venal than a natural human tendency to improve on a good story. But Jung's theory of archetypes operating through the collective unconscious is in no way dependent upon its veracity. The Solar Phallus Man will, like J. J. Honegger, disappear into history, but the theory of archetypes will survive as long as it retains its explanatory and descriptive power.

Jung's Biology

Noll makes three criticisms of Jung's biological thinking which, taken cumulatively in conjunction with the exploded case of the Solar Phallus Man, in Noll's opinion, effectively dispose of Jung's archetypal theory once and for all. These criticisms are as follows: (1) that, like Freud, he accepted Haeckel's biogenic law; (2) that he abandoned twentieth-century biology in order to embrace a nineteenth-century Romantic view of Nature rooted in German *Naturphilosophie*; and (3) that he was a teleologist in his conception of evolutionary processes (i.e. he believed there to be some intention behind them guiding them in the direction of the evolution of the human psyche), whereas no neo-Darwinian will go along with this (i.e. they adopt the 'blind watchmaker' view that evolution is undirected and purely the consequence of 'natural selection').

There is a strange omission in this list of 'errors' and that is the one criticism which can be most tellingly advanced against Jung, at least against the earliest formulations of his theory, namely, that, like Freud, he subscribed to a Lamarckian view of heredity (i.e. the idea that a characteristic acquired in the lifetime of an individual could be genetically transmitted to the next generation). One wonders if Noll overlooked this line of attack because Lamarck was French and not 'Germanic'. However, I have dealt with this objection on pages 36–8 in the present volume and so I will confine myself to Noll's three criticisms.

Noll makes a great deal of the fact that Jung's evolutionary thinking was influenced by Ernst Haeckel (1834–1919). Haeckel was Professor of Zoology at the University of Jena and dominated German evolutionary biology throughout the second half of the nineteenth century. Because Haeckel propounded the now discredited 'biogenic law' that 'ontogeny recapitulates phylogeny' and because Jung evidently embraced this idea, Noll feels that this effectively discounts anything that either of them had to say about the evolutionary role of biology in psychology.

Where both Haeckel and Jung adopted a stance at variance with contemporary biology was in the emphasis they placed on the no longer acceptable idea that the development of the individual (ontogeny) closely follows and recapitulates the evolutionary history of the species (phylogeny). That they were wrong about this does not invalidate their view that anatomy and psychology share a common basis in evolutionary biology. Nor does the fact that Jung's ideas about psychological development throughout the human life cycle were influenced by Haeckel's biogenic law invalidate, as Noll wishes us to believe, Jung's hypothesis of a collective unconscious subject to the laws of Darwininan biology.

But so determined is Noll to discredit the hypothesis of a collective unconscious as mystical '*völkisch*' twaddle that he will not tolerate Jung's assertion that the collective unconscious is biologically based. What has become apparent from my public correspondence with him in the pages of the *Times Higher Educational Supplement* is that he cannot bear to admit that if one drops the Haeckelian overtones, the biological (Darwinian) basis of the concept remains entirely valid. There is no need to postulate

Lamarckian or Haekelian processes in the evolution of the phylogenetic psyche, since the Darwinian explanation in terms of natural selection is adequate to account for it. Rather than acknowledge this, Noll has attempted to lay down a smoke-screen over the whole issue by making the insulting and outrageous suggestion that I, and others like me, do not know the difference between 'evolution' and 'natural selection'. For the record, I, like other evolutionary psychiatrists, use both terms in the way that Darwin used them in his masterpiece *The Origin of Species by Means of Natural Selection.*

In his essay 'The Structure of the Unconscious', Jung says: 'Every man is born with a brain that is profoundly differentiated, and this makes him capable of very various mental functions, which are neither ontogenetically developed nor acquired . . . This particular circumstance explains, for example, the remarkable analogies presented by the unconscious in the most remotely separated races and peoples [which is evidenced by] . . . an extraordinary correspondence between the themes and forms of autochthonous myths. The universal similarity of human brains leads us then to admit the existence of a certain psychic function, identical with itself in all individuals; we will call it the *collective psyche*' (CW7, paras 453–454). This statement is fully compatible with the Darwinian position.

Where Jung moves on to less secure ground is in his assertion that 'there are also collective psyches limited to race, tribe, and family, at a level that is less deep than that of the "universal" collective psyche' (CW7, para. 454). It is doubtful that these shallower collective psyches are genetically determined.

The position which, to my mind, is both biologically and psychologically unexceptionable is as follows: the *collective psyche* is the psychological potential of humanity which is encoded in the brain. The *personal psyche* is what the individual makes of the collective psyche in the course of ontological development. Intermediate between these is what Joseph Henderson (1991) calls the *cultural psyche,* which incorporates the shared unconscious assumptions of every family, neighbourhood and nation. The cultural psyche is not genetically transmitted in the manner of the collective psyche: it is the product of traditional influences over the actualization of archetypal imperatives arising from the collective psyche through the development of generations of individuals living out their lives in a given geographical location. This provides an explanation for the Romantic illusion that it is 'the soil' that is responsible for the formation of national, '*völkisch*' characteristics.

One of the important consequences of Jung's familiarity with Haeckel's work was the insight that the whole life cycle is a developmental process with an inherent agenda determined by genetics – that the life of the individual is at the same time the life of the species. In this he anticipated Waddington's (1957) 'epigenetic law' by several decades.

Noll's suggestion that Jung abandoned twentieth-century biology in order to embrace a nineteenth-century *Naturphilosophie* is summarized by the following paragraph: 'With the creation of his religious cult and its transcendental notions of a collective unconscious in 1916 Jung had already left the scientific world and academia, never to really return'. His adoption of the theory of 'dominants' or 'archetypes' completed this break, asserts Noll, and united him with Goethe and Carus and the 'morphological idealists of the Romantic or metaphysical schools of Naturphilosophie that reigned supreme between 1790 and 1830 in German scientific circles' (*The Aryan Christ*, 1997, p. 269).

Noll follows enthusiastically in the wake of Henri Ellenberger, travelling into that hinterland of Jung's thinking inhabited by Goethe, Schopenhauer, Nietzsche, and the Romantic idealists. But unlike Ellenberger he uses the information thus gleaned not to augment our appreciation of Jung's contribution but in order to condemn him. He gives Jung no credit for having moved beyond the nature-philosophers but insists that because he was influenced by many of their ideas, 'Jung's psychological theory is placed squarely within the tradition of speculative or metaphysical Naturphilosophie due to their commonly shared fundamental concepts such as *Einheit* (unity), *Stufenfolge* (succession of stages of gradual development), *Polarität* (polarity, or the interplay of opposing vital forces), *Metamorphose* (metamorphosis), *Urtyp* (archetype), and *Analogie* (analogy).' Thus, because Jung makes use of these concepts in his thinking, it follows, insists Noll, that his psychology is 'a twentieth-century regression or degeneration to nineteenth-century Naturphilosophen' (p. 272).

At no time does Noll consider the possibility that the nature-philosophers themselves had legitimate insights into nature and into biological processes, even if these were superseded by twentieth-century biology. The notions of metamorphosis and the succession of stages of gradual development are at the heart of modern developmental psychology and its conceptions of human epigenesis. The notion of polarity, or the interplay of opposing forces, is central to the modern physiological concept of homeostasis and to the science of cybernetics. The notion of the archetype is, as we have seen, indeed compatible with the 'innate psychological mechanisms' of evolutionary psychology, and the notion of analogy is indispensable to understanding the symbolism of dreams. If Noll considers that, in order to be compatible with twentieth-century science, modern psychology must deprive itself of these concepts, purely because they were thought of in the nineteenth century, he is adopting a position which it is hard to reconcile with his self-proclaimed status as an 'historian of science'.

Because Jung did not subscribe to the 'blind watchmaker' view of evolution, and because the evidence provided by the case of the Solar Phallus Man is far from watertight, Noll argues that the hypotheses of the archetype and the collective unconscious are totally discredited. This does not follow. Jung was perfectly within his rights to argue that there is some implicit intention behind the creation of the universe and the evolution of the human psyche. That this view is decisively rejected by biologists such as Richard Dawkins does not mean that it is wrong. (In my experience, a number of evolutionary biologists are closet teleologists.) Nor does it affect the fact that the archetypes can be understood as biological entities that evolved non-teleologically through natural selection. What matters is that Jung was one of the few psychologists of stature in the twentieth century to reject the *tabula rasa* theory of human psychological development and to replace it with a psychological theory that accepted the profound influence of phylogenetic factors on ontogenetic development.

Though Noll does not take advantage of Jung's early Lamarckian sympathies in order to strengthen his attack, he nevertheless insists that on all other grounds 'Jung's theories simply cannot fit in with the wider body of twentieth-century scientific theory' (p. 272). I hope that I have demonstrated that this is not true.

I have felt it necessary to discuss Noll's adversarial stance to Jung at such length because there can be no doubt that the uncritical acclaim with which Noll's books have been received has done considerable damage to Jung's reputation and to the professional status of analytical psychology. I hope that this second edition of my book may go some way to redress the balance.

POSTSCRIPT

It is not possible to give a complete outline of Jungian psychology in a volume of this size, and critics will find much that I have left out or treated too superficially. Jung was a prolific writer, and his articles and books make up eighteen large volumes of the *Collected Works*. There are, in addition, two volumes of his letters, one volume of correspondence with Freud, his memoir *Memories, Dreams, Reflections*, his chapter in *Man and His Symbols* and a number of seminars, not all of which have been published. Rather than attempt a précis of all this material, I have endeavoured to give the reader a feeling for the nature of the man and his work by tracing through his life – and the life cycle of our species – what I see as certain crucial threads. In doing so I have quoted as copiously as space will allow from Jung's own writings, citing the volume and paragraph in the *Collected Works* from which the quotation is drawn (for instance, *CW* 8, para. 788). Page references are given for all quotations from *Memories, Dreams, Reflections*. The reader is warmly recommended to read this extraordinary work in its entirety.

In recent years it has become fashionable to distinguish between different 'schools' of Jungian psychology, which are designated 'classical', 'developmental' and 'archetypal' according to the emphasis that each places on different aspects of Jung's thought. While such distinctions have a certain descriptive value, there is a danger that they may lead to an exaggeration of the differences between these various approaches and to an underestimation of the degree to which they overlap. Awareness of this danger has prompted me to present the concepts of 'classical' Jungian psychology in a 'developmental' perspective, while at the same time paying proper respect to the creative importance of the imagination, which is the particular emphasis of the 'archetypal' school. I have not, however, sought – except briefly in relation to the anima and animus – to describe the various revisions and developments of Jungian theory that have been proposed in the last three decades. Those who are interested in these matters are referred to Andrew Samuels's encyclopaedic *Jung and the Post-Jungians*.

My own 'personal equation' has caused me to stress the biological foundations of Jungian theory as well as its application to the developmental problems of childhood and adolescence. These concerns are dealt with at greater length in my *Archetype: A Natural History of the Self* (1982).

The implications of Jungian psychology for dream interpretation are examined in *Private Myths: Dreams and Dreaming* (1996), for symbolism in *Ariadne's Clue: A Guide to the Symbols of Humankind* (1998), for the therapeutic alliance in *An Intelligent Person's Guide to Psychotherapy* (1998), and for contemporary psychiatry in *Evolutionary Psychiatry: A New Beginning* (1996) which I wrote in collaboration with John Price. The issue of Jung's alleged anti-Semitism is discussed in my *Jung* (1994).

Other recommendations for further reading in relation to the ideas developed in this book are listed under the appropriate chapter headings. Publication details will be found in the bibliography.

Those in need of a dictionary of Jungian terms will be helped by the glossary at the end of *Memories, Dreams, Reflections*. A more detailed exposition is to be found in *A Critical Dictionary of Jungian Analysis* by Andrew Samuels, Bani Shorter and Fred Plaut.

BIBLIOGRAPHY

Adler, A. (1927) *The Practice and Theory of Individual Psychology.* Harcourt, New York.
Adler. G. (1948) *Studies in Analytical Psychology.* Routledge & Kegan Paul, London.
—— (1961) *The Living Symbol: A Case Study in the Process of Individuation.* Routledge & Kegan Paul, London.
Alain-Fournier (1913) *Le Grand Meaulnes.* Translated by Frank Davison. Penguin Books, Harmondsworth.
Berry, P. (ed.) *Fathers and Mothers: Five Papers on the Archetypal Background of Family Psychology.* Spring Publications, Zürich.
Bleuler, P. E. (1911) *Dementia Praecox, oder die Gruppe der Schizophrenien.* Translated by J. Zinkin (1950) as *Dementia Praecox, or the Group of Schizophrenias.* New York.
Bolen, J. S. (1979) *The Tao of Psychology: Synchronicity and the Self.* Harper & Row, New York.
—— (1984) *Goddesses in Everywoman: A New Psychology of Women.* Harper & Row, New York.
Bowlby, J. (1951) *Maternal Care and Mental Health.* WHO, Geneva.
—— (1958) 'The Nature of the Child's Tie to His Mother', *International Journal of Psycho-Analysis,* 39, pp. 350–73.
—— (1969) *Attachment and Loss, Volume I: Attachment.* Hogarth Press and The Institute of Psycho-Analysis, London.
—— (1979) *The Making and Breaking of Affectional Bonds.* Tavistock Publications, London.
Bradway, K. (1982) 'Gender Identity and Gender Roles: Their Place in Analytic Practice', in *Jungian Analysis,* edited by Murray Stein. Open Court, La Salle and London.
Brome, V. (1978) *Jung: Man and Myth.* Macmillan, London.
Bühler, C. (1935) *From Birth to Maturity: An Outline of the Psychological Development of the Child.* London and New York.
Buss, D. M. (1995) 'Evolutionary psychology: a new paradigm for

psychological science', *Psychological Enquiry*, Vol. 6, No. 1, pp. 1–30.
Campbell, J. (1949) *The Hero with a Thousand Faces.* Pantheon, New York.
Crews, F. 'The Unknown Freud', *New York Review of Books*, 18 November 1993, pp. 55–66.
—— 'The Revenge of the Repressed', *New York Review of Books*, Part I, 17 November 1994, pp. 54–60; Part II, 1 December 1994, pp. 49–58.
Edinger, E. F. (1972) *Ego and Archetype: Individuation and the Religious Function of the Psyche.* Putnam, New York.
—— (1985) *Anatomy of the Psyche: Alchemical Symbolism in Psychotherapy.* Open Court, La Salle, Illinois.
Eibl-Eibesfeldt, I. (1971) *Love and Hate.* Methuen, London.
Eliade, M. (1964) *Shamanism: Archaic Techniques of Ecstasy.* Routledge & Kegan Paul, London.
—— (1975) *Birth and Rebirth (or Rites and Symbols of Initiation).* Harper, New York.
Ellenberger, H. F. (1970) *The Discovery of the Unconscious.* Basic, New York.
Elms, A. (1994) *Uncovering Lives: The Uneasy Alliance of Biography and Psychology.* Oxford University Press, New York.
Erikson, E. H. (1950) *Childhood and Society.* Norton, New York.
Eysenck, H. J. (1952) *The Scientific Study of Personality.* Routledge & Kegan Paul, London.
Fordham, M. (1969) *Children as Individuals.* Hodder & Stoughton, London.
Frazer, J. G. (1926) *The Worship of Nature* (The Gifford Lectures, University of Edinburgh, 1924–57). New York.
Freud, S. (1900) *The Interpretation of Dreams.* In *The Standard Edition of the Complete Psychological Works of Sigmund Freud.* The Hogarth Press and The Institute of Psycho-Analysis, London (hereafter S.E.), IV and V.
—— (1914) *On the History of the Psycho-Analytic Movement.* S.E. XIV.
—— (1933) *New Introductory Lectures on Psycho-Analysis.* S.E. XXII.
Gilbert, P. (1989) *Human Nature and Suffering.* Lawrence Erlbaum Associates, Hove and London, Hillsdale, NJ.
Goldstein, K. (1939) *The Organism.* American Book Co., New York.
Guggenbühl-Craig, A. (1981) *Marriage, Dead or Alive.* Spring Publications, Dallas.
Hannah, B. (1977) *Jung: His Life and Work.* Michael Joseph, London.
—— (1981) *Encounters with the Soul: Active Imagination as Developed by C.G. Jung.* Sigo Press, Santa Monica.
Harding, M. E. (1933) *The Way of All Women.* Harper & Row, New York, 1975.
—— (1964) *The Parental Image.* G. P. Putnam, New York.
Harlow, H. F., and Harlow, M. K. (1965) 'The Affectional Systems', in A. M. Schrier, H. F. Harlow and F. Stollnitz (eds) *Behaviour of Nonhuman Primates.* Academic Press, London.

Henderson, J. (1991) 'C.G. Jung's psychology: additions and extensions'. *Aspects of Analytical Psychology*, 36, 4, pp. 429–42.
Henderson, J. L. (1967) *Thresholds of Initiation*. Wesleyan University Press, Middleton, Connecticut.
Herzog, E. (1966) *Psyche and Death*. Hodder & Stoughton, London.
Hillman, J. (1967) *Insearch: psychology and Religion*. Hodder & Stoughton, London.
—— (1985) *Anima: An Anatomy of a Personified Notion*. Spring Publications, Dallas.
Hochheimer, W. (1969) *The Psychotherapy of C. G. Jung*. Barrie & Rockliffe, London.
Homans, P. (1979) *Jung in Context: Modernity and the Making of a Psychology*. University of Chicago Press, Chicago and London.
Huizinga, J. (1970) *Homo Ludens: A Study of the Play Element in Culture*, revised edition. Temple Smith, London.
Hutt, C. (1972) *Males and Females*. Penguin Books, Harmondsworth.
Jacobi, J. (1942) *The Psychology of C. G. Jung*. Routledge & Kegan Paul, London.
—— (1967) *The Way of Individuation*. Hodder & Stoughton, London.
Jaffé, A. (1970) *The Myth of Meaning in the Work of C. G. Jung*. Hodder & Stoughton, London.
Jones, E. (1961) *The Life and Work of Sigmund Freud*, abridged in one volume. Basic, New York.
Jung, C. G. (1990) *Analytical Psychology, Seminars*, Vol. 3. Routledge, London.
Jung, C. G. The majority of quotations in the text are taken either from *The Collected Works of C. G. Jung* (1953–78), edited by H. Read, M. Fordham and G. Adler and published in London by Routledge, in New York by Pantheon Books (1953–60) and the Bollingen Foundation (1961–7) and in Princeton, New Jersey (1967–78), or from *Memories, Dreams, Reflections* (1963) published in London by Routledge & Kegan Paul and in New York by Random House. Sources of quotations from *The Collected Works* are indicated by the volume number followed by the number of the paragraph from which the quotation is taken, e.g., *CW* 10, para. 441. Quotations from *Memories, Dreams, Reflections* are indicated by the page number thus: *MDR*, p. 111.
—— (1962) *Commentary on the Secret of the Golden Flower*, translated by C. F. Baynes. Collins and Routledge & Kegan Paul, London.
Jung, E. (1957) *Animus and Anima*. Spring Publications, New York.
Kenton, L. (1986) 'All I Ever Wanted Was a Baby' (in *A Celebration of Babies*, edited by S. Emerson). Blackie, London.
Leonard, L. S. (1982) *The Wounded Woman: Healing the Father–Daughter Relationship*. Swallow Press, Athens, Ohio and Chicago.
Levinson, D., Darrow, C. N., Klein, E. B., Levinson, M. H. and McKee, B. (1978) *The Seasons of a Man's Life*. Knopf, New York.
Lorenz, K. (1970) *The Enmity Between Generations and its Possible Causes*. The Nobel Foundation, Stockholm.

—— (1977) *Behind the Mirror: A Search for a Natural History of Human Knowledge.* Methuen, London.
McGuire, W. (1974) *The Freud/Jung Letters.* The Hogarth Press and Routledge & Kegan Paul, London.
Macmillan, M. (1997) *Freud Evaluated: The Completed Arc.* The MIT Press, Cambridge, Mass., and London, England.
Maslow, A. H. (1967) *Towards a Psychology of Being.* Van Nostrand, Princeton.
Monick, E. (1987) *Phallos: Sacred Image of the Masculine.* Inner City Books, Toronto.
Nesse, R. M. (1987) 'An evolutionary perspective on panic disorder and agoraphobia', in *Ethology and Sociobiology,* Vol. 8, 3S, pp. 73–84.
Neumann, E. (1973) *The Child: Structure and Dynamics of the Nascent Personality.* Hodder & Stoughton, London.
Noll, R. (1992) *Vampires, Werewolves and Demons: Twentieth Century Reports in the Psychiatric Literature.* Brunner/Mazel, New York.
—— (1994) *The Jung Cult: Origins of a Charismatic Movement.* Princeton University Press, Princeton, NJ.
—— (1997a) *The Aryan Christ: The Secret Life of Carl Jung.* Random House, New York.
—— (1997b) 'A Christ Named Carl Jung' from *At Random,* No. 18, (Fall).
Papadopoulos, R. K., and Saayman, G. S. (eds) (1985) *Jung in Modern Perspective.* Wildwood House, London.
Parkes, C. M. (1973) 'Factors Determining the Persistence of Phantom Pain in the Amputee', *Journal of Psychosomatic Research,* 17, pp. 97–108.
Parsons, J. E. (ed.) (1980) *The Psychobiology of Sex Differences and Sex Roles.* Hemisphere, Washington; McGraw-Hill, New York.
Parsons, T., and Bales, R. F. (1955) *Family, Socialization and Interaction Process.* Free Press, Chicago, Illinois.
Perera, S. B. (1981) *Descent of the Goddess.* Inner City Books, Toronto.
Progoff, I. (1953) *Jung's Psychology and Its Social Meaning.* Routledge & Kegan Paul, London.
Riesman, D. (1952) *The Lonely Crowd.* Yale University Press, New Haven.
Russell, B. (1946) *A History of Western Philosophy.* George Allen & Unwin, London.
Samuels, A. (1985) *Jung and the Post-Jungians.* Routledge & Kegan Paul, London.
—— (ed.) (1985a) *The Father: Contemporary Jungian Perspectives.* Free Association Books, London.
Samuels, A., Shorter, B. and Plaut, F. (1986) *A Critical Dictionary of Jungian Analysis.* Routledge & Kegan Paul, London.
Sears, E. (1986) *The Ages of Man: Medieval Interpretations of the Life Cycle.* Princeton University Press, New Jersey.
Shamdasani, S. (1998) *Cult Fictions: C. G. Jung and the Founding of Analytical Psychology.* Routledge, London and New York.

Sharp, D. (1988) *The Survival Papers: Anatomy of a Mid-Life Crisis.* Inner City Books, Toronto.
Shorter, B. (1987) *An Image Darkly Forming: Women and Initiation.* Routledge & Kegan Paul, London.
Staude, J.-R. (1981) *The Adult Development of C. G. Jung.* Routledge & Kegan Paul, London.
Stein, M. (ed.) (1982) *Jungian Analysis.* Open Court, La Salle, Illinois, and London.
—— (1983) *In Midlife: A Jungian Perspective.* Spring Publications, Dallas, Texas.
Stevens, A. (1982) *Archetype: A Natural History of the Self.* Routledge & Kegan Paul, London; William Morrow & Co., New York.
—— (1986) *Withymead: A Jungian Community for the Healing Arts.* Coventure/Element Books, London.
—— (1989) *The Roots of War: A Jungian Perspective.* Paragon House, New York.
—— (1994) *Jung.* Oxford University Press.
—— (1996) *Private Myths: Dreams and Dreaming.* Penguin, London.
—— (1998) *An Intelligent Person's Guide to Psychotherapy.* Gerald Duckworth & Co., London.
—— (1998) *Ariadne's Clue: A Guide to the Symbols of Humankind.* Allen Lane, London and Princeton University Press, NJ.
Stevens, A. and Price, J. (1996) *Evolutionary Psychiatry: A New Beginning.* Routledge, London.
Storr, A. (1972) *The Dynamics of Creation.* Secker and Warburg, London.
—— (1973) *Jung.* Fontana/Collins, London.
—— (1988) *The School of Genius.* André Deutsch, London.
Thompson, R. (1968) *The Pelican History of Psychology.* Penguin Books, Harmondsworth.
Tiger, L. (1969) *Men in Groups.* Random House, New York.
Tinbergen, N. (1951) *The Study of Instinct.* Oxford University Press, London.
Tuby, M. *The Search and Alchemy.* Guild Lectures No. 210. The Guild of Pastoral Psychology, Colmore Press, London.
Ulanov, A. B. (1981) *Receiving Woman: Studies in the Psychology and Theology of the Feminine.* Westminster Press, Philadelphia.
van der Post, L. (1975) *Jung and The Story of our Time.* Pantheon Books, New York.
van Gennep, A. (1960) *The Rites of Passage.* Routledge & Kegan Paul, London.
von Franz, M.-L. (1970) *The Problem of the Puer Aeternus.* Spring Publications, New York and Zurich.
—— (1975) *C. G. Jung: His Myth in Our Time.* Hodder & Stoughton, London.
—— (1986) *On Dreams and Death.* Shambhala, Boston and London.
Waddington, C. H. (1957) *The Strategy of the Genes: A Discussion of Some Aspects of Theoretical Biology.* George Allen & Unwin, London.

Webster, R. (1997) *Why Freud Was Wrong: Sin, Science and Psychoanalysis.* HarperCollins, London.
Wehr, D. S. (1988) *Jung and Feminism: Liberating Archetypes.* Routledge, London.
Wehr, G. (1987) *Jung: A Biography.* Shambhala, Boston and London.
Wenegrat, B. (1984) *Sociobiology and Mental Disorder.* Addison-Wesley, Menlow Park, California.
Whiting, B. (ed.) (1963) *Six Cultures: Studies of Child Rearing.* Wiley, New York.
Whitmont, E. C. (1969) *The Symbolic Quest.* Barrie & Rockliffe, London.
—— (1983) *Return of the Goddess: Femininity, Aggression and the Modern Grail Quest.* Routledge & Kegan Paul, London.
Whyte, L. L. (1979) *The Unconscious Before Freud.* Julian Freedman, London.
Wickes, F. G. (1966) *The Inner World of Childhood.* Appleton-Century, New York.
Winnicott, D. W. (1977) *The Maturational Process and the Facilitating Environment.* International University Press, New York.
Wolff, T. (1956) *Structural Forms of the Feminine Psyche.* Students' Association of the C. G. Jung Institute, Zürich.

INDEX

READ MORE IN PENGUIN

In every corner of the world, on every subject under the sun, Penguin represents quality and variety – the very best in publishing today.

For complete information about books available from Penguin – including Puffins, Penguin Classics and Arkana – and how to order them, write to us at the appropriate address below. Please note that for copyright reasons the selection of books varies from country to country.

In the United Kingdom: Please write to *Dept. EP, Penguin Books Ltd, Bath Road, Harmondsworth, West Drayton, Middlesex UB7 ODA*

In the United States: Please write to *Consumer Sales, Penguin Putnam Inc., P.O. Box 12289 Dept. B, Newark, New Jersey 07101-5289.* VISA and MasterCard holders call 1-800-788-6262 to order Penguin titles

In Canada: Please write to *Penguin Books Canada Ltd, 10 Alcorn Avenue, Suite 300, Toronto, Ontario M4V 3B2*

In Australia: Please write to *Penguin Books Australia Ltd, P.O. Box 257, Ringwood, Victoria 3134*

In New Zealand: Please write to *Penguin Books (NZ) Ltd, Private Bag 102902, North Shore Mail Centre, Auckland 10*

In India: Please write to *Penguin Books India Pvt Ltd, 11 Community Centre, Panchsheel Park, New Delhi 110017*

In the Netherlands: Please write to *Penguin Books Netherlands bv, Postbus 3507, NL-1001 AH Amsterdam*

In Germany: Please write to *Penguin Books Deutschland GmbH, Metzlerstrasse 26, 60594 Frankfurt am Main*

In Spain: Please write to *Penguin Books S. A., Bravo Murillo 19, 1º B, 28015 Madrid*

In Italy: Please write to *Penguin Italia s.r.l., Via Benedetto Croce 2, 20094 Corsico, Milano*

In France: Please write to *Penguin France, Le Carré Wilson, 62 rue Benjamin Baillaud, 31500 Toulouse*

In Japan: Please write to *Penguin Books Japan Ltd, Kaneko Building, 2-3-25 Koraku, Bunkyo-Ku, Tokyo 112*

In South Africa: Please write to *Penguin Books South Africa (Pty) Ltd, Private Bag X14, Parkview, 2122 Johannesburg*

READ MORE IN PENGUIN

A CHOICE OF NON-FICTION

Jane Austen: A Life Claire Tomalin

'I cannot think that a better life of Jane Austen than Claire Tomalin's will be written for many years . . . a truly marvellous book' *Mail on Sunday*. 'As near perfect a Life of Austen as we are likely to get . . . Tomalin presents Austen as remarkably clever; sensitive, but unsentimental' *Daily Telegraph*

A Wavering Grace Gavin Young

'By far . . . the most moving account of Vietnam to be written in recent years' Norman Lewis. 'This delicate, terrible and enchanting book . . . brings the atmosphere of Vietnam so near that you can almost taste and smell it' *The Times*

Clone Gina Kolata

On July 5 1996 Dolly, the most famous lamb in history, was born. It was an event of enormous significance, for Dolly was a clone, produced from the genetic material of a six-year-old ewe. Suddenly, the idea that human beings could be replicated had become a reality. 'Superb' J. G. Ballard, *Sunday Times*

Huxley Adrian Desmond

T. H. Huxley (1825–95), often referred to as 'Darwin's Bulldog', became the major champion of the theory of evolution and was crucial to the making of our modern Darwinian world. 'Nobody writes scientific biography like Adrian Desmond, and this account of Huxley's progress . . . is his best so far' *The Times Literary Supplement*

Cleared for Take-Off Dirk Bogarde

'It begins with his experiences in the Second World War as an interpreter of reconnaissance photographs . . . his awareness of the horrors as well as the dottiness of war is essential to the tone of this affecting and strangely beautiful book' *Daily Telegraph*

READ MORE IN PENGUIN 

A CHOICE OF NON-FICTION

Time Out Film Guide Edited by John Pym

The definitive, up-to-the-minute directory of every aspect of world cinema from classics and silent epics to reissues and the latest releases.

Four-Iron in the Soul Lawrence Donegan

'A joy to read. Not since Bill Bryson plotted a random route through small-town America has such a breezy idea for a book had a happier (or funnier) result' *The Times*. 'Funny, beautifully observed and it tells you things about sport in general and golf in particular that nobody else thought to pass on' *Mail on Sunday*

Nelson Mandela: A Biography Martin Meredith

Nelson Mandela's role in delivering South Africa from racial division stands as one of the great triumphs of the twentieth century. In this brilliant account, Martin Meredith gives a vivid portrayal of the life and times of this towering figure. 'The best biography so far of Nelson Mandela' Raymond Whitaker, *Independent on Sunday*

In Search of Nature Edward O. Wilson

'*In Search of Nature* makes such stimulating reading that Edward O. Wilson might be regarded as a one-man recruitment bureau for tomorrow's biologists . . . His essays on ants tend to leave one gasping for breath, literally speaking . . . Yet he is equally enchanting in his accounts of sharks and snakes and New Guinea's birds of paradise' *The Times Higher Education Supplement*

Reflections on a Quiet Rebel Cal McCrystal

This extraordinary book is both a vivid memoir of Cal McCrystal's Irish Catholic childhood and a loving portrait of his father Charles, a 'quiet rebel' and unique man. 'A haunting book, lovely and loving. It explains more about one blighted corner of Ireland than a dozen dogged histories' *Scotsman*

READ MORE IN PENGUIN

LITERARY CRITICISM

The Penguin History of Literature

Published in ten volumes, *The Penguin History of Literature* is a superb critical survey of the English and American literature covering fourteen centuries, from the Anglo-Saxons to the present, and written by some of the most distinguished academics in their fields.

New Bearings in English Poetry F. R. Leavis

'*New Bearings in English Poetry* was the first intelligent account of the work of Eliot, Pound and Gerard Manley Hopkins to appear in English and it significantly altered critical awareness . . . Leavis gave to literary criticism a thoroughness and respectability that has never since been equalled' Peter Ackroyd, *Spectator*. 'The most influential literary critic of modern times' *Financial Times*

The Uses of Literacy Richard Hoggart

Mass literacy has opened new worlds to new readers. How far has it also been exploited to debase standards and behaviour? 'A vivid inside view of working-class culture and one of the most influential books of the post-war era' *Observer*

Epistemology of the Closet Eve Kosofsky Sedgwick

Through her brilliant interpretation of the readings of Henry James, Melville, Nietzsche, Proust and Oscar Wilde, Eve Kosofsky Sedgwick shows how questions of sexual definition are at the heart of every form of representation in this century. 'A signal event in the history of late-twentieth-century gay studies' Wayne Koestenbaum

Dangerous Pilgrimages Malcolm Bradbury

'This capacious book tracks Henry James from New England to Rye; Evelyn Waugh to a Hollywood as grotesque as he expected; Gertrude Stein to Spain to be mistaken for a bishop; Oscar Wilde to a rickety stage in Leadsville, Colorado . . . The textbook on the the transatlantic theme' *Guardian*

READ MORE IN PENGUIN

LITERARY CRITICISM

The Practice of Writing David Lodge

This lively collection examines the work of authors ranging from the two Amises to Nabokov and Pinter; the links between private lives and published works; and the different techniques required in novels, stage plays and screenplays. 'These essays, so easy in manner, so well-built and informative, offer a fine blend of creative writing and criticism' *Sunday Times*

A Lover's Discourse Roland Barthes

'May be the most detailed, painstaking anatomy of desire we are ever likely to see or need again ... The book is an ecstatic celebration of love and language ... readers interested in either or both ... will enjoy savouring its rich and dark delights' *Washington Post*

The New Pelican Guide to English Literature Edited by Boris Ford

The indispensable critical guide to English and American literature in nine volumes, erudite yet accessible. From the ages of Chaucer and Shakespeare, via Georgian satirists and Victorian social critics, to the leading writers of the twentieth century, all literary life is here.

The Structure of Complex Words William Empson

'Twentieth-century England's greatest critic after T. S. Eliot, but whereas Eliot was the high priest, Empson was the *enfant terrible* ... *The Structure of Complex Words* is one of the linguistic masterpieces of the epoch, finding in the feel and tone of our speech whole sedimented social histories' *Guardian*

Vamps and Tramps Camille Paglia

'Paglia is a genuinely unconventional thinker ... Taken as a whole, the book gives an exceptionally interesting perspective on the last thirty years of intellectual life in America, and is, in its wacky way, a celebration of passion and the pursuit of truth' *Sunday Telegraph*

READ MORE IN PENGUIN

POLITICS AND SOCIAL SCIENCES

The Unconscious Civilization John Ralston Saul

In this powerfully argued critique, John Ralston Saul shows how corporatism has become the dominant ideology of our time, cutting across all sectors as well as the political spectrum. The result is an increasingly conformist society in which citizens are reduced to passive bystanders.

A Class Act Andrew Adonis and Stephen Pollard

'Will Britain escape from ancient and modern injustice? A necessary first step is to read and take seriously this ... description of the condition of our country. Andrew Adonis and Stephen Pollard here destroy the myth that Britain is a classless society' *The Times Higher Education Supplement*

Accountable to None Simon Jenkins

'An important book, because it brings together, with an insider's authority and anecdotage, both a narrative of domestic Thatcherism and a polemic against its pretensions ... an indispensable guide to the corruptions of power and language which have sustained the illusion that Thatcherism was an attack on "government"' *Guardian*

Structural Anthropology Volumes 1–2 Claude Lévi-Strauss

'That the complex ensemble of Lévi-Strauss's achievement ... is one of the most original and intellectually exciting of the present age seems undeniable. No one seriously interested in language or literature, in sociology or psychology, can afford to ignore it' George Steiner

Invitation to Sociology Peter L. Berger

Without belittling its scientific procedures Professor Berger stresses the humanistic affinity of sociology with history and philosophy. It is a discipline which encourages a fuller awareness of the human world ... with the purpose of bettering it.

READ MORE IN PENGUIN

PHILOSOPHY

Brainchildren Daniel C. Dennett

Philosophy of mind has been profoundly affected by this century's scientific advances, and thinking about thinking – how and why the mind works, its very existence – can seem baffling. Here eminent philosopher and cognitive scientist Daniel C. Dennett has provided an eloquent guide through some of the mental and moral mazes.

Language, Truth and Logic A. J. Ayer

The classic text which founded logical positivism and modern British philosophy, *Language, Truth and Logic* swept away the cobwebs and revitalized British philosophy.

The Penguin Dictionary of Philosophy Edited by Thomas Mautner

This dictionary encompasses all aspects of Western philosophy from 600 BC to the present day. With contributions from over a hundred leading philosophers, this dictionary will prove the ideal reference for any student or teacher of philosophy as well as for all those with a general interest in the subject.

Labyrinths of Reason William Poundstone

'The world and what is in it, even what people say to you, will not seem the same after plunging into *Labyrinths of Reason* . . . holds up the deepest philosophical questions for scrutiny in a way that irresistibly sweeps readers on' *New Scientist*

Metaphysics as a Guide to Morals Iris Murdoch

'This is philosophy dragged from the cloister, dusted down and made freshly relevant to suffering and egoism, death and religious ecstasy . . . and how we feel compassion for others' *Guardian*

Philosophy Football Mark Perryman

The amazing tale of a make-believe team, *Philosophy Football* is the story of what might have happened to the world's greatest thinkers if their brains had been in their boots instead of their heads . . .

READ MORE IN PENGUIN

LANGUAGE/LINGUISTICS

Language Play David Crystal

We all use language to communicate information, but it is language play which is truly central to our lives. Full of puns, groan-worthy gags and witty repartee, this book restores the fun to the study of language. It also demonstrates why all these things are essential elements of what makes us human.

Swearing Geoffrey Hughes

'A deliciously filthy trawl among taboo words across the ages and the globe' *Observer*. 'Erudite and entertaining' Penelope Lively, *Daily Telegraph*

The Language Instinct Stephen Pinker

'Dazzling . . . Pinker's big idea is that language is an instinct, as innate to us as flying is to geese . . . Words can hardly do justice to the superlative range and liveliness of Pinker's investigations' *Independent*. 'He does for language what David Attenborough does for animals, explaining difficult scientific concepts so easily that they are indeed absorbed as a transparent stream of words' John Gribbin

Mother Tongue Bill Bryson

'A delightful, amusing and provoking survey, a joyful celebration of our wonderful language, which is packed with curiosities and enlightenment on every page' *Sunday Express*. 'A gold mine of language-anecdote. A surprise on every page . . . enthralling' *Observer*

Longman Guide to English Usage
Sidney Greenbaum and Janet Whitcut

Containing 5000 entries compiled by leading authorities on modern English, this invaluable reference work clarifies every kind of usage problem, giving expert advice on points of grammar, meaning, style, spelling, pronunciation and punctuation.

READ MORE IN PENGUIN

PSYCHOLOGY

Closing the Asylum Peter Barham

'A dispassionate, objective analysis of the changes in the way we care for the mentally ill. It offers no simple solutions but makes clear that "care in the community" is not so easy to implement as some seem to believe' *The Times Educational Supplement*

Child Behaviour Dorothy Einon

Covering the psychology of childcare, this book traces every key theme of child behaviour from birth to adolescence. Dorothy Einon discusses what, at any age, it is reasonable to expect of a child, how to keep things in perspective, and the most interesting and rewarding aspect of parenthood – bringing up a happy, well-adjusted child.

Bereavement Colin Murray Parkes

This classic text enables us to understand grief and grieving. How is bereavement affected by age, gender, personal psychology and culture? What are the signs of pathological grieving which can lead to mental illness? And how can carers provide genuine help without interfering with the painful but necessary 'work' of mourning?

Edward de Bono's Textbook of Wisdom

Edward de Bono shows how traditional thinking methods designed by the 'Gang of Three' (Socrates, Plato and Aristotle) are too rigid to cope with a complex and changing world. He recognizes that our brains deserve that we do better with them, and uses his gift for simplicity to get readers' thoughts to flow along fresh lines.

The Care of the Self Michel Foucault
The History of Sexuality Volume 3

Foucault examines the transformation of sexual discourse from the Hellenistic to the Roman world in an enquiry which 'bristles with provocative insights into the tangled liaison of sex and self' *The Times Higher Education Supplement*